Forensic Aspects of Driver Perception and Response

By

Paul L. Olson

Lawyers & Judges Publishing Company, Inc.

Lawyers & Judges Publishing Company, Inc.

P.O. Box 30040
Tucson, AZ 85751-0040
(520) 323-1500
(602) 323-1500
FAX (520) 323-0055

Olson, Paul,
Forensic aspects of driver perception and response / by Paul Olson.
p. cm.
Includes bibliographical references and index.
ISBN 0-913875-22-8
1. Liability for traffic accidents—United States—Trial practice. 2. Trial practice—United States. 3. Traffic accidents—United States. 4. Traffic accident investigation. 5. Automobile driving–Physiological aspects. I. Title
KF8925.T7057 1996
346.7303'22—dc20
[347.306322] 96-6158
CIP

ISBN 0-913875-22-8
Printed in the United States of America
10 9 8 7 6 5 4 3

Table of Contents

Chapter 4

Chapter 5

Preface

Driver perception and perception-response time are two issues of considerable importance to accident reconstructionists. They are also areas that I have spent a considerable portion of my professional life researching. The knowledge I have gained from my own work, combined with that of a number of other individuals, provides a data base that I believe is beneficial to those whose business is investigating accidents and drawing conclusions concerning causality. Like others who do research for a living I have published my work, and like others who publish I tend to think that the obligation ends there. My experience as a consultant in litigation, however, has made it painfully apparent that there is a significant communication barrier. Clearly, relevant information in these areas is not making it to the people in the front lines, at least not in sufficient quantity and/or in a way that is comprehensible.

The natural thing, I suppose, is to blame reconstructionists for being ill informed and failing their duty to keep up to date in their field. This argument is defeated by the facts. The many reconstructionists I have met and come to know over the years are bright people who are eager to learn as much as they can about their chosen field. The problem, I believe, is that the authoritative writings in areas such as perception and perception-response time appear in journals and other sources that are probably not within the usual scope of a typical reconstructionist's reading. Even if they were, the applicability of the data and its limitations in a particular case may not be clear to someone from a different discipline. In the end, it is incumbent upon the researcher to disseminate findings in a way that will benefit the end user. In that sense, the communication failure is my fault and that of others who have worked in the field. This book is an attempt to rectify that problem.

I have two aims for this book. The first is technical accuracy. The second, and perhaps more important aim is to create a book that will be useful to persons having a need for the information it contains, but whose training is very different from my own. To that end I have presented background material and research results, and attempted to show how the research data relate to the real-world events with which the reconstructionist must cope. I have also tried to point out the limitations of the data, and the assumptions upon which they are based.

It has been my experience that authors tend to assume that people will seize upon their work and read it cover to cover in wide-eyed wonder. I didn't. It may not a bad idea to read this book cover to cover, but I anticipate that most people will probably attack it piecemeal. That being the case, I have tried to organize the book, and the individual chapters, in a way that will assist those who only have the time to read a bit here and there. As one aid to this approach I have included an overview at the end of each chapter. This is probably a good starting point for the browser who is trying to determine whether it is worthwhile to read the entire chapter.

Lack of information is the major frustration I have experienced in trying to put this work together. Far too often it has been necessary to use qualitative rather than quantitative terminology, or to suggest that the readers are on their own when it comes to producing hard numbers for some situation. An awareness of the limitations of available data is probably just as important as an awareness of the data itself, but readers who expect to find solutions to all their problems within these covers are fated to be disappointed. In part the problem lies in the complexity of the human animal and the variety of situations that end up in litigation. In part, unfortunately, it is due to lack of necessary research. The latter problem is unlikely to be resolved in the near future.

Nothing as complex as a book can be a one-person effort. That is certainly true in this case. Many people provided generous assistance and, I sincerely believe, helped produce a far better work than would have been the case were it truly a solo effort.

First and foremost among those persons is my ever-patient and long-suffering wife. For the better part of a year she has found me hunched over the computer in the late evening hours and asked "working on the book?" The response, normally in the form of a grunt, was taken as affirmative and I was left to my labors. She tolerated the laptop computer that seemed to follow us everywhere, even on vacations, and grew somewhat used to seeing me bent over it when rational people would have been enjoying themselves. If it was a relief to me to see the end product packaged up and off to the publisher, it must have been much more to her. More than any other single item or individual, her support, tolerance and understanding made this book possible.

Special thanks are due to Gary Cooper and Weldon Greiger who took their valuable time to review the manuscript and offer many helpful suggestions. This is a much better product because of their efforts. Obviously, the author alone bears responsibility for any flaws that remain.

Weldon Greiger also helped with the photography. His skill, experience and patience was invaluable in preparing these important figures.

The art work in the book is by Sandra Olson. Those who suspect nepotism would be correct, since Sandra is the author's daughter. More important, she is a skilled graphic artist, whose efforts greatly improved the appearance and usefulness of the many figures throughout the book.

Finally, I would like to express my appreciation to Steve Weintraub of Lawyers and Judges Publishing Company. It was Mr. Weintraub who first contacted me about writing a book. This had the effect of getting me moving on a project that had long been in the back of my mind. He and his staff also provided a great deal of assistance and encouragement throughout the birth process.

Forensic Aspects of Driver Perception and Response

By
Paul L. Olson

Chapter 1

Introduction: Human Factors in Accident Reconstruction

Introduction to Human Factors

To most people the aftermath of a motor vehicle collision appears to be little more than a mass of crumpled metal. A reconstructionist can often make sense of the wreckage and, combining that analysis with other information, describe with some accuracy what happened before, during, and after the crash. The opinions arrived at in this process can be of great importance in a case at law.

The information upon which the reconstructionist relies in carrying out this task is largely drawn from the fields of engineering and physics. All of which makes excellent sense. However, motor vehicle collisions involve people as well. It frequently happens that human performance is a central issue in litigation. Accordingly, reconstructionists are often called upon to offer opinions in that area. The relevant data come from several disciplines, but primarily experimental psychology and human factors.

In the fields of engineering and physics the characteristics of materials have long been an area of scientific study. The information obtained is vital input for engineers who have an obvious interest in designing bridges that will not collapse, and other devices that perform as expected. In many systems, at all levels of complexity, humans are used as key control elements. In that case it makes just as much sense to have information about human performance capabilities as it does that of the metal, plastics, etc. that go into the system. A major difference is that designers generally have some options in the matter of materials. If more strength is required in a mechanical component, for example, the engineer normally has alternatives such as altering dimensions or using other materials. No such luxury exists in dealing with humans. If there is a mismatch between the capabilities of the operator and the demands of the machine it is the latter that must yield. The basic rule is that if reliance is to be placed on humans to carry out important control functions the device in question absolutely must take into account the strengths and limitations of the population from which the operators will be drawn.

The discipline specifically concerned with obtaining, disseminating and applying human performance data in this context is human factors. One of the most important roles of the human factors professional is to carry out research on human performance capability, seeking to obtain information useful in the design of all kinds of devices with which humans must interact.

History

One of the distinguishing characteristics of humans is the use of tools. In essence, a tool becomes part of the user, expanding that individual's capabilities. In prehistoric times tools improved the ability of humans to do the things necessary to survive, such as building shelters, securing food, or dealing with enemies. Tools remain very much part of our lives today, with their use extending far beyond the basic necessities of existence. Then as now, the more effective the tool, the more it improves the user's ability to carry out chosen tasks. The effectiveness of a tool is determined by a number of factors, but certainly one of the most important is the degree to which it conforms to the physical characteristics and capabilities of the user. Take the example of a club. In all likelihood the first of these were just pieces of wood or bone. They were probably two to three feet long and of a weight that allowed them to be carried for some time without undue fatigue and still do a reasonable club-type job. In time it was discovered that lashing a rock to the end of a relatively slender stick produced a far more effective club. It was easier to carry and dealt a more powerful blow for the same weight. Some might say that this was a neat piece of engineering, making use of basic principles of physics. That may be true, but the people of that time knew nothing of engineering or physics. The developments were based on what made best use of their capabilities in solving the problems that they faced. Tools developed using this fundamental principle of human factors contributed to making humankind ascendant over other animals that were bigger, faster and stronger.

On a basis of this description human factors is one of the oldest of scientific/engineering disciplines. As an organized area of inquiry, however, it started during World War II, when the military, particularly the Army Air Force, became concerned that some of the new machines of war were threatening to outstrip the ability of humans to exercise effective control. Hot new aircraft, as one example, experienced many crashes, which were routinely blamed on pilot error. Indeed, post-crash investigations often revealed that a pilot did something wrong or failed to do something in a timely fashion. Pilots, on the other hand, complained about such things as basic controls that were grouped too close together, making it unnecessarily difficult to actuate a particular one. Sometimes the positions of important controls were changed from one aircraft to another, or even on different models of the same aircraft, for no apparent reason. For a pilot who flew model A on some occasions and model B on others, such changes greatly increased the probability of error. Sometimes emergency procedures took more time to carry out than was typically available when the emergency occurred. In time it became apparent to some high military officials that the pilots had a point. A number of individuals, most of whom were experimental psychologists, were set to work to find out what might be done to improve matters. The body of research they generated laid the foundation for the profession.

In early years the field was often called "applied experimental psychology." Many of the practitioners, however, were not psychologists, so the term "human engineering" came into use. Perhaps because this seemed to imply that it was the humans who were being altered, the term "human factors," or sometimes "human factors engineering" was adopted. In the United States human factors is still the preferred description. In most of the rest of the world the term "ergonomics" is used, and in recent years its use in the US has increased rapidly. The expression "ergonomically designed" has recently enjoyed extensive use in advertising. Businesspersons clearly hope to convince people who know little or nothing about the field to regard such products as somehow superior to the other kind. Recently the Human Factors Society in the US bowed to the inevitable and added Ergonomics to its name.

Human Factors in Product Evaluation and Development

It may seem ironic that a common product evaluation technique today is the same one that has been used since the dawn of time, i.e., for designers to try it out themselves. The fact is that for many types of products this approach provides a direct feedback loop that works fairly well. After all, the engineers and designers are people who are probably not very different from the end user in many cases. In addition, any engineer or designer worthy of the name knows that a product must do its job well in the hands of the intended user and not present unnecessary risks. In a competitive marketplace products that fail these basic tests tend not to do well. Since the designers and engineers involved in development want the product of their efforts to succeed in a competitive environment, they are motivated to pay attention to human factors issues, even if they have no familiarity with the discipline. Finally, these people are in a good position to decide what can and should be done to correct problems in a cost-effective manner.

For all its virtues this approach has substantial deficiencies. Sometimes ego gets in the way of objective evaluation, and designers have difficulty understanding why the product of their genius should cause problems for anyone else. Especially with more complex systems, it often happens that the designer does not or cannot participate in the evaluation process, or does not do so under all realistic conditions. In World War II the fact that the people who were designing high-performance aircraft typically did not fly them often placed designers and pilots at loggerheads, and was a major factor in initiating the first organized research in the field.

Personal evaluation can also produce misleading results when carried out by persons lacking an appropriate technical background. For example, a personal evaluation approach is commonly employed by experts in assessing visibility matters for purposes of litigation. The logic seems to be: "I have normal vision. If I recreate the accident situation with some care, what I can see would be the same as anyone with normal vision could see." Conducting a reenactment of some kind is not a bad idea, and the thinking contained within the quotations seems reasonable, but it is naive for reasons that will become apparent as one progresses through this book.

The use of personal evaluation is also unscientific in that information is not pursued in an organized fashion and is typically not reported in a way that either allows it to be evaluated by qualified professionals or makes it readily available to others facing similar problems. Human factors work should be all of these things. The goal of the profession is to develop a body of information about human performance that will enable engineers and designers to fully understand this key component in their system and arrive at sound designs from the start. It takes time to develop the necessary body of information, but that will not be accomplished with the personal evaluation approach.

With roots extending back to the early 1940s, the profession of human factors is over 50 years old at the time this book goes to press. Genuine progress has been made in that time, sometimes, unfortunately, despite apathy or active opposition from representatives of other disciplines on design teams. Still, much remains to be done, and serious deficiencies persist in many areas. For individuals with an interest in the subject, Casey's book *Set Phasers on Stun* (1993), is a fascinating collection of stories of failures in design at the human-machine interface.

Applicability of Human Factors to Accident Reconstruction

Motor vehicles are part of a closed-loop system, the other components of which are a driver and a road. The driver functions not only as a controller, but also as a planner, establishing destination, timetable and route. As a controller the driver utilizes information already in memory, coupled with feedback from the driving environment and from the vehicle itself to make progress toward the ultimate destination and avoid conflicts with other road users and roadway elements.

Collisions represent a system failure, the cause of which may be found in any component or combination of components.

One of the important roles of the reconstructionist is to evaluate available evidence associated with a particular collision to assess responsibility. This requires not only extensive training, but an open mind as concerns contributing factors. There was a time not all that long ago when virtually all collisions were blamed on the driver. Indeed, in that era one would-be comedian opined that the only defective component in the automotive transportation system was the nut that holds the steering wheel. This attitude was pervasive and had unfortunate consequences. In my youth and in the city of my birth I recall decorative lighting standards being installed along one of the important roads. In front of each was placed three concrete posts, the obvious purpose of which was to protect the light poles from errant vehicles. They were probably effective in that respect. They also represented a deadly hazard to the occupants of those vehicles. Attitudes have changed since then. It's hard to imagine someone suggesting, either by word or deed, that a lighting fixture is of greater value than a human life. Today it is generally acknowledged that the design of both vehicles and roadways can cause crashes or worsen their consequences. It is also generally acknowledged that these design flaws should be avoided, in so far as practical. In addition, we've come to accept that even a dumb mistake on the part of a driver does not deserve physical punishment that it is within our power to prevent.

The change in attitude does not mean that driver error can be dismissed as a factor in motor vehicle collisions. The most comprehensive study of causative factors in the United States (Treat, 1980), found that the driver was the sole factor in 57% of collisions and was a contributing factor in 94%. These statistics should be ever borne in mind by any investigator dealing with issues of driver performance. In our litigious society the search for deep pockets sometimes leads to attempts to build an association between a particular collision and an alleged defect that strain credulity to the limit. Certainly, some cases are fairly clear. If, for example, a pedestrian wearing dark clothing manages to get in front of a vehicle going 65 mph in an unlighted area at night he or she will almost certainly become a statistic, and through no fault of the driver. On the other hand, sometimes the question of liability becomes a bit iffy. Suppose a driver crosses a clearly-marked edge line, also at night, and rear ends a truck stopped on the shoulder that had only its running lights showing. Is it reasonable to blame the truck driver? Typically, the argument will be that the truck driver was negligent in not placing the required warning devices and/or activating the flashers. Perhaps so. It may also be reasonable to argue that the driver of the car was probably not paying a whole lot of attention at the time.

Cases fall in two categories, those where there is a solid "yes" or "no" concerning the alleged cause and effect relationship, buttressed by scientific and/or engineering data. The other category is "maybe yes, maybe no." First category cases are often clear enough to all concerned so that the need for experts is minimal. That leaves the other category for the experts to puzzle over most of the time. One of the problems is that collision-producing failures actually attributable to the vehicle and/or road often look like and, through a superficial examination of the facts, will be attributed to the driver(s). A more thorough examination may show otherwise. Because a basic obligation of the expert is to provide accurate and complete information to the client, the reconstructionist must be able to sort these out, difficult as it may be in some cases. Doing so requires extensive knowledge in several subject areas, including those covered in this book.

Human Variability

Psychologists have been quoted as saying that variability is the one constant characteristic in human performance. This is an example of what some people call "academic humor," and may help explain why college professors are sometimes perceived as a dull lot. The subject matter, however, is deadly serious to anyone concerned with the assessment of human performance. People differ from one another on every imaginable performance continuum. There is also a great deal of variability within individuals. My golfing partner, as one example, averages 200 yards off the tee to my 150. Of course, not every drive of his will be 200 yards straight down the fairway, and sometimes my drives will be further or straighter than his. There are great differences in raw ability from one individual to the next, and great differences in how a given individual will respond to an identical situation on different occasions. Human variability is a recognized fact that is, sadly, often ignored by accident investigators when offering opinions concerning the performance of a particular individual.

Variability is manifest in distributions of performance that plot out in characteristic ways. The distribution with which most people are familiar is the normal, bell-shaped curve, known to statisticians as a Gaussian distribution (see Figure 1.1). Many human characteristics produce plots that look more or less like this one. A basic problem is how to describe in fairly simple terms data characterized by scatter like that shown in Figure 1.1. One approach is to employ so-called measures of central tendency. The best known of these is the average ("mean" to statisticians), which is simply the sum of all scores represented in the distribution divided by the number of entries. Another is the median. The median is the 50th percentile point of the distribution, or that point on either side of

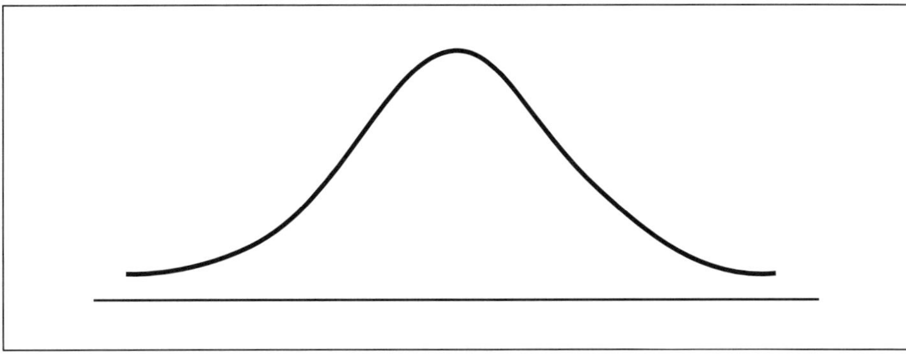

Figure 1.1 *Illustration of a normal (Gaussian) distribution.*

which lie half of the scores in the data set. In a true normal distribution such as that depicted in Figure 1.1 the average and median correspond.

The average and median are useful for quick comparisons of different groups. Suppose, for example, someone ran an experiment comparing a new method of teaching math with the standard method. At the end of the term the students' performance was compared based on the final exam. If you were told that, on average, the students in the new method group scored seven points better than the students in the control group on a test where the maximum possible score was 100 points you might be impressed. On the other hand, if you saw the distributions of scores of the two groups and they looked like the distributions in Figure 1.2 you might be less impressed, since it is obvious that the scores of the great majority of students in the experimental group were within the range of scores of students in the control group. You might be still less impressed if you found that a couple of students in the experimental group aced the test, and their high scores pulled the average up to create the seven-point difference.

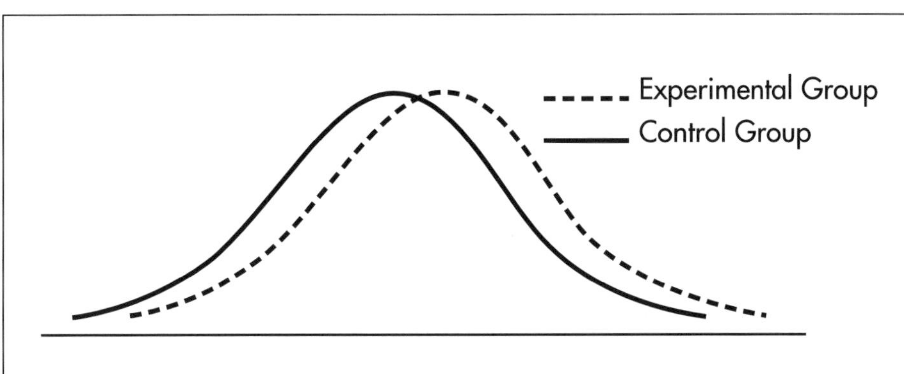

Figure 1.2 *Hypothetical distributions of final test scores for students in experimental and control math classes.*

It is important to remember that the average is but a single point in a distribution. The average tells us nothing about the scatter in performance, the shape of the distribution, or how that distribution relates to other distributions that may be of interest. In addition, the average is of virtually no help in predicting what can be expected from one randomly-selected individual. Consider the two curves in Figure 1.3. The tall, skinny distribution might represent the distribution of scores of professional golfers on a given course, the other that of amateurs on the same course. Knowing the average scores recorded in the past puts you in a much better position to estimate the performance of professionals than it does amateurs because there is far less variability among professionals. Still, it would take a brave (or foolish) person to confidently predict the score of a given pro on a given day just knowing the average.

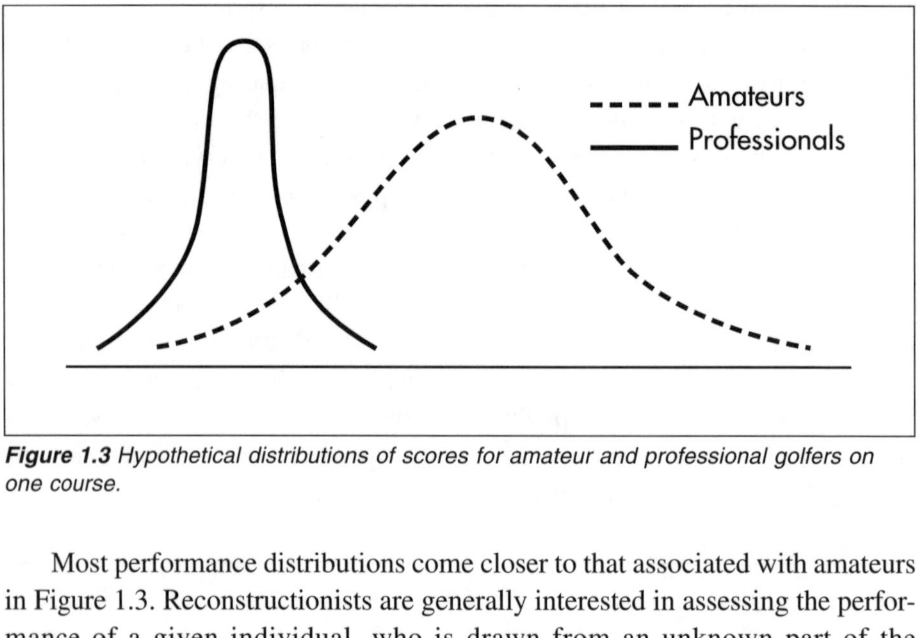

Figure 1.3 *Hypothetical distributions of scores for amateur and professional golfers on one course.*

Most performance distributions come closer to that associated with amateurs in Figure 1.3. Reconstructionists are generally interested in assessing the performance of a given individual, who is drawn from an unknown part of the distribution of interest. In such cases the average is virtually useless as a guide and may be seriously misleading. Because of this difficulty other indices have been developed that better relate individual performance to a distribution of performances. For purposes of the material to be covered in this book the most useful of these is the concept of percentile.

A percentile is a point on a distribution at and below which fall a given percentage of the values of interest. One such point has already been discussed, the median or 50th percentile. Assume for the moment that the distribution of major-league batting averages is as shown in Figure 1.4. A batting average at the

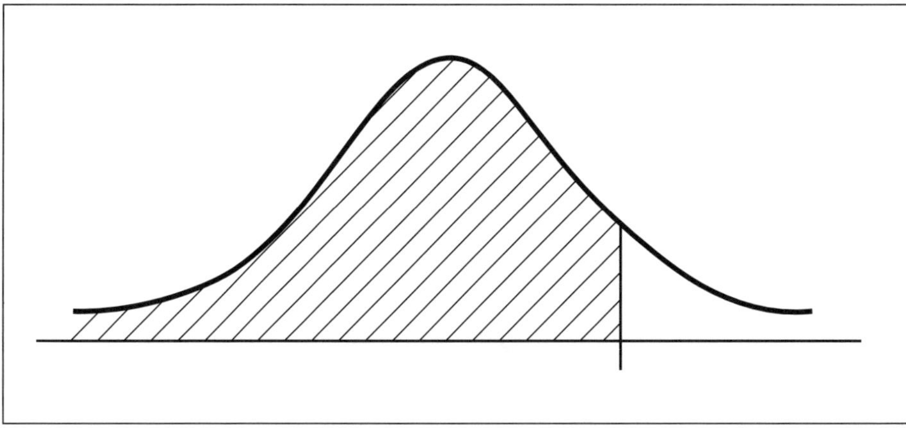

Figure 1.4 *Distribution illustrating the relationship of the 85th percentile to a distribution of performances.*

eighty-fifth percentile (represented by the vertical line to the right of the figure) would be equal to or better than 85% of the other batting averages (represented by the darkened area in the figure). Percentiles can often provide intuitive understandability to individuals who have little or no grasp of the subject matter. Tell a baseball illiterate that a given player has a lifetime batting average of, say .295 and they will likely say "that's nice," but may walk away thinking that .295 doesn't sound all that great. Tell them instead that his lifetime batting average puts him at the 90th percentile of all major leaguers and a context has been established that makes the player's ability immediately obvious.

Percentiles also facilitate inter-group comparisons, permitting descriptions of generalized differences, but also indications of the degree to which relevant distributions overlap. For example, Salthouse and Somberg (1982), carried out a study comparing the ability of older and younger subjects on a time-accuracy task. The 85th percentile performance level of the younger subjects was 0.325 second. That is, 85% of the younger subjects responded correctly in 0.325 second or less. The 85th percentile performance level for the older subjects was 0.405 second. Is this just another illustration of the so-called geezer gap? In a sense it is. It should be noted, however, that 74% of the older subjects responded correctly within 0.325 second. Clearly, there is a very great overlap in the young-old performance distributions on this task. Comparisons like these provide much better information about individual and group performance relative to defined populations than does the average.

An individual interested in offering an opinion concerning the reasonableness of a person's behavior must compare what is known of that person's behavior with the range of "reasonable" behavior for the dimension of concern. For example, an investigation may determine that a particular driver took X seconds to respond to a given situation. This performance is then compared to the range of "reasonable" times for that situation. This is illustrated in Figure 1.5, where the range of reasonable performance is represented by the bell curve. So long as the subject individual's performance falls within the continuum defined as "reasonable" then their performance was reasonable.

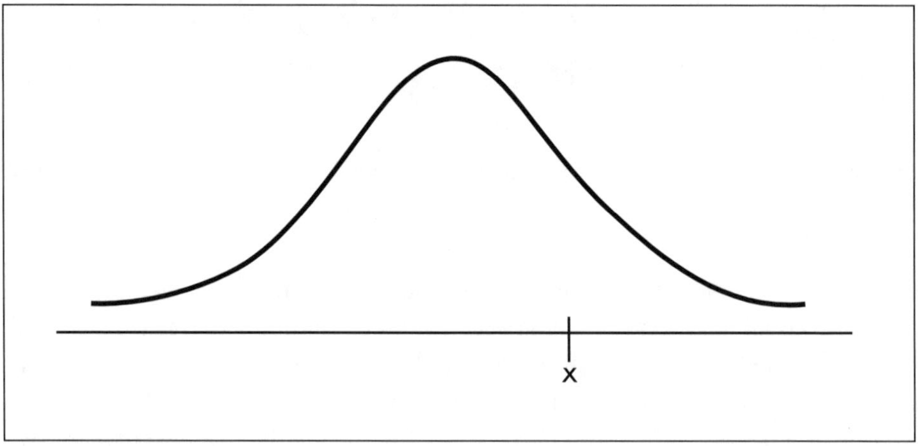

Figure 1.5 *Illustration of the location of one individual's performance relative to the range of "reasonable" performances.*

Rarely would the expert actually work with a performance continuum as shown in Figure 1.5. Instead, typically, the performance of the subject individual is compared with a single percentile value. For example, research may indicate that the 95th percentile value for perception-response in a given situation is Y. So long as the perception-response time for the individual is no greater than Y it is considered reasonable. Why the 95th percentile? Why not choose the 100th percentile? As a practical matter, covering all scores in a distribution greatly increases the range and will result in the inclusion of some that no one is likely to consider "reasonable." Consider perception-response time as an illustration. Taking all possible recorded times will result in the inclusion of some that are very long, due to the individual being distracted or inattentive, and some of infinite length, where the individual was literally asleep at the switch. The higher percentile cut offs are arbitrary, admittedly, but necessary. By the same token, the fact that a given individual's performance is only just beyond what has been set as the statistical limit for "reasonable" does not automatically provide justification for branding it as unreasonable. Good judgment is required of the expert when tinkering around the limits of available data.

The choice of a higher percentile cut off is also dependent on conventional practices in different fields. In traffic engineering the use of the 85th percentile is common. In other areas the 90th and 95th percentiles are used. Much depends on the quality of the data and the cost of including more extreme values in design. It's also a question of how much data to include that can still be considered "reasonable." Both the 85th and 95th percentile will be referred to in describing test results in this book. Where appropriate data are available the 95th percentile will be the basic reference. In part this is convention, in part this is because experience suggests that it is a realistic cut off.

One final bit of statistical jargon will be helpful, the standard deviation. Researchers will often report their results in terms of averages and standard deviations. Mathematically the standard deviation is the root-mean square of the deviations from the average. The general equation is:

$$\text{sd} = \sqrt{\frac{\Sigma(x^2)}{n}} \qquad 1.1$$

Where:

x = deviations from the average
n = total number of items

The standard deviation is a measure of scatter in a distribution. One reason it is valuable is because of its relationship to percentiles in a normal distribution. Table 1.1 shows the the relationship between the standard deviation and area under the normal curve. Each cell entry represents the percentage of area under the normal curve accounted for on one side of the average. For example, 1.0 standard deviation includes about 34% of the population either above or below

Table 1.1 Areas of the Normal Curve

Decimals	Whole Numbers			
	0	1	2	3
0.0	.0000	.3413	.4773	.4986
0.1	.0398	.3643	.4821	.4990
0.2	.0793	.3849	.4861	.4993
0.3	.1179	.4032	.4893	.4995
0.4	.1554	.4192	.4918	.4997
0.5	.1915	.4332	.4938	.4998
0.6	.2257	.4452	.4953	.4998
0.7	.2580	.4554	.4965	.4999
0.8	.2881	.4641	.4974	.4999
0.9	.3159	.4713	.4981	.4999

Adapted from: Arkinh and Colton, (1939). *An Outline of Statistical Methods* (4th Edition), New York, Barnes and Noble.

the average. Therefore, ± one standard deviation includes about 68% of the population. Suppose you were reviewing the results of a study and noted that the average score for some condition was 50, with a standard deviation of 10. From Table 1.1 you would determine that ± two standard deviations includes 95% of the population; thus 95% of the scores fell between 30 and 70. Other helpful statistics can be calculated from the information in Table 1.1. Suppose you were told that your score on a given test was 1.5 standard deviations above the average. Looking at Table 1.1 tells you that 1.5 standard deviations includes 43% of the population. Since your score is above average you add the 50% below the average and determine that your score was at the 93rd percentile.

Not all variables plot out as normal distributions. This commonly happens if there is a limit at one end or the other of the continuum being considered. Income is one such example. There is a minimum income (0 dollars) but no maximum. The plot of income looks approximately like Figure 1.6, with most people receiving modest incomes and a relatively few very high incomes. The result is known as a skewed distribution. The fact that the tail of the distribution

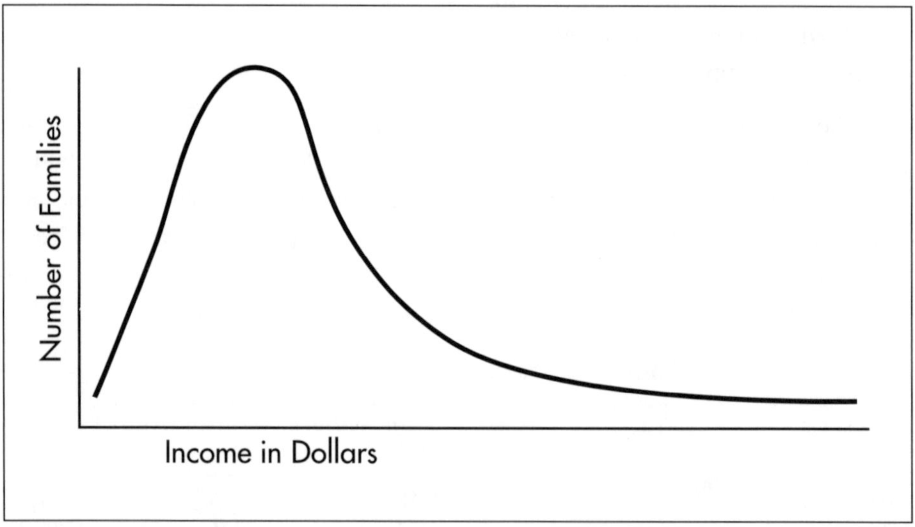

Figure 1.6 *Approximation of the distribution of family income in the United States, illustrating a positively-skewed distribution.*

in this case is pointed toward high values leads to it being described as positively skewed. Perception-response time also produces a positively-skewed distribution because there is a limit to how fast people can respond, but no limit to how slowly they can respond. This effect will be observed in data presented in Chapter 9.

The average and median part company in a skewed distribution. The median is still the 50th percentile. The average, however, is much affected by the extreme values in a distribution and becomes less useful as a measure of central tendency as the degree of skewness increases. Based on 1990 census data for example, average annual household income in Michigan (adjusted to 1993 dollars) was $42,700, while the median was $33,300, a difference of more than $9,000.

In sum, an investigator must be aware that humans are highly variable in their performance on virtually any task. Judgments concerning the performance of a given individual must be based on an understanding of the range of reasonable performance for the matter at hand. The issue is not how the individual compares to some "average" or "representative" norm, but whether their performance falls within the range associated with representative individuals performing the task in question.

Chapter Overview

This chapter has provided an introduction to the area of human factors and sought to indicate how that discipline can be of benefit in accident reconstruction. In addition the chapter discussed the issue of variability in human performance, which will apply to both of the major topics to be covered in this book. The following are the principal points covered:

- Human factors is a scientific discipline concerned with the interrelationship of humans and devices of all kinds, as well as the operating environment of those devices.
- The primary role of the human factors specialist is to develop, disseminate and apply information concerning human performance capability. This information can be used in the design of all types of devices with which humans must interact. The intent is to maximize system output as well as the safety and comfort of those humans who can be affected by the system.
- Human factors input can supply valuable scientific information to accident reconstruction whenever issues of driver performance are being considered.
- There is great variability from person to person on virtually any performance continuum. There is also often great variability in performance within a given individual from one occasion to the next. The reconstructionist cannot judge a particular individual's

performance based on some presumed "average," but rather on the entire range of reasonable performance of the dimension being considered.

References

Casey, S. (1993). *Set Phasers on Stun.* Santa Barbara, California. Aegean Publishing Company.

Salthouse, T. A. and Somberg, B. L. (1982). Time-Accuracy Relationships in Young and Old Adults. *Journal of Gerontology, 37*(3), 349-353.

Treat, J. R. (1980). A Study of Precrash Factors Involved in Traffic Accidents. Ann Arbor, Michigan. *The HSRI Research Review.* May-August.

Section I
Vision and Perception

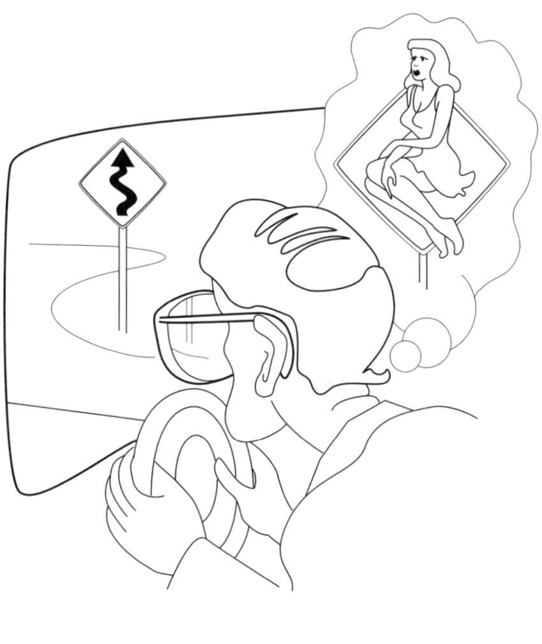

Chapter 2

The Fundamentals of Vision in Driving

Introduction

Vision is undoubtedly the main source of information necessary to the operation of an automobile. An estimate one commonly finds in the literature is that 90% of essential driving-related information is acquired visually. This may overstate the case, because other senses are important as well. Steering and the control of speed and braking would be difficult if not impossible without the kinesthetic senses, whose receptors are located in the muscles and joints of the body. They provide the inputs so that we know how far the steering wheel has been turned without looking at it, how much force is being exerted on the brake pedal, and they allow us to make fine adjustments in the position of the accelerator. The difference is that we do not have the conscious awareness of kinesthesis that we do of vision. Still, no one will question that vision plays a critical role both in moment-to-moment vehicle control operations and in acquiring information necessary for future actions.

Vision is used to acquire basic information such as where the road is going, one's position on the road, and the location and actions of other vehicles. It is the sense of choice for signals that originate from vehicles (e.g., brake application, turn signals) and the signs and signals placed by traffic engineers. Thus, an understanding of the fundamentals of vision is important to someone seeking to assess causation in traffic crashes.

This chapter will begin with some definitions that will prove helpful throughout the book. It will then cover two topics. The first is the fundamentals of how the visual system works, which is concerned with the structure of the eye and certain related matters. Vision, of course, is a means for humans to acquire information. How humans process information is probably just as important as how it is acquired in the first place, and this will be the second topic covered.

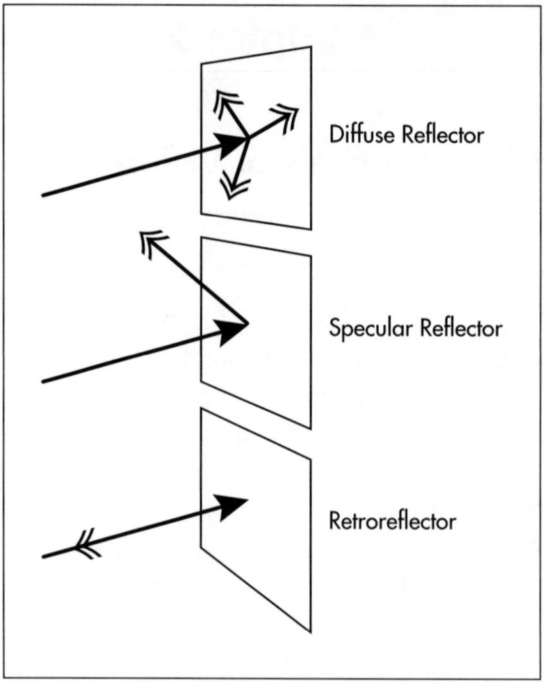

Figure 2.1 *Schematic illustrations of diffuse, specular, and retroreflective surfaces.*

Definitions

This and other chapters in the book will make occasional reference to certain terms that are basic to vision and visibility. Unnecessary complexity will be avoided so far as possible, but it would be helpful to the reader to have a grasp of the meaning of this terminology.

Light-Reflecting Surfaces

Of the light reaching any surface, some is absorbed and some is reflected. Clearly, only the latter is useful in making the object visible. The behavior of light when it reaches an object and the consequent appearance of that object to an observer depends to a considerable extent on the type of surface the object has. Classified by how they reflect light, there are three types of surfaces with which this book will be concerned, diffuse, specular and retroreflective. These are illustrated in Figure 2.1 and described below.

Diffuse Reflectors

A diffuse reflector is characterized by a rough texture that reflects light more or less equally in many directions. As a consequence, even though the light source might be highly directional (e.g., the headlights on a car) the object will appear to have the same brightness when viewed from many different angles. Most objects of concern to the accident investigator are diffuse reflectors, including the clothing worn by pedestrians and the roadway surface. The reflectivity of a diffuse surface is typically given as the percentage of the total light reaching the surface that is reflected. For example, high-quality white writing paper reflects 80-90% of the light reaching it. The reflectivity of dark clothing worn by a pedestrian might be only 3-5%.

Specular Reflectors

As contrasted with a diffuse reflector, a specular reflector has a microscopically smooth surface. A common example is a mirror. Light encountering a specular reflector is reflected at an angle equal and opposite to the angle at which it entered. Because of this characteristic, an object having a specular surface may not be visible unless it is oriented in such a way that light is reflected toward the eyes of the observer. As noted above, a road surface is a diffuse reflector. Rainfall can fill in the voids, however, making the surface a specular reflector. This is why the appearance of the road surface can change so dramatically in the rain. To illustrate, Figure 2.2 shows two photographs of the same street, the top photograph taken during dry weather, the bottom photograph during rainfall. The effects of rainfall on pavement reflectivity will be discussed in some detail in Chapters 4 and 5.

Retroreflectors

A retroreflector is a surface having unique and very useful properties. Its optical characteristics are a bit like a specular reflector, but with a critical difference. Light encountering a retroreflector is reflected back toward the source with minimal scatter. As a result, assuming that the observer's eye is relatively close to the light source, a retroreflector appears much brighter than does a diffuse reflector under identical conditions. Retroreflectors occur in nature, as in the eyes of some animals. Indeed, some of the first retroreflectors used in highway applications were called cats-eye reflectors. Retroreflectors are widely used to make signs visible and legible at night. They are also used as vehicle markers and road delineators. Because of their widespread use in roadway and vehicle applications the visibility of such devices may become an issue in a case under investigation. Therefore, it would be helpful to understand some of the basic characteristics of retroreflectors.

There are a number of measures that are used in describing the performance of retroreflectors, but for the purposes of the discussion in this book, only two are of interest. These are illustrated in Figure 2.3. One is the entrance angle, which is formed between the surface of the retroreflector and the entering beam of light. The other is the observation angle, which, for any distance between the light

Figure 2.2 *Two photographs showing the effect of rainfall on the reflective characteristics of a road surface.*

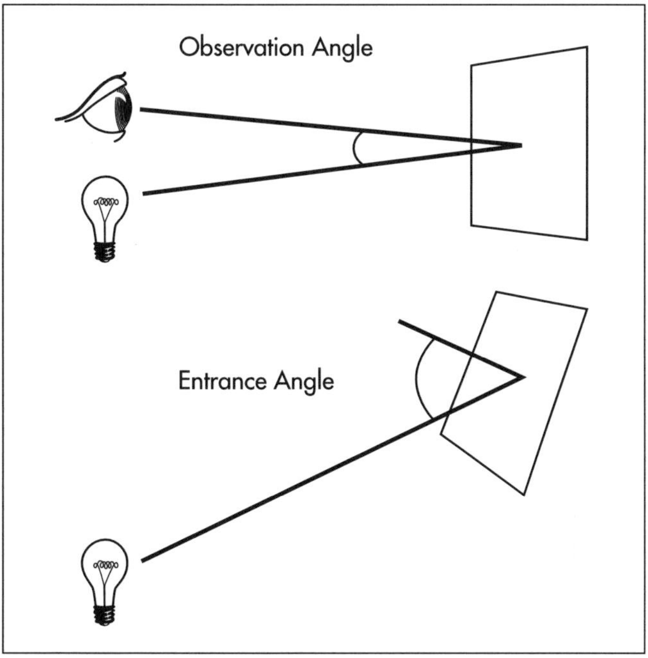

Figure 2.3 *Illustration of entrance and observation angles as applied to retroreflectors.*

source and retroreflector, is determined by the separation between the light source and receptor (e.g., the eye of the observer).

The performance of a retroreflector is maximum when the entrance angle is close to 0° (i.e., the light beam is perpendicular to the retroreflector's surface). Performance is reduced as the entrance angle is increased. The shape of this function depends on the optical characteristics of the material, and there are substantial differences from one material to another. To illustrate, taking a material commonly used in signing applications, if its measured brightness at an entrance angle of -4° is taken as 100%, its measured brightness at an entrance angle of 30° is 60-70% (assuming an observation angle of 0.2°), and at an entrance angle of 45° its measured brightness would be only about 20-30%. (A small negative entrance angle, typically -4°, is used rather than 0° to avoid specular reflections from the surface of the retroreflector.)

The performance of a retroreflector is very sensitive to changes in observation angle. For the same product used as an example in the preceding paragraph, if measured brightness at 0.2° is taken as 100% (assuming an entrance angle of -4°), its measured brightness at 0.33° is about 75%, its measured brightness at 0.5° is about 40%, and its measured brightness at 1.0° is about 10%. To put this in perspective, the observation angle (averaged for both headlamps) for the driver of a typical automobile, with the target close to the edge of the road, would be about 0.2° at a distance of about 700 feet. On large trucks, due to the greater vertical separation distance between the driver's eyes and the headlamps, the observation angle at any given distance is typically about twice as large as on passenger cars. Thus, other factors being equal, retroreflectors appear less bright to the driver of a truck than they do to the driver of a car.

Miscellaneous Visibility-Enhancing Materials

Fluorescent Materials

Fluorescent materials have the capability of converting electromagnetic energy in the near infra red to visible wavelengths. As a result they appear much brighter than would a surface of the same color that was not fluorescent. The fluorescent characteristic is activated by ultra violet wavelengths. Since there is normally no ultra violet around in the hours of darkness, the fluorescent characteristic confers no benefit to visibility at night.

Fluorescent materials are widely used where maximum daytime visibility is sought. They appear in the vests worn by construction workers, certain signs, and the slow-moving vehicle symbol commonly attached to vehicles such as farm equipment. One problem with fluorescent materials is that they have a relatively short life expectancy (about two years) when under continuous exposure to the elements. This is of concern for applications such as the slow-moving vehicle symbol sign. Experience suggests that users install them on equipment because it is required and typically pay no further attention. The benefits from use of fluorescent materials are lost long before the equipment must be replaced.

Luminous Materials

Certain materials have the ability to absorb electromagnetic energy and emit light in visible wavelengths after the energy source has been removed. These are commonly referred to as luminous materials. They have been used for a variety of applications for a number of years, including garments designed to enhance nighttime visibility. Unlike retroreflectors, luminous sources do not require that a light source be directed toward them to make them appear bright.

There are two major problems with luminous materials for application in roadway settings. One is that their output is fairly weak. Someone wearing a garment with luminous components would probably be visible in a totally dark setting. Add in some clutter or glare and the visibility-enhancing capability of these sources becomes questionable. The other problem is that the materials emit visible light for only a fairly short time. If a luminous source was left out in the sun all day, for example, then taken into a dark room, it would look quite bright at first, then begin to fade. After 30-60 minutes there would be essentially nothing left. For these reasons luminous materials are not practical for use in roadway settings.

Photometry

For a variety of applications it is very useful to be able to measure light. The measurement of light, known as photometry, has developed into a very complex specialty with its own terminology. Fortunately, the information in this book does not require a high level of sophistication on the part of the reader as concerns the units of light measurement. An understanding of certain key terms will suffice nicely.

What we call "light" is electromagnetic energy. Electromagnetic energy is emitted by many sources and spans a very broad spectrum as defined by wavelength (see Figure 2.4). At one end are cosmic rays having wavelengths of 10^{-15} meter, at the other is the output of AC circuits having wavelengths of many kilometers. We cook with electromagnetic energy (microwaves), use them in medicine (X rays), and they form a vital part of our communications via radio

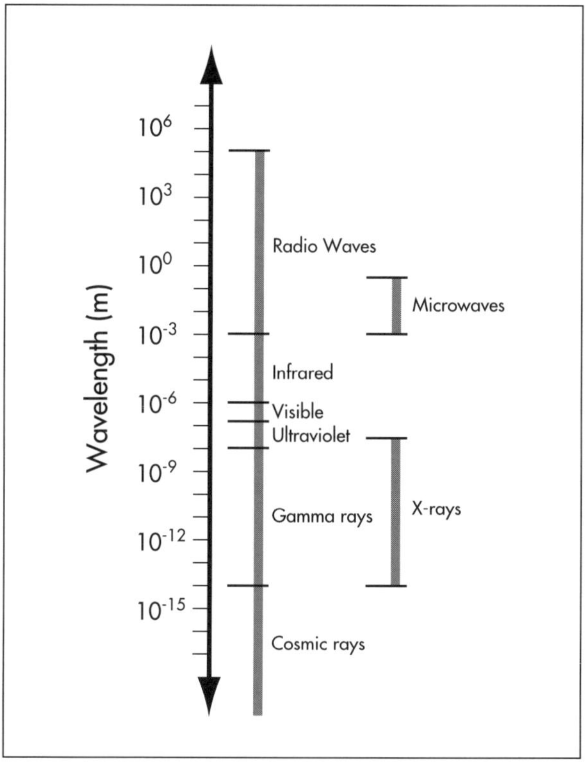

Figure 2.4 *The electromagnetic spectrum.*

and television. Perhaps the most vital aspect of electromagnetic energy to humans comes from the fact that our eyes respond to it at certain wavelengths, roughly from 400 to 700 nanometers (a nanometer, nm, is one billionth, 10^{-9}, of a meter). The eye is not equally sensitive to all portions of the visible portion of the spectrum. Peak sensitivity depends on the level of illumination. It is about 550 nm at high levels and about 500 nm at low levels. This change in sensitivity to wavelength as a function of the level of illumination is known as the Purkinje shift. It can be noticed during the twilight period when green grass seems to become brighter than red flowers.

There are three categories of light measurement that are most important. These are:

1. source output (luminous intensity)
2. the amount of light reaching a surface (illuminance)
3. the amount of light reflected from a surface (luminance)

Luminous Intensity

In describing the units of luminous intensity it is easiest to start by imagining a point light source at the center of a sphere having a radius of r = 1. Also, assume that the source radiates equally in all directions, providing uniform illuminance at all points on the surface of the sphere. Luminous intensity is the density of luminous flux (time rate of flow of light) in a given unit solid angle. A unit solid angle is a cone-shaped space extending outward from the center of the sphere whose area on the surface of the sphere is equal to the radius. The unit solid angle is also called the steradian.

The unit used to refer to total light output from a source is the lumen (lm). A lumen is the total light output from a given source per unit time (per second). It is a measure of flux (F), which is defined as the time rate of flow of visually evaluated energy. Since there are 4π steradians contained within a sphere, a uniformly radiating source has an intensity equal to F/4π.

Generally, we are interested in the light emitted in a particular direction. Here the basic measure is lumens per unit solid angle in that direction. The alternative unit, and the one that will generally be employed in this book, is candela (cd). A source of one candela will produce one lumen of luminous flux per steradian. Therefore, a one candela source will produce 4π (12.57) lumens.

Originally the candela unit was based on the output of a candle of specific composition, burned under carefully controlled conditions. The need for greater precision led to a different standard, based on a blackbody radiator operated at a specific temperature. What was undoubtedly a gain in scientific accuracy led to a loss in intuitive understandability. Still, one can get a rough idea of a candela from the output of a common candle.

Illuminance

Illuminance is the density of luminous flux incident on a surface. Probably the most familiar measure is foot candles (ft-c), which is lumens per square foot. The metric equivalent is lumens per square meter, or lux. One foot candle equals 10.76 lux.

A source of one candela will provide one foot candle of illuminance at a distance of one foot. Illuminance decreases as the square of the distance from the source. This is known as the distance-squared law, which may be written as:

$$I = \frac{c}{d^2} \qquad 2.1$$

Where:

I = illuminance in foot candles
c = source output in candelas
d = distance from source to surface in feet

For example, a source that yields 1 foot candle at distance X will yield 1/4 foot candle at distance 2X and 1/16 foot candle at distance 4X.

Luminance

Light reflected from a surface yields the sensation of brightness. The photometric term is luminance. Brightness is a subjective impression that varies depending on factors such as the background of the object and the level of dark adaptation. Luminance is measured in English units as foot-Lamberts (ft-L) and in metric units as candelas per meter squared (cd/m^2). A surface that reflected all the light reaching it and reflected light uniformly in all directions, would have a luminance of one ft-L when the illuminance was one ft-c. One ft-L equals 3.425 cd/m^2.

Table 2.1 is a summary of the photometric concepts and terms just discussed.

Table 2.1 Summary of Photometric Terms

Condition	Photometric Term	Measures
Light from a source	Luminous intensity	Candela (cd) Lumens (lm)
Light reaching a surface	Illuminance	Foot candles (ft-c) Lux
Light reflected from a surface	Luminance	Foot Lamberts (ft-L) Candelas per meter squared (cd/m^2)

Measurement of Visual Performance

In the section to follow frequent reference will be made to visual acuity. It will be helpful for the reader to understand the concept. Static acuity is defined simply as a measure of the ability to distinguish fine detail in a stationary target. There are four distinct types of visual acuity, each of which relates to the ability to discriminate a different aspect of detail. These are described as follows, with typical tests being illustrated in Figure 2.5.

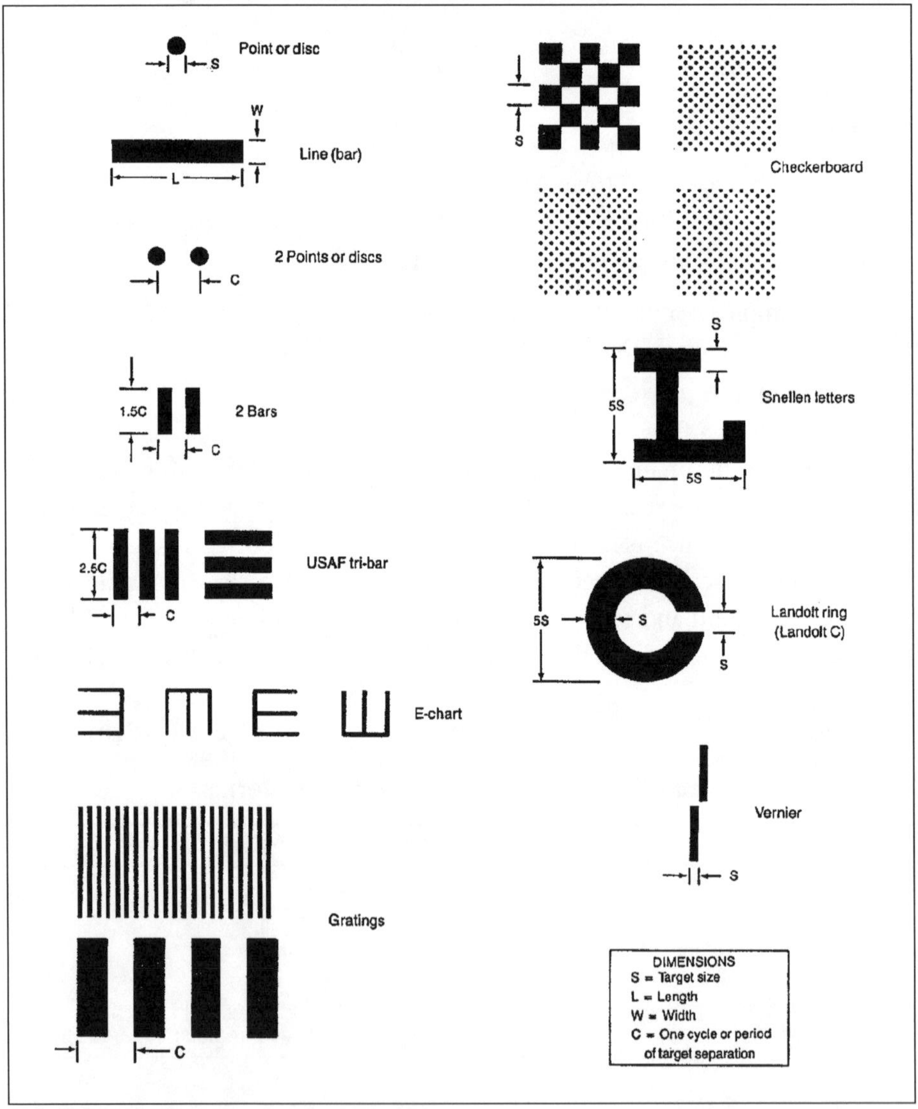

Figure 2.5 *Targets used in measuring various types of visual acuity. Reproduced with Permission from: Farrell, R.J. and Booth, J.M. (1975)* Design Handbook for Imagery Interpretation Equipment. *Document D180-19063-1.*

1. Minimum visibility, which is the ability to detect a point source of light such as a star.
2. Minimum perceptibility, which is the ability to detect small objects against a homogeneous background. Examples are the small black dot, disc or bar on a white background or white letters on a dark background.
3. Minimum separability, which is the ability to see that two or more objects very close together are separate. Examples are two or more parallel bars, sine-wave gratings, two discs, and checkerboards.
4. Minimum distinguishability, which is the ability to distinguish discontinuities or irregularities in object contours. An example is vernier acuity.

Most acuity tests (the exception being minimum visibility) are based on the size of the smallest pattern detail that can be discriminated, measured in minutes of arc of visual angle subtended at the eye. "Normal" visual acuity is assumed to be the ability to resolve a target detail of one minute of arc at 20 feet. A person who can just resolve one minute of detail on a test chart at a distance of 20 feet or 6 meters is said to have an acuity of 20/20 (6/6 in metric notation). A score of 20/40 (6/12 in metric notation), which is a typical minimum level of acuity for obtaining a driver's license, means that the person can barely read at 20 feet what someone with 20/20 acuity could read at 40 feet. As a practical matter it also means they can read highway signs at about half the distance of someone with 20/20 acuity. Occasionally one will hear 20/20 acuity referred to as perfect vision. It's not. There are many people, especially among the younger population whose acuity measures much better than 20/20.

There are a number of other measures of visual performance, many of which do not correlate highly with static acuity, but may be meaningful in the driving context. Some of those that are of interest in night driving are:

- Low-luminance acuity (acuity measured under conditions of relatively low illumination).
- Low-contrast acuity (acuity measured using a gray on white symbol rather than black on white).
- Glare susceptibility (acuity or target detection capability measured in the presence of glare).
- Glare recovery (how long it takes to recover from a glare exposure).
- Low-contrast target detection threshold (ability to detect a target whose luminance is only slightly different from its background).

There has been some interest in adding tests like these to the standard driver's license screening. At present, however, measures such as those listed are rarely taken, except for experimental purposes.

Structure and Performance of the Eye

Structure

Structurally, the eye can be compared to a simple camera. Except for a shutter, both have the same essential elements. Each has a lens system to focus an image on the light-sensitive layer. Each has a means for adjusting focus to accommodate to objects both near and far away. Each also can to some extent control the amount of light allowed to enter as a means for adjusting to different lighting conditions. Finally, the sensitivity of the light-sensitive layer can be changed as a further means of adjusting to different lighting conditions.

Figure 2.6 is a diagram of the eye, with some of the principal parts labeled. A description of each follows:

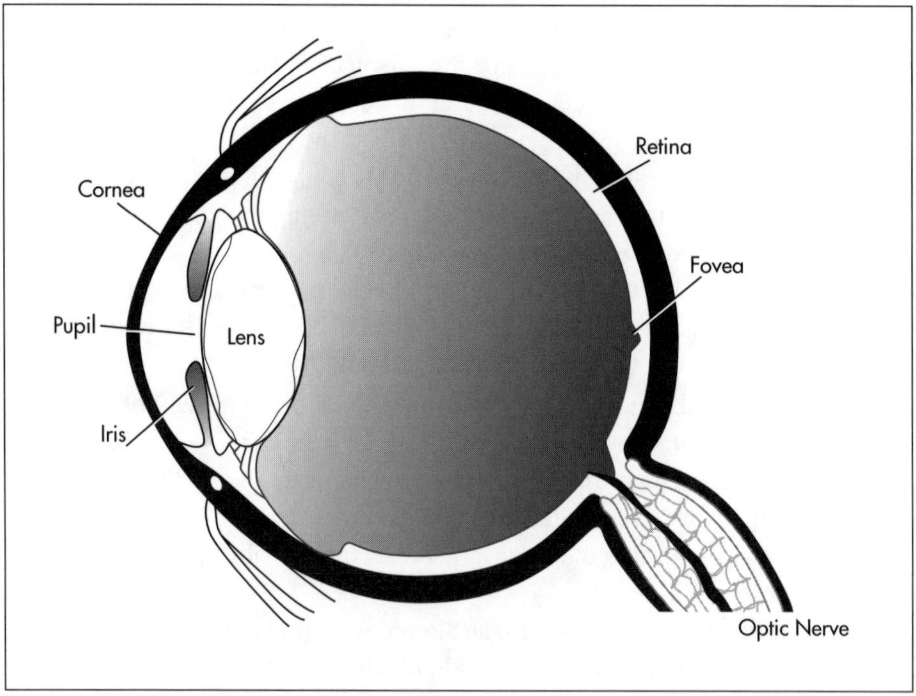

Figure 2.6 *Diagram of the human eye.*

The cornea is the transparent front surface of the eye through which light enters. The cornea and the lens work together to bring incoming light to a focus on the retina. The cornea actually does the bulk of the work of refracting (bending) the light. The lens helps in this job, but its most important function is to accommodate to objects at different distances.

As shown in Figure 2.7, light rays from a distant object are essentially parallel, while those from a nearby object are diverging slightly. If the optical system is set for distant objects the image of a nearby object will not be brought to a focus on the light-sensitive layer and will be seen as blurred. In a camera this effect is compensated for by moving the lens further from the film plane. In the eye it is accomplished by changing the refracting power of the lens. This is possible because the lens is flexible. It is suspended in a network of muscles that can cause it to become fatter or thinner, thus altering its focal length. When focusing on a distant object the lens is relatively flat, with minimal refracting power. When focusing on a nearby object, however, the lens becomes more spherical, increasing its refracting power as an aid in bringing the diverging rays of light to a sharp focus.

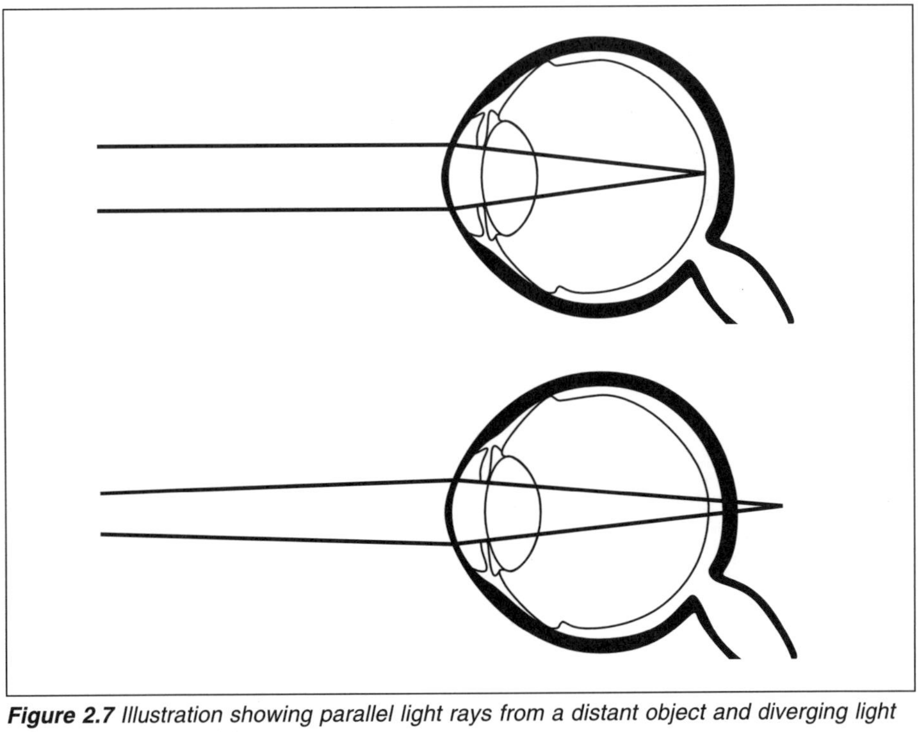

Figure 2.7 *Illustration showing parallel light rays from a distant object and diverging light rays from a nearby object.*

The lens continues to add layers of cells throughout life. Since it cannot grow larger it becomes more dense and less flexible instead. As a consequence the eye gradually loses its ability to focus up close, a condition called presbyopia. As a result, the near point (the shortest distance from the eye at which sharp focus can be achieved) moves further and further away. For many people this condition leads to an eventual need for reading glasses or bifocals, typically in the 40s or early 50s. Presbyopia can be an annoyance for older drivers, who often find that the dash panel display is out of focus for both the near and far portions of their eyeglasses. It is probably not a safety factor, however. The lens also becomes somewhat yellow with age, reducing the level of illumination reaching the retina, particularly from the blue end of the spectrum.

The iris is the colored portion of the eye. It is a ring of muscle that functions to control the size of the opening in front of the lens (the pupil), regulating the amount of light that can enter. It is one of two mechanisms (the other is the ability of the receptor cells in the retina to adjust their sensitivity) that allow the eye to function (adapt) through a very broad range of lighting conditions. In the eye of a young adult the pupil can open to a maximum diameter of about 7.5 mm in darkness and constrict to as little as 2.5 mm in bright light. This yields about a nine-fold range of intensity control. This is, however, less than 10% of the range of light levels at which the eye can function. Thus, the iris plays a minor role in adaptation. Its main role may be to provide a quick response capability to sudden changes in light levels, since retinal adaptation is relatively slow.

The iris also becomes less flexible with age, with the result that the maximum pupil diameter is gradually reduced. The maximum opening of the pupil goes from a diameter of about 7.5 mm at age 20 to about 4.8 mm at age 85 (Birren, et al., 1950). Under low-luminance conditions this means that about 2-1/2 times more light is getting by the iris in a 20 year old eye, compared to an 85 year old eye. This condition, called senile myosis, is a significant factor in the loss of visual capability at night associated with aging.

The retina covers about two-thirds of the interior of the eye and contains the light-sensitive cells. At its center there is a slight depression called the fovea. It is upon the fovea that we cause to be imaged that which we are trying to see as well as possible. The portion of the retina outside of the fovea is referred to simply as the periphery. The light-sensitive cells are connected to nerves, which are gathered together and depart the eye in the optic nerve. There are no receptor cells at the exit point of the optic nerve, hence no vision. This is commonly referred to as the "blind spot." The blind spot in each eye is in a different part of the visual field, so there is coverage. Even with one eye, however, there is no awareness of the blind spot because the brain fills in the missing information. A special test is necessary to appreciate the existence of the blind spot. One such test is shown below. Hold the page about a foot from your eyes. Close one eye and look at the opposite X (left X for the right eye and vice versa). Move the page closer or further away until the peripheral X disappears. It will then be imaged on the blind spot.

X **X**

There are two types of receptor cells, rods and cones. These receptors differ functionally as well as in their distribution throughout the retina. Table 2.2 is a summary of the most important differences between the rods and cones.

Table 2.2: Principal Differences Between Rods and Cones

Cones	Rods
Wavelength sensitive (provide color vision).	Not wavelength sensitive (no color vision).
Functional at higher light levels.	Functional at lower light levels.
Only receptor in fovea. Also found in rest of retina, except for extreme periphery.	Not found in fovea. Distributed throughout rest of the retina.
Relatively few interconnections.	Numerous interconnections.

The Functioning of the Visual System at Different Levels of Illumination

The human eye is capable of responding to illumination through a range of ten to eleven log units. This is illustrated in Figure 2.8 from Grether and Baker (1972). The adjustments the visual system makes to changes in illumination are referred to as adaptation. Reducing illumination levels results in dark adaptation, increasing illumination results in light adaptation. In Figure 2.8 adaptation luminance is shown in foot Lamberts on a logarithmic scale. As noted in Table 2.2, only the cones function at high luminance levels. This is referred to as photopic vision. As light levels decrease the cones become more sensitive. About four log units below the upper level of visual tolerance, at a luminance level of approximately two foot Lamberts, the rods begin to function together with the cones. The range of luminance levels at which rods and cones are both functioning is referred to as mesopic vision. Rods and cones continue to function together as luminance is decreased about another 3.5 log units. Finally, at a level approximating that of average earth viewed in a full moon, the cones cease to function. Rod vision alone is called scotopic vision.

Where is someone adapted while driving at night? The only data currently available are those of Olson, et al. (1990). In this test adaptation levels were measured on a dark, rural road under three conditions, i.e., with no illumination,

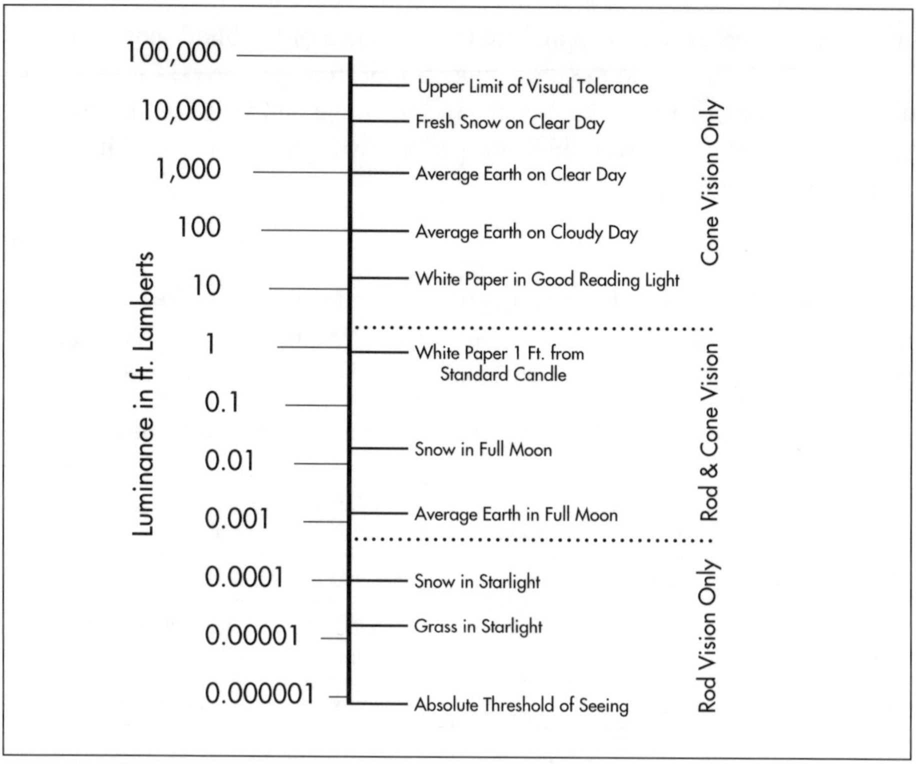

Figure 2.8 *Range of luminance values to which the eye responds.*

low beams only, and high beams. The adaptation levels were 0.005 ft-L with no illumination, 0.3 ft-L using low beams, and 1.7 ft-L with high beams. Comparing these results with the ranges shown in Figure 2.8 show adaptation without lighting was at the low end of the mesopic zone at the time the test was carried out. Turning on the low beam headlights altered adaptation to a luminance level approximately one hundred times higher, at the upper end of the mesopic zone. Changing to the high beams pushed adaptation to photopic levels.

There are some practical lessons in the adaptation level study. These can be summarized as follows:

- Contrary to what some people seem to think, night driving is not done using exclusively rod vision. Not even close. Cones, and the fovea, are still active.
- At least in areas where there is little or no artificial illumination, the adaptation level for the driver of a car at night is probably much higher than it would be for someone not in a car. This means that the eyes of someone outside the car are more sensitive, and they are better able to see things not within the beam of the car's headlamps. Therefore,

observations about what could be seen made by someone on foot at the scene are inherently suspect. Visibility estimates relating to a driver at night must be made from inside a vehicle, with the headlights on, to ensure a proper adaptation level.

- Comparing the low-beam adaptation level to that associated with moonlight in Figure 2.8 makes it clear that the driver's eyes are adapted to too high a level for moonlight to be of much use. This does not rule out moonlight as an aid in revealing high-contrast objects at a distance, something a prudent investigator should check. The optimism sometimes seen regarding moonlight as an aid to drivers is generally misplaced.

The process of dark adaptation takes time. How much time depends on a number of variables, but is primarily determined by the level to which the eye is originally adapted and the new level to which it must adapt. For example, if an individual walks from bright sunlight into a photographic darkroom, a half hour or more may be required to reach maximum sensitivity. Reversing the process (light adaptation) is typically more rapid than dark adaptation through the same range of luminance values. In an extreme case such as that described above full light adaptation may require ten minutes.

In typical driving situations the changes to which a driver must adapt are much less drastic than those described above. As a consequence, adaptation times are much shorter. Adaptation problems are sometimes experienced in situations such as driving from bright sunlight into a tunnel or from a brightly lighted commercial area into an adjacent unlighted area. However, the most common stimulus that can alter driver dark adaptation is the headlights of oncoming cars. From the driver's point of view it can be difficult to separate the unpleasantness and loss of visibility associated with headlight glare from its after effects. Sometimes a driver can see so much better after the glaring vehicle has passed that the lesser effect of adaptation change goes unnoticed. Ottander (1963) measured readaptation time after moderate levels of headlamp glare and found it to be a maximum of two seconds. Ottander used European style headlamps, which are less glaring than those used in the US. Mortimer and Olson (1974) measured visibility to various targets in two-car meeting situations using US-style low-beam headlamps. Based on the time it took subjects to record maximum visibility distances after passing the other car, readaptation time was about ten seconds. Readaptation time is increased by more severe conditions, such as higher levels of glare and longer exposure. Readaptation time is longer for older drivers than for younger drivers.

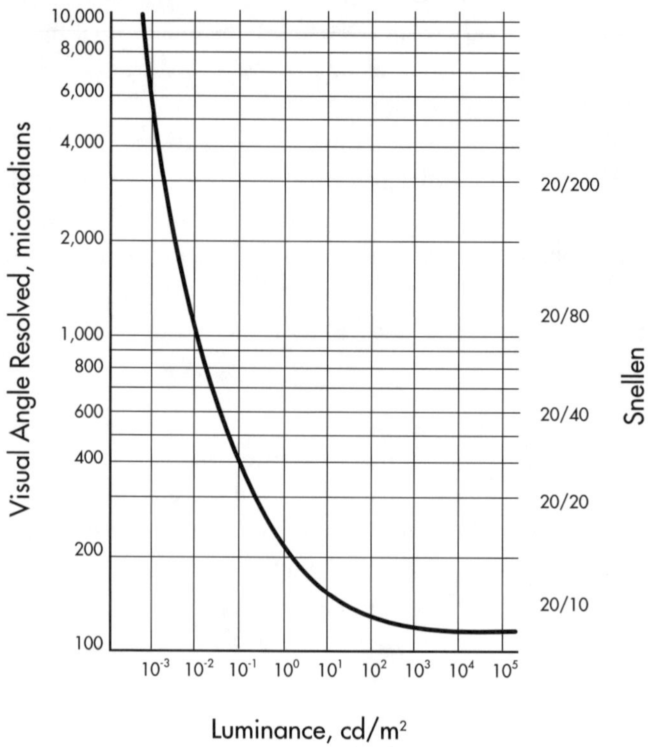

Figure 2.9 *Relationship between acuity and adaptation luminance.*

The performance of the visual system is not constant at all levels of illumination. We are clearly designed as daytime animals. Visual performance as measured by indices such as acuity falls off as illumination levels are reduced below those normally associated with daytime. This is illustrated in Figure 2.9 (from Cole, 1972). As shown in this figure, acuity is maximum, and relatively constant, at adaptation levels of about 1,000 cd/m^2 (about 300 foot-Lamberts) and higher. At adaptation levels below those values acuity begins to decrease. At adaptation levels associated with night driving in areas where there is little artificial illumination, acuity will be significantly below maximum. For a young person whose daytime acuity is 20/20, acuity at adaptation levels associated with night driving on unlighted roads would be in the range of 20/25 to 20/30. With aging the loss in acuity under low-luminance conditions becomes more severe. A person who was 70 or older would typically have an acuity in the range of 20/40 or worse under the conditions just described.

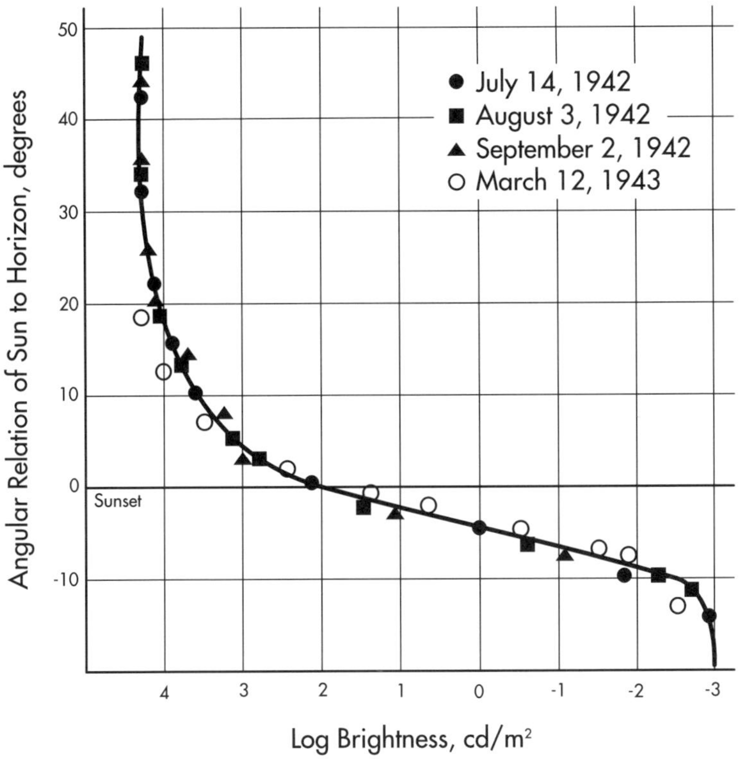

***Figure 2.10** Relationship between sun angle and luminance on the surface of the earth. Bebbe-Center, J.G., Carmichael, L. and Mead, L.C. (1944).* Daylight Training of Pilots for Night Flying, *Aeronautical Engineering Review, 3, 9-29.*

The range of luminance values to which drivers are typically exposed has been measured by several investigators. Representative data (from Beebe-Center, et al., 1944) are given in Figure 2.10. To collect these data a disc target was placed on a flat surface (i.e., facing straight up) and luminance measurements were taken at intervals on four days at different times of the year. The luminance values range from a maximum of slightly over 10,000 cd/m^2 (about 3,000 ft-L) to a minimum of about 0.001 cd/m^2 (about 0.0003 ft-L).

Note in Figure 2.10 how measured luminance begins to decrease when the sun angle approaches 25° above the horizon. By sunset the luminance has dropped to about 1% of that measured in full daylight. The drop in luminance continues after sunset, through the period of twilight, finally leveling off when the sun reaches about 18° below the horizon. It is interesting to note that there is a much greater range in luminance values after sunset than there is before.

Twilight is a period of about 90 minutes duration from sunrise/sunset to a sun altitude of -18°. Investigating accidents that occur in this time frame, especially in the first half hour or so after sunset, poses special problems. Some understanding of the terminology and characteristics associated with this period would be helpful.

By definition, sunrise/sunset occurs when the upper edge of the sun disc appears to be exactly on the horizon. Due to refraction caused by the atmosphere the sun is actually about one-half degree below the horizon at this time. Calculated sunrise/sunset times such as one might obtain from the US Weather Service or other sources are based on the visual appearance of the sun. They also assume a flat horizon.

There are three periods of twilight. The first, civil twilight, extends from sunrise/sunset to a sun angle of -6°. When the sun is at -6° there will be substantial skylight, particularly in that portion of the sky closest to the sun (assuming the sky is clear), but it will be dark enough on the face of the earth that headlights are required for a driver to see objects on the road. Drivers who are eastbound at dawn or westbound at sunset are under a significant handicap in the period of civil twilight because the bright sky alters their dark adaptation, making it more difficult for them to detect and identify unlighted objects on the road ahead.

The period when the sun angle is -6° to -12° is called nautical twilight. At a sun angle of -12° there will still be a discernible glow in the sky closest to the sun (again assuming a clear sky), but it will be quite dark on the face of the earth. The third phase is called astronomical twilight, which includes sun angles of -12° to -18°. At a sun angle of -18°, as indicated in Figure 2.9, there is full darkness. The sun moves roughly 1° every 5 minutes in the latitudes of the US, so each twilight period takes about half an hour, and the entire period extends to about an hour and a half.

For the accident investigator civil twilight is a particular problem, because in less than half an hour illumination goes from essentially daylight levels to the point where drivers need their headlights to see. There is actually a greater change in illumination levels in that half-hour period than there is in the two hours before sunset or after sunrise. Due to the very rapid changes in illumination during civil twilight eyewitnesses are likely to sharply disagree about how dark it was at the time of the event in question. The accuracy of the investigating officer's estimate of the time of collision becomes very important, since as little as five minutes either way can make a difference in driver visibility. When a time of collision has been established investigations must be carried out within a matter of a few minutes of the target time to stay within an appropriate envelope of illumination. Cloud cover will have a much larger effect on illumination, and consequently on visibility, than at any other time of day. If getting illumination levels right in an investigation during civil twilight is a problem, duplicating cloud cover is a major challenge.

It is very helpful for the investigator to be able to determine sun position with some precision at the location and time of interest. This information can be used to assess the lighting conditions at the time, but is also of great value in planning an on-site investigation. There are normally two times during the year when sun altitude and azimuth match. These occur at equal intervals on either side of the summer or winter solstice. For example, if the subject collision occurred two months after the summer solstice, there would be an identical sun condition two months before the summer solstice. Determining the exact sun position at the time of the event in question and the best matching date requires some help. There is software available for personal computers that can provide the desired information for any point on earth. Input required is latitude and longitude (which can be obtained from an atlas), difference in hours from Greenwich mean time, (+5 to +8 hours during standard time in the continental US), and date and time of occurrence. The output varies with the software, but these programs will calculate sun and moon position (altitude and azimuth), moon phase, and generally a great deal of other information as well. Note that the software assumes a flat horizon. Actual sunset will be earlier and sunrise later if there are hills or mountains in the way. This effect will have to be determined by an on-site inspection. There are a number of such packages that will run on an IBM-compatible machine. To the author's knowledge, there is only one available for a Macintosh. It is called MacAstro and is available as shareware.

Implications for Vision Due to the Structure of the Eye

The response characteristics of the rods and cones, and their distribution in the retina, have important implications for visual performance. When the cones are functioning, i.e., under photopic and mesopic conditions, we see most clearly things that are imaged on the fovea. Things imaged in the periphery are seen less well, the clarity of the image falling off very rapidly in proportion to its angular separation from the fovea. This effect is illustrated in Figure 2.11, which shows acuity in peripheral areas of the retina at different levels of adaptation luminance. Foveal vision is at 0 degrees in this figure. For example, at an adaptation luminance of 3.2 cd/m^2 (about 1 foot-Lambert), which is at the top of the mesopic zone in Figure 2.8, if a person's acuity for objects seen foveally is 20/20, acuity for objects imaged at five degrees from the fovea will be about 20/60. Overall visual performance drops as adaptation luminance is decreased, as discussed earlier and illustrated in Figure 2.9. Foveal performance, however, remains

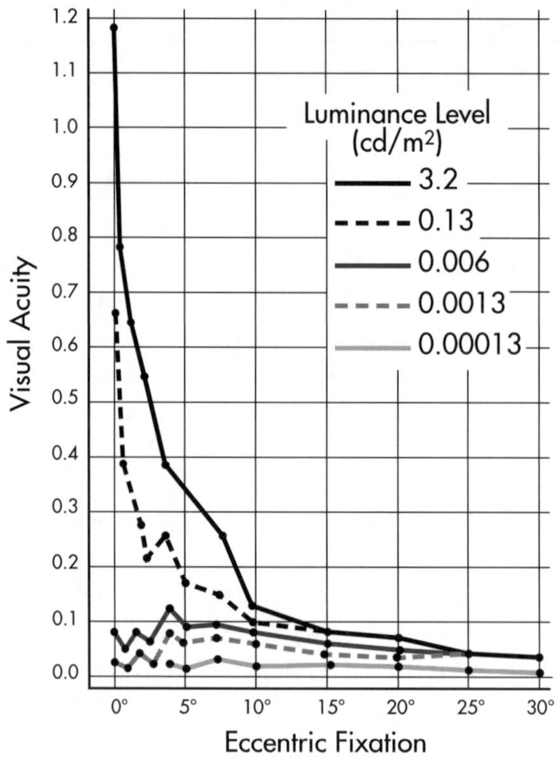

***Figure 2.11** Relationship between eccentric fixation and acuity. Credit line: Reproduced with permission from: Mandelbaum, J. and Sloan, 1947.* American Journal of Ophthalmology, *30, 581-588. Published by the Ophthalmic Publishing Company.*

greatly superior to that of the periphery at luminance levels in which the cones are functioning. At the three lowest luminance levels shown in Figure 2.11 this situation is reversed. This is simply an indication that the cones have ceased to function, the consequence being that the fovea is blind.

The limited size of the foveal area, combined with the relatively poor visual performance characteristic of the peripheral area, must be kept in mind when assessing visibility during an accident investigation. Figure 2.12 is a photograph of an ordinary street scene taken through the windshield of an automobile. The black dot represents the approximate area covered by the fovea. Because this area is so small relative to the entire visual field, detection typically occurs in the periphery. The eyes may then be shifted to bring the detected object into sharp focus in the fovea as part of the identification process. However, in order to be detected, an object in the periphery must have greater attention-gaining

Figure 2.12 *Photograph of driving scene indicating the approximate area covered by the fovea.*

characteristics (conspicuity) than if its image had fallen on the fovea. Other factors being equal, the further from the fovea the image of an object falls, the less likely it is to be detected at any given point in time, and the more likely it is to be overlooked altogether. Investigators who are evaluating visibility in a particular accident scenario have the advantage of knowing what they are looking for and where it is located. The normal response is to look directly at the target object, i.e., fixate it foveally. This is not fair to the driver whose visibility is purportedly being assessed because, unlike the investigators, that individual did not have the what and where information beforehand, and the object likely appeared initially in the peripheral area. At the least such evaluations should include assessments of peripheral detection. This can be accomplished simply by looking directly up the lane in use while approaching the scene so that the target object is imaged on the peripheral retina. For the investigator it is still an expected object and, consequently, will be detected at a substantially greater distance than if it was not expected. What this exercise will accomplish is make the investigator more aware of the differences in target conspicuity when its image falls in the periphery rather than the fovea of the eye.

The Processing of Visual Information

The reader may have noticed that it is possible to drive a familiar route and afterwards remember almost nothing about the details of the trip. This doesn't mean that what they say about the decline in your mental facilities is really true. It is simply a normal consequence of the way in which humans process information. In recent years researchers in cognitive psychology have made substantial progress in understanding the way humans process information. The area is quite complex. For our purposes, however, only some general principles need be covered.

At any given point in time there may be a great deal of information available to a driver from the various senses. All of this must be expeditiously sorted out in some reasonable way so that any necessary actions can be made in a timely fashion. Clearly, we do this successfully almost always without any special awareness of a particular "process." There are times, admittedly, when we are in a near-overload condition, as when trying to find our way through a strange community in heavy traffic, when the time-sharing characteristic and limitations of the information-processing system become evident.

Figure 2.13 is a schematic diagram of the information-processing system. The process is initiated by inputs from sense organs such as the eye, which go to

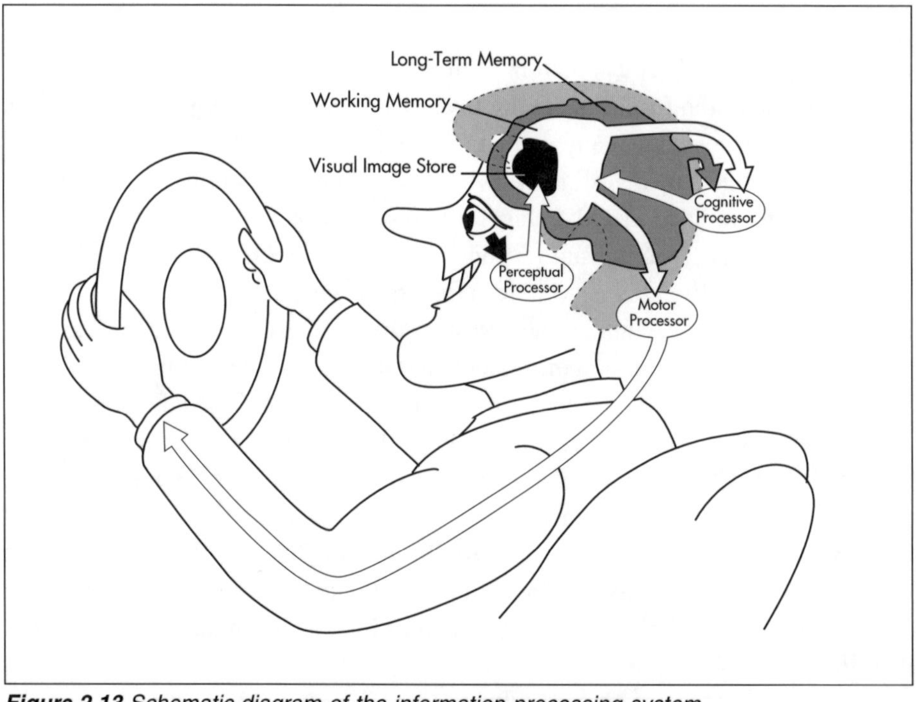

Figure 2.13 *Schematic diagram of the information-processing system.*

perceptual processors, where they are coded and transmitted to sensory image stores. The sensory image stores are part of so-called working memory. Working memory consists of parts of long-term memory that are activated for the purpose at hand. There is a cognitive processor that takes the information in the sensory image stores, along with information from long-term memory to arrive at an action decision. A simple sequence would be as follows: The image of a red signal light ahead impinges on the retina. The light pattern is translated to nerve impulses that go to a perceptual processor and then to a visual image store. The cognitive processor takes that information together with information from long-term memory concerning the meaning of the signal and its implications in terms of behavior. This is fed back into working memory, which informs the motor processor, which in turn issues the necessary commands to bring about the required physical response. Once the action is initiated, further input from the visual and kinesthetic systems is processed in a similar fashion to ensure that the goal initially decided on is realized.

Information contained in the image stores and working memory normally decays very rapidly once the need is past. This explains the inability to recall details of a routine trip mentioned earlier. It also helps to explain the discrepancies often noted in eyewitness testimony. For the eyewitness the events immediately preceding a crash are processed as routine information and may not be retained in long-term memory with any accuracy. The same would be true of happenings afterwards, where concern with the crash witnessed and its consequences may overwhelm memory traces of post-crash events. Eyewitness testimony relies on future recall of information processed in the working memory. Limited retention, hence poor reliability is to be expected. Where objective information and eyewitness testimony disagree, the former should be given greater weight.

Conventional wisdom has long held that humans are serial processors of information. That is, we can deal with only one thing at a time. This is a bit oversimplified. Certain overlearned tasks, such as tying one's shoes, can be carried out in parallel with other things. Fundamentally, however, it is accurate to regard the cognitive system as parallel in the recognition stage and serial in the action stage. That is, we can be aware of multiple things but can do only one thing at a time. This is difficult for many people to accept because it seems contrary to experience. We can drive at an acceptable level of safety, converse with passengers or on a cellular telephone, and attend to signs, signals, the actions of other vehicles, etc. all at the same time. Or so it seems. What is actually occurring is a skilled form of time sharing. The system works so long as the combined demands stay within the resource capabilities of the operator.

Since we are typically processing some information all the time the action channel is normally occupied. What we do next or what causes us to interrupt what we are doing so that something else can be accomplished depends on a condition being perceived in the first place, and perceived as being of sufficiently high priority to warrant immediate attention as well. The characteristics of objects or conditions that are likely to capture our attention have been identified. In general, the eye is attracted toward areas that contain a great deal of information, such as concentrations of signs, lights, people, etc. (Mackworth and Morandi; 1967; Notton and Stark, 1971: Yarbus, 1967); objects that differ greatly from their backgrounds in terms of brightness, color, texture, etc. (Thomas, 1968); flickering or flashing stimuli (Thomas, 1968, 1969); objects of large size (Thomas, 1968); and objects that are moving (Thomas, 1968). Most people would probably agree that the characteristics listed are those that make something conspicuous.

The term "conspicuity" is sometimes used when referring to the ability of a given object or condition to capture attention. Conspicuity is defined as those characteristics of an object or condition that determine the likelihood that it will come to the attention of an observer. The fact that something may be present in the visual field does not necessarily mean that it will be detected, because it may have less conspicuity than other visible features. This is especially true in areas where there is a great deal of information available. In an urban center, for example, particularly at night, not only is there much to be concerned with as a driver (e.g., vehicles, pedestrians, and various signs and signals), but it would not be unusual for the most conspicuous features of the environment to be something like advertising signs, which at best are irrelevant to the driving task.

The serial nature of information processing at the action stage, combined with the structural characteristic of the eye that provides maximum performance in only a small area (the fovea) places the human operator at a disadvantage in coping with unexpected events that may be initiated at almost any point in a very broad visual field. First, the event must come to the attention of the observer, even though its image will probably initially fall in the peripheral portion of the retina and be relatively inconspicuous as a consequence. In addition, it must compete for action channel space with other sources of information. In assessing the reasonableness of a given driver's behavior the investigator must keep these limitations in mind.

Chapter Overview

The purpose of this chapter is to provide a foundation of information concerning the operation and limitations of the human visual information processing system. The following are the key points covered:

- The appearance of a surface is largely determined by the way in which it reflects light. There are three types of reflective surfaces, diffuse, specular and retroreflective. Most of the objects with which the accident investigator will have to deal have diffuse characteristics.
- Road surfaces are diffuse reflectors. In the rain, however, they become specular reflectors. This has a marked effect on their overall appearance and the effectiveness of light sources.
- The units of light measurement most necessary to accident investigation are those concerned with: (1) Source output, known technically as luminous intensity. The photometric units are lumen and candela. (2) The amount of light reaching a surface, or illuminance. The photometric units are foot-candle and lux. (3) The amount of light reflected from a surface in a specific direction, or luminance. The photometric units are foot-Lambert and candela per meter squared.
- Acuity is a measure of the ability of the eye to resolve fine detail. Acuity that allows an individual to resolve detail of one minute of arc at 20 feet yields a score of 20/20. An individual who can see at 20 feet what someone with 20/20 acuity can see at 40 feet, has an acuity of 20/40.
- Except for a shutter system, the human eye is constructed much like a simple camera, with a lens system, a means for controlling the amount of light that can enter, a means for adjusting for viewing distance, and a light-sensitive layer of variable sensitivity.
- The retina is the layer of the eye that contains the light-sensitive receptors. There are two types of receptors in the eye, rods and cones. They differ in function and distribution throughout the retina.
- The cones operate at higher levels of illumination and are color sensitive. The central portion of the retina, called the fovea, is composed entirely of cones. Cones are also found outside the fovea, although their numbers diminish as the distance from the fovea increases.
- The rods operate at lower levels of illumination and are not color sensitive. Rods are found throughout the retina, except for the fovea.

- The function and distribution of the two types of receptors has implications for visual performance. At levels of illumination where the cones are functioning, vision is best in the fovea, with a rapid fall off in the peripheral areas. All driving is done at levels of illumination in which the cones are functioning.
- Due to the function and distribution of the receptors and the small size of the fovea, the detection of unexpected objects probably occurs in the periphery most of the time. The eyes will then be shifted to bring the detected object into focus in the foveal area as part of the identification process.
- When detection occurs in the periphery the target object's conspicuity must be greater than if it occurred in the fovea, due to the lesser quality of vision in the periphery.
- The eye is designed for optimum performance at relatively high levels of illumination. Visual performance is reduced as illumination decreases. This effect is more pronounced with increasing age.
- Human information-processing capability is distinctly limited. While we have the capability of being aware of multiple things, we can act on only one thing at a time.
- The serial nature of information processing means that an unexpected event must compete with information already being processed in order to gain the attention of the individual. The likelihood of it doing so successfully depends on its conspicuity.

References

Beebe-Center, J. G., Carmichael, L. & Mead, L. C. (1944). Daylight Training of Pilots for Night Flying. *Aeronautical Engineering Review.* 3, 9-29.

Birren, J. E., Casperson, R. C. and Botwinick, J. (1950). Age Changes in Pupil Size. *Journal of Gerontology. 5,* 267-271.

Cole, B. L. (1972). Visual Aspects of Road Engineering. ARRB Proceedings. 6(1), 102-148.

Grether, W. F. and Baker, C. A. (1972). Visual Presentation of Information. In: Van Cott, H. P. and Kinkade, R. G. (Eds.) *Human Engineering Guide to Equipment Design.* New York, N.Y. McGraw-Hill Book Company.

Mackworth, N. H. and Morandi, A. J. (1967). The Gaze Selects Informative Details Within Pictures. *Perception and Psychophysics, 2*, 547-552.

Mandelbaum, J. and Sloan, L. L. (1947). Peripheral Visual Acuity: With Special Reference to Scotopic Illumination. *Journal of Ophthalmology, 30,* 581-588.

Mortimer, R. G. and Olson, P. L. (1974). Development and Use of Driving Tests to Evaluate Headlamp Beams. Ann Arbor, MI. The Highway Safety Research Institute. Report No. UM-HSRI-HF-74-14.

Notton, D. and Stark, L. (1971). Eye Movements and Visual Perception. *Scientific American, 224*(6), 34-43.

Ottander, C. (1963). Adaptation Time After Glare. In: Ingelstam, E. (Ed.) *Lighting Problems in Highway Traffic.* New York, N.Y. MacMillan Co. 111-119.

Thomas, E. L. (1968). Movements of the Eye. *Scientific American, 219*(2), 88-95.

Thomas, E. L. (1969). Search Behavior. *The Radiologic Clinics of North America, 7*, 403-417.

Yarbus, A. L. (1967). *Eye Movements and Vision*, New York, Plenum Press.

Chapter 3

Driver Perception

Introduction

Chapter 2 dealt in part with the eye. The eye is one of the sense organs with which humans are equipped. It is certainly important for accident investigators to have some knowledge of how the eye works. It is equally important, however, to understand that the input of sensory organs such as the eye represents only the first step in a complex process, the end product of which is called perception. This chapter will provide a brief introduction to the subject of perception. The reader will find that it is an intriguing subject, but it is also important to anyone concerned with the assessment of human performance. The chapter also deals with two perception-related issues, identification of closing speed and motorcycle conspicuity.

Perception as Contrasted to Sensation

Definition

A useful definition of perception has been offered by Hochberg (1988), who says that the term refers most generally to our sensory experiences of the world, and of the people, objects, and events that comprise it. He goes on to say that the term refers as well to the process by which an internal representation of the world is obtained from sensory information about objects and events in the world.

There are two definitions here. The first merely points out that the term perception is used casually to refer to sensory experience in general and is often used interchangeably with terms such as seeing and hearing. The second part of the definition is more technical, and a major area of interest to experimental psychologists. Basic to this part of the definition is the notion that perception is the end product of a process in which sensation is the starting point.

The Nature of Perception

A camera is a passive device. Within the limits of the film medium it simply records the patterns of light that impinge upon the light-sensitive surface. The eye is like that as well; the difference being that we are not directly aware of the images that are registered on the retina. The information those images represent is transmitted to the brain. There is a certain amount of processing that takes place prior to its reaching the level of consciousness. This is not mere meddling; it turns out that the processing that goes on is generally very helpful. A couple of simple examples will serve to illustrate the point. If you hold a pencil vertically at arm's length in front of you, each eye receives a somewhat different image of that pencil. This is because your eyes are separated horizontally by about 2.5 to 3.0 inches. The result is that your right eye sees further around the right side of the pencil than does your left eye and vice versa. From this one might reasonably expect that the appearance of the pencil would be somewhat less clear when viewed with two eyes than if it were viewed with one eye. Instead, the perception is of three dimensions, in that the pencil appears to stand out from its background. This cue to distance, and relative distance, is very useful in everyday life. Similarly, a sound originating from one side reaches one ear roughly a millisecond before it reaches the other ear. Logically, it would appear that this would result in a slightly muddied impression of the sound. Not at all. Instead the perception is one of directionality. This cue to the origin of sound probably saved more than one of our ancient ancestor's necks by giving them a slight advantage in determining the direction from which a predator was coming. For all of us the cue is valuable with regularity in indicating where to start looking when identifying some sound source.

In sum, the perceptual system is anything but a passive participant in the business of information processing. Sensory information is analyzed and interpreted so that what we perceive is organized in a way that generally assists in coping with the myriad bits of data with which we are often confronted.

Visual Illusions

Demonstrating the processing of visual information by the perceptual system is easy, and fun, via illusions. Three simple examples will suffice. Look at Figure 3.1. There are two pairs of horizontal lines and a diagonal line. The lines in each of the horizontal pairs are of the same length, and should be so perceived. Now look at Figure 3.2. Nothing has changed physically about the lines shown in Figure 3.1, but perceptually they appear different. In the case of the horizontal lines the upper line appears significantly longer than the lower one. In addition, the two sections of the diagonal line do not appear to line up. The additional visual information in Figure 3.2 has the effect of changing the perception of the items in Figure 3.1. Interestingly, the perceptions cannot be altered based on investigation. You can satisfy yourself intellectually that nothing has changed with the lines from Figure 3.1 to Figure 3.2, but your perceptual system will stubbornly insist otherwise.

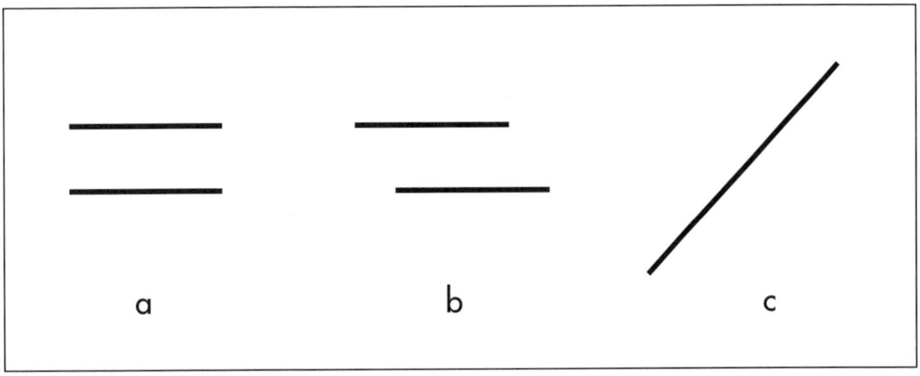

Figure 3.1 *Parallel lines and a diagonal line.*

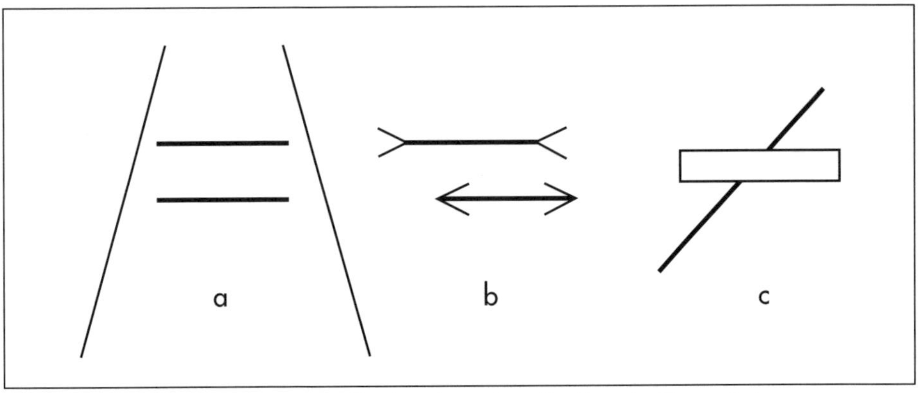

Figure 3.2 *Illustration of common illusions based on the lines in Figure 3.1.*

Literally hundreds of visual illusions have been described. Most seem to have no obvious counterpart in the real world, but some do. One example is on the left side of Figure 3.2. Suppose you were standing on a sidewalk, looking parallel to its edges, as depicted in Figure 3.3. There are two objects on the sidewalk, and the further one comes closer to filling the space between the edges. One can say with some confidence that more distant object is longer than the nearer one. What the illusion illustrates is that this knowledge is not arrived at by exercise of the intellect but reflects "automatic" processing by the perceptual system.

Visual illusions have been employed by artists and architects for thousands of years. The ancient Greeks have achieved renown for their skill in creating beautiful colonnaded structures. Much less well known is the fact that the sides of the columns are not parallel. Rather they taper out at the top to compensate for the effects of perspective. Arnheim (1965) cites one fairly extreme example of the use of illusion in architecture, concerning the Plazzo Spada in Rome. When

Figure 3.3 *Photograph of a sidewalk and two objects. Which object is longer?*

Franceso Borromini was given the commission in 1635 his idea was to have a deep architectural vista tapering off in a vaulted colonnade. Unfortunately, the site available to him was of limited size. A visitor to the Plazzo Spada stands in the courtyard and looks into a colonnade. The perception is one of a long tunnel, flanked by columns, and leading to an open space in which is located a large statue of a warrior. Investigation shows how wrong the perception is. The front arch is 19 feet high and ten feet wide, the back arch, which is only 28 feet away, is ten feet high and three feet wide. The side walls converge, the floor rises, the ceiling slopes down, and the intervals between the columns diminish. The statue, when reached, is found to be relatively small. According to Arnheim, distortion of perspective was commonly employed by medieval architects (although not nearly to the same degree as Borromini in this case) as a means of enhancing the apparent depth of churches.

From the perspective of the human operator, it is clear that what he/she perceives to be the case is what counts. Often the challenge of the accident investigator is to determine whether an apparent misperception on the part of a driver was reasonable under the circumstances. It is clear that perception can be altered by design, whether the design is deliberate or comes about by happenstance. Later in this chapter the discussion will be concerned with some dangerous perceptual situations. At this point it is reasonable to ask whether perceptual principles might be employed to alter driver behavior in ways that promote safety.

Very little use has been made of the potential that design might affect driver perceptions and thus driver behavior. One example of an application is commonly found at toll booths. Drivers who have been traveling at high speed for a while sometimes do not slow sufficiently in the approach to the toll area. It has been found helpful to paint stripes or place rumble strips at ever closer intervals in the approach area as a means of exaggerating apparent speed. The same technique is sometimes used on ramps where experience has shown that drivers tend to go too fast.

Some research shows that it might be possible to manipulate driver perceptions in useful ways. In one example Shinar (1977) showed subjects photographs of pairs of curves. The curves in each pair were similar in geometry, but differed in accident history. The subjects tended to judge the high-accident curves as closer, wider and more visible than the low-accident curves. They did not perceive the high-accident curves as more dangerous, and they did not indicate that they would slow down any more for them. In a related study Shinar, et al. (1975) showed that a driver's perception of the radius of a curve could be altered through placement of delineators.

There might be a lesson here. If we knew enough about how drivers perceive driving situations and arrive at judgments of safe speed then it may be possible to alter design in a way that will cause drivers to travel at speeds that are appropriate for the facility in question. The question then becomes whether drivers will eventually discover the subterfuge and the more reckless among us return to their former ways. It's not possible to answer that question at the present, but it does seem worthwhile to further explore the manipulation of driver perception as a means for improving traffic safety.

Difficulties in Perception While Driving

Certain situations in driving produce misperceptions on the part of drivers. These in turn sometimes lead to delayed or inappropriate responses. Frankly, most of these "perceptual traps" that are roadway related are designed into the system. This is not to suggest villainy or ineptness on the part of highway engineers. Rather these often come about due to cost constraints or other compromise-inducing situations. Sometimes something that looks good on paper simply doesn't work as well when realized in concrete.

Figure 3.4 *Photograph of a roadway illustrating a perceptual trap.*

Problems in roadway design and the application of signs and signals are encountered with some frequency. A right-hand exit ramp near the start of a left curve, as one example, may lure some drivers onto the ramp at speeds far in excess of what is safe. The practice of extending the right edge line, in dashed form, across the entrance to a ramp is helpful in reducing this type of error.

Drivers rely on a variety of cues as indicators of where the road is going. Look at the road shown in Figure 3.4. The primary road curves sharply to the left about in the center of the photograph. Yet the alignment of the trees, utility poles, and the connecting road all suggest that the road continues straight for some considerable distance further. Signing can help in warning of a condition such as that shown. A better (although more costly) solution is to destroy the illusion by breaking the apparent continuity between the main and connecting roads. This could be accomplished by altering the alignment of the connecting road in the approach so that it does not appear to line up with the main road.

Positive Route Guidance

A discussion of perceptual problems in road design leads naturally to the subject of positive route guidance. Positive route guidance is a systematic procedure for supplying information to drivers using basic principles of human factors. In the words of Alexander and Lunenfeld (1975):

> "Positive guidance is based on the premise that a driver can be given sufficient information about a hazard where he needs it and in a form he can use to enable him to avoid an accident. This concept involves an analysis of the information needed by the driver to perform the driving task safely and efficiently. It includes determination of needed information, appropriate traffic control devices, their location, and the format of the information presented."

Positive route guidance is more than a philosophy about how things ought to be done. The several papers that have been written since 1975 provide detailed descriptions of how problem areas should be approached. They review driver information needs, expectancy, and performance characteristics, provide formats for gathering and evaluating information, and review numerous examples of applications of positive route guidance.

An adequate discussion of positive route guidance goes beyond the scope of this book. Subsequent to the 1975 paper, there have been a number of reports issued by the Federal Highway Administration on the subject of positive route guidance (e.g., Post, et al., 1977, 1981; Alexander and Lunenfeld, 1986; Hostetter and Lunenfeld, 1982; Lunenfeld, 1980; Parker and Zegeer, 1989; Lunenfeld and Alexander, 1990). Persons interested in an in-depth understanding of the subject would find these reports worth reading.

Positive route guidance represents a major contribution of human factors to highway design and traffic engineering. Its applicability to real-world problems in road design, signing and the use of traffic control devices has been widely accepted and has led to significant improvements in these areas.

Perception of Closing Speed

A critical skill for drivers is the assessment of closing speed. It is used in judging the adequacy of gaps in traffic for such basic maneuvers as crossing, merging and passing. The fact that drivers generally perform these maneuvers successfully suggests that they can make these judgments with some accuracy. In fact, judgment of closing speed is something that available research indicates that humans do very poorly. Drivers survive in situations that seem to call for this skill only because they have learned that a gap is adequate when the approaching vehicle appears to be at least a certain distance away. If that vehicle's speed is greatly different than assumed trouble may result because humans cannot discern closing speed with any accuracy until the gap has closed to a dangerous extent.

The problem lies in the cues that are used in judging closing speed. An important cue to distance is the angular size of an object. Thus, if an object such as a car appears tiny, we know it is far away. Change in image size is a cue to change in distance. That is, if the object seems to be getting larger, that means the distance is closing. Of course, there is nothing unusual about closing on another vehicle while driving. What is unusual, and potentially very dangerous, is closing at a high rate of speed. An important cue here is *rate* of change of image size. That is, if the object seems to be getting larger fast, that indicates a high closing speed. The difficulty here is that this cue depends not only on closing speed, but on separation distance.

A simple example will serve to make it clear why this happens. Imagine that a vehicle first comes into view when it is 1,000 feet away. Unknown to the observer initially is that it is stopped. As the distance closes by one half (i.e., from 1,000 to 500 feet) the image size of the vehicle doubles. Reduce the distance by one half again (i.e., from 500 to 250 feet) and the image size doubles again, but in half the time. This process continues with the image size doubling each time the distance is halved, as illustrated in Figure 3.5. A rapid change of image size only becomes evident when the separation distance has closed to a considerable extent.

Clearly, this is a potentially dangerous perceptual limitation. Due to the general scarcity of other cues, it is probably much more dangerous at night. Sometimes reference is made to the "moth effect," when people drive into the rear of lighted vehicles at night. The assumption seems to be that drivers are drawn to lights like a moth to a flame. When an intoxicated individual runs into the rear of a police car with all its lights going, this may not be an unreasonable explanation. People who are not intoxicated run into stopped or slow-moving vehicles on occasion, however, sometimes leading investigators to conclude that they must have been very inattentive to have failed to see it. Detection is not the problem. As will be discussed starting in Chapter 9, the driver must not only see something, but must understand what it is and what it is doing. It is the latter failing that may cause someone to approach so close to another vehicle as to be unable to avoid a collision, or to pull out in front of another vehicle that just happens to be going at a much higher speed than other traffic on that road.

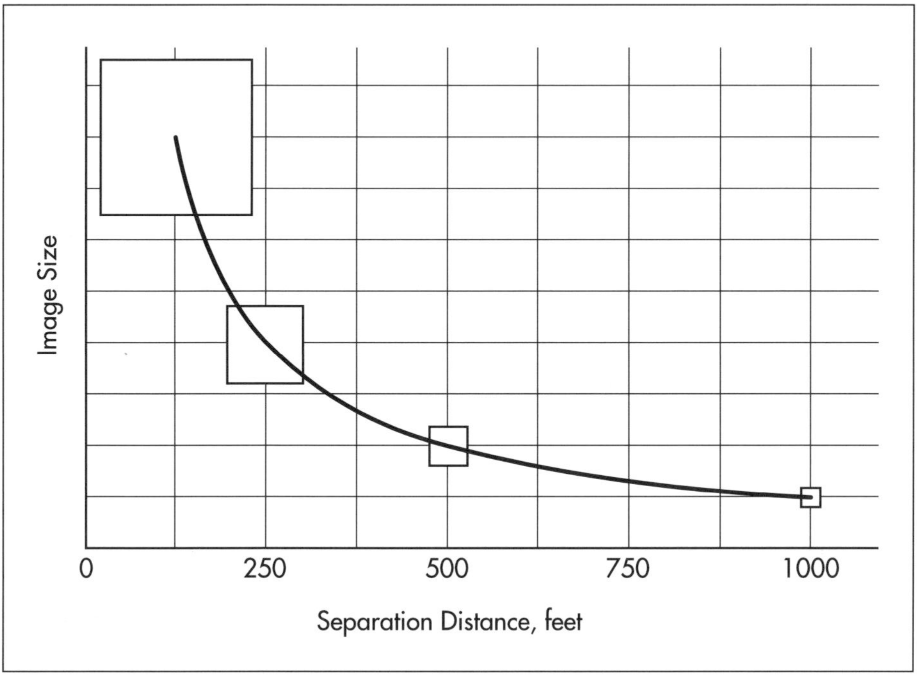

Figure 3.5 *The relationship between viewing distance and image size.*

In terms of arriving at some estimate of driver capability in making these judgments, there is limited research available. All of it has been carried out under conditions where the subjects were aware of the nature of the test, hence the results illustrate best possible performance. Clearly, a driver's expectations are violated when he/she encounters a vehicle that is stopped or moving much slower than other traffic. Driver expectancy will be discussed in some detail in Chapter 4. For the moment suffice it to say that when a driver's expectancies are violated the probability that a situation will be correctly identified is significantly reduced and the time required to make a correct identification is significantly increased.

A comprehensive review of the literature up to that time concerning the ability of people to discern spacing changes and relative speed is provided in Mortimer, et al, (1974). In the car-following simulations carried out as part of that work it was determined that drivers did moderately well in determining whether the space between theirs and a lead vehicle was opening or closing, but appeared to make little use of relative velocity information, basing their responses on perceived headway.

Plotkin (1976) has reported research on the ability of subjects to discern closing speed. In a controlled study he found that the limit of human perception was 25 to 30 milliradians per second. In equation form the results can be expressed as follows:

$$V \geq \frac{0.0275s^2}{w} \qquad 3.1$$

Where:

V = velocity in feet per second
0.0275 = perception limit in radians per second
s = distance between vehicles in feet
w = width of stopped vehicle in feet

This equation can be used to illustrate the maximum capability of people to judge closing speed. Bearing in mind that the subjects were fully informed of the purpose of the investigation, their expectancy was different from that of a driver who has no reason to believe that the vehicle ahead is stopped or going slower than normal. This says that the constant of 0.0275 radians/second would be significantly greater when applied to real-world situations. How much greater is, unfortunately, a matter of conjecture.

In sum, the ability of persons to judge the speed of another vehicle, whether traveling in the same or opposite direction, is limited even under controlled test conditions. In the real world, when the situation is counter to what the individual expects from that other vehicle, it will certainly be much worse.

Motorcycle Conspicuity

The term "motorcycle conspicuity" refers to a hypothesis that a motorist seeking to make a maneuver across other traffic lanes is more likely to fail to detect an approaching motorcycle than a car or truck. Apparently the first mention of this possibility was in a paper by Lehmann (1957). Since that time a great number of papers have appeared dealing with the subject in one way or another. Some of these were statistical analyses, but most of them reported research seeking to improve the conspicuity of the motorcycle and/or its operator.

There are several pieces of evidence suggesting a special problem in conspicuity for motorcycles. The most often cited is the fact that the offending motorist typically claims not to have seen the motorcycle or not to have seen it in time. There is also solid statistical evidence showing that motorcycles are more likely to be involved in certain types of two-vehicle collisions than are automobiles. Table 3.1 presents typical data, in this case based on 929 car-motorcycle and 36,711 car-car crashes that occurred in Texas in 1986. The table considers only crashes in which the vehicles were initially going in opposite directions, and is organized based on what each involved vehicle was doing pre crash.

Table 3.1 A Comparison of Precrash Maneuvers in Daytime Car-Motorcycle and Car-Car Collisions in Which the Vehicles were Initially Going in Opposite Directions

Car Maneuver	Motorcycle Maneuver	% Car-Motorcycle Crashes	% Car-Car Crashes
Straight	Straight	3.7	3.1
Backing	Straight	0.1	
Straight	Backing	<0.1	
Total		**0.1**	**0.5**
Stopped	Straight	0.1	
Straight	Stopped	<0.1	
Total		**0.1**	**0.2**
Turn Right	Straight	<0.1	
Straight	Turn Right	<0.1	
Total		**0.1**	**<0.1**
Turn Left	Straight	17.1	
Straight	Turn Left	1.7	
Total		**18.8**	**10.4**
Stopped	Backing	<0.1	
Backing	Stopped	0.2	
Total		**0.2**	**0.8**
Turn Left	Turn Right	0.1	
Turn Right	Turn Left	0.1	
Total		**0.2**	**0.2**
Turn Left	Turn Left	<0.1	0.1
Overall Total		**23.1**	**15.2**

From: Olson, 1989

Of all the maneuver categories listed in Table 3.1, the one that stands out is the case where the motorcycle is going straight and the car makes a left turn. This is ten times the percentage of cases where the car is going straight and the motorcycle makes a left turn. The same pattern, i.e., motorcycle going straight and the car making a left turn shows up, although not as strongly, when examining data for right-angle meetings and cases where the vehicles are going in the same direction. This marked difference in involvement for motorcycles is intriguing. The question is why does it come about?

For many investigators the answer is that motorcycles are harder to see, perhaps because they have such a small profile when viewed from the front. This is buttressed by the "I-didn't-see-it" explanation. But, the "I-didn't-see-it" statement is evidence for a problem in motorcycle conspicuity only if it is unique to crashes involving motorcycles, or at least heard more often in such cases. The explanation is hardly unique to motorcycle crashes. Right-of-way violations are one of the most common precursors of multi-vehicle collisions. Of all the reasons why someone would deliberately violate the right of way of another driver in a way likely to result in a collision, failure to detect has to be at or near the top of the list. There are no data on the relative frequency with which the explanation is used in car-motorcycle and car-car crashes.

Thus, there is some reason to believe that motorcycle conspicuity may not be a unique problem with motorcycles. If not, how does one explain the crash-involvement statistics? There are several possible explanations, some of which have been subject to investigation, some of which have not. One, for which there is much data, is blockages. Here the possibility is that because motorcycles are small when viewed from the front, they are easily blocked from a driver's view by other vehicles in the traffic stream, road-related hardware, and even things associated with the vehicle, such as roof-support pillars. Two excellent studies have examined the blockage issue (Hurt, et al., 1981, and Williams and Hoffman, 1977). Both studies found that in about half of cases where there was a violation of the motorcycle's right of way there was a blockage of the driver's view of the motorcycle at some time prior to collision.

Other possible causes may be in speed-spacing judgment errors or even in the attitudes of motorcyclists themselves. It may even be that motorcycle conspicuity *is* a significant problem. The point is that no one knows for certain. At the present state of knowledge there is no basis for blaming the motorcycle alone for the statistical abnormalities that are evident in the data.

Chapter Overview

Sensation is but the first step in a complex process through which humans receive information about the world about them. The end result of this process is called "perception." This chapter has provided a brief overview of perception as applied to motor vehicle operation. The following are the principal points covered:

- The term perception refers to the mental impressions that result from a process that starts with the stimulation of one of the sensory organs. Sensation is organized, integrated and interpreted by the higher centers in ways that are generally helpful in dealing with multiple and complex stimuli.

- Perceptual illusions are displays that alter our impressions of some object or condition. Illusions have long been used by artists and architects to achieve ends that are visually pleasing.
- Illusions exist in the driving environment as well and sometimes cause difficulties for drivers.
- Illusions are used profitably in certain traffic situations, primarily to cause drivers to believe they are going faster than is actually the case, in an effort to make them slow for a hazard such as a toll booth.
- There is some evidence that illusions can be employed in other traffic situations to alter driver behavior in ways that should lead to increased safety. One example is in the design of curves. It may be possible to design curves so that the radius is perceived as being smaller than it actually is. This should cause drivers to slow more than they would otherwise. Little work has been done to explore this possibility.
- Positive route guidance is an application of human factors principles to traffic engineering that has come to be widely accepted as an effective means of analyzing driver information needs and finding practical solutions to problem areas in the highway system.
- Drivers have a very limited capability for discerning the relative speed relationship between theirs and another vehicle. For this reason situations in which an approaching vehicle is traveling much faster than expected or a lead vehicle is traveling much slower than expected pose a danger. By the time the perceptual cues to the relative speed become apparent, it may be too late for the driver to take effective action.
- Motorcycle conspicuity is a hypothesis that says that a motorcycle is less likely to be detected than a car by a motorist seeking to make a maneuver across its path. While crash statistics show a pattern of over-representation for motorcycles in certain types of two-vehicle crashes, the main support for the hypothesis comes from the frequent statement of drivers to the effect that they did not see the motorcycle.
- The "I-didn't-see-it" explanation is not evidence for a problem in conspicuity with motorcycles because drivers say the same thing after collisions involving all types of vehicles. There are alternative explanations for the crash statistics in such things as blockages and speed-spacing judgment errors. The contribution of these as factors in motorcycle crashes should be further explored.

References

Alexander, G. J. and Lunenfeld, H. (1975). Positive Guidance in Traffic Control. Washington, D. C. U.S. Department of Transportation. Federal Highway Administration. Office of Traffic Operations.

Alexander, G. J. and Lunenfeld, H. (1986). Driver Expectancy in Highway Design and Traffic Operations. Washington, D. C. U.S. Department of Transportation. Federal Highway Administration. Office of Traffic Operations. Report No. FHWA-TO-86-1.

Arnheim, R. (1965). *Art and Visual Perception.* Berkeley. The University of California Press.

Hochberg, J. (1988). Visual Perception. In: Atkinson, R. C., Herrnstein, R. J., Lindzey, G. and Luce, R. D. (Eds.) *Stevens' Handbook of Experimental Psychology.* New York. John Wiley & Sons.

Hostetter, R. S. and Lunenfeld, H. (1982). Planning and Field Data Collection. Washington, D. C. U.S. Department of Transportation. Federal Highway Administration. Office of Traffic Operations. Report No. FHWA-TO-80-2.

Hurt, H. H., Ouellet, J. V. and Thom, D. R. (1981). Motorcycle Accident Cause Factors and Identification of Countermeasures. Warrendale, PA. Society of Automotive Engineers Technical Paper 810190.

Lehmann, K. (1957). Zur Ursachenforschung bei Strassenverkersunfaellen. *Zeitschrift fuer Verkehssicherheit,* 1-2, 32.

Lunenfeld, H. (1980). Evaluation of Traffic Operations, Safety and Positive Guidance Projects. Washington, D. C. U.S. Department of Transportation. Federal Highway Administration. Office of Traffic Operations. Report No. FHWA-TO-80-1.

Lunenfeld, H. and Alexander, G. J. (1990). A Users' Guide to Positive Guidance (3rd Edition). Washington, D. C. U.S. Department of Transportation. Federal Highway Administration. Office of Traffic Operations. Report No. FHWA-SA-90-017.

Mortimer, R. G., Hoffman, E. R., Poskocil, A., Jorgeson, C. M., Olson, P. L. and Moore, C. D. (1974). Studies of Automobile and Truck Rear Lighting and Signaling Systems. Ann Arbor. The Highway Safety Research Institute. Report No. UM-HSRI-HF-74-25.

Olson, P. L. (1989). Motorcycle Conspicuity Revisited. *Human Factors.* 31(2), 141-146.

Parker, M. R. and Zegeer, C. V. (1989). Traffic Conflicts for Safety and Operations. McLean, Virginia. U.S. Department of Transportation. Federal Highway Administration. Report No. FHWA-IP-88-027

Plotkin, S. C. (1976). *Accident and Product Failure Analysis.* Oakland, California. Syllabus.

Post, T. J., Robertson, H. D., Price, H. E., Alexander, G. J. and Lunenfeld, H. (1977). A Users' Guide to Positive Guidance. Washington, D. C. U. S. Department of Transportation, Federal Highway Administration.

Post, T. J., Alexander, G. J. and Lunenfeld, H. (1981). A Users' Guide to Positive Guidance (2nd Edition). Washington, D. C. U. S. Department of Transportation, Federal Highway Administration. Report No. FHWA-TO-81-1.

Shinar, D. (1977). Driver Visual Limitations, Diagnosis and Treatment. Bloomington, Indiana. Indiana University Institute for Research in Public Safety. Final Report No. DOT-HS-5-1275.

Shinar, D., Rockwell, T. H. and Malecki, J. (1975). Rural Curves: Designed for the Birds? Or the Effect of Changes in Driver Perception on Rural Curve Negotiation. Ann Arbor. Paper presented at the 8th summer meeting of the Transportation Research Board.

Williams, M. J. and Hoffman, E. R. (1977). The Influence of Motorcycle Visibility on Traffic Accidents. Melbourne, Australia. University of Melbourne, Department of Mechanical Engineering.

Chapter 4

Visibility When Driving at Night

Introduction

From the discussion in Chapter 2, it should be clear that humans are not designed to be creatures of the night. The human eye functions best at relatively high levels of illumination. Visual performance is significantly below maximum at the levels of adaptation associated with night driving. In order for us to be able to function adequately while driving at night, relatively high levels of illumination are required. In the context of motor vehicle operation, this illumination may be provided by fixed lighting installations, by the vehicle's headlamps, or by a combination of the two.

There are street-lighting installations of such high quality that they make headlamps unnecessary, except possibly as vehicle markers. These are the exception, however. Many installations are of lesser quality, characterized by lower levels of illumination overall and considerable variation in pavement luminance from one area to another. Such systems can be deceptive, with the capacity to hide significant hazards in the dark areas. The problems associated with visibility in areas where there is significant fixed lighting are discussed in greater detail in Chapter 6.

There is no question that wide use of high-quality fixed-lighting systems is desirable. They are, unfortunately, costly to install and operate. As a result most people drive most of their nighttime miles on roads that are unlighted, or lighted at levels that make the illumination provided by the vehicle's headlamps necessary. This chapter is concerned with the visibility provided by motor vehicle headlamps. It will discuss the different types of equipment in use today, some problems in design, and the performance that can be expected.

Target Contrast and its Importance

Definition

Contrast is defined as characteristics of a scene that cause an object to appear distinct from its background. At higher levels of illumination contrast can be provided by such things as differences in color, pattern, shading, texture, and brightness. When operating a motor vehicle at night generally only brightness contrast is available.

The human eye responds to contrast. Bluntly stated, it's the only way we can perceive that something is there. It seems to be generally assumed that the function of lighting systems is to illuminate potential hazards so they can be seen. Not so. The job that lighting systems must accomplish is to create contrast between the target object and its background. Automobile headlamps generally work by making the target object brighter than its background, as shown in the top photograph in Figure 4.1. Fixed lighting systems may do that, or they may brighten up the background so that the target can be seen in silhouette, as shown in the bottom photograph in Figure 4.1.

Calculating Contrast

Contrast can be expressed quantitatively. Unfortunately, there is no universally agreed upon way of doing so. Authors sometimes talk of a contrast value without stating how it was derived, adding to the confusion. The following is presented to assist investigators who may wish to calculate contrast themselves or are faced with having to interpret calculations prepared by others.

Of the various ways in which contrast may be quantified, perhaps the simplest is a ratio describing the luminance relationship between the object and its background. For example, if the luminance of the target is 8 units and the luminance of the background is 2 units the contrast ratio is 4 to 1. The following equations are alternative ways to calculate contrast:

$$\mathrm{C} = \frac{(L_{\mathrm{d}} - L_{\mathrm{b}})}{L_{\mathrm{b}}} \qquad 4.1$$

Where:

L_d = the luminance of the detail (target object) and
L_b = the luminance of the background

$$\mathrm{C} = \frac{(L_{\mathrm{g}} - L_{\mathrm{l}})}{L_{\mathrm{g}}} \qquad 4.2$$

Where:

L_g = greater luminance and
L_l = lesser luminance

Figure 4.1 *Two photographs of a pedestrian seen in direct illumination from vehicle headlamps and as a silhouette against a bright background.*

$$C = \frac{(L_g - L_l)}{L_l} \qquad 4.3$$

Where:

L_g = greater luminance and
L_l = lesser luminance

The use of equation 4.1 will yield positive values from zero to infinity for cases in which the target has greater luminance than its background and values from 0 to -1 for cases in which the target has lower luminance than its background. This equation is recommended by some because they feel the contrast values that result represent relative visibilities. Sometimes reference will be made to positive and negative contrast, meaning that the target has greater or lesser luminance than its background, respectively. That terminology comes from the use of equation 4.1. Referring back to Figure 4.1, the top photograph illustrates positive contrast, the bottom photograph negative contrast.

Equations 4.2 yields numerical values between 0 and 1 regardless of whether the object has higher or lower luminance than its background. Equation 4.2 is felt to be useful in situations where there is no clear distinction between object and background.

Equation 4.3 yields values from 0 to infinity. It is an alternative to equation 4.2 that is often used when the object is brighter than its background.

The Reflectivity of Objects in the Real World

Brightness contrast may be achieved when the target and background are receiving different illuminances, when the background is greatly removed from the target, when the background contains light sources, or when the target and background have different reflectivity. Under the conditions of night driving, differences in illuminances generally only occur in cases that allow the target to be seen in silhouette. For example, a streetlamp or other sources may increase the luminance of the road or structures behind a pedestrian, making it possible to see him/her as a dark object against a light background, as depicted in the bottom photograph in Figure 4.1. Obviously, the sources are also illuminating the pedestrian, but on the side away from the observer.

Headlamps, on the other hand, illuminate the target on the side facing the observer, but they also illuminate the background. If the background is distant relative to the target sufficient contrast may be developed simply because the illuminance reaching the target is so much greater than that reaching the background. As a consequence of the way headlamps are designed, it often happens this does not work until the car is so close to the target that a collision is a real possibility. As will be discussed in some detail later in this chapter, the main power of the low-beam system is directed down and to the right. This means that the highest levels of illuminance fall on the lower portion of the target, where the background (typically the road surface) is relatively close. If both have about the same reflectivity there will be little contrast and little probability that the target will be detectable by the driver.

The best chance for good contrast under night driving conditions is from differences in reflectivity in target and background. A pedestrian wearing light-colored garments will generally be detected at a greater distance than one wearing dark clothing. A pedestrian wearing retroreflective garments will be detected at a still greater distance.

The most comprehensive information on the reflectivity of roadway backgrounds has been reported by Bhise, et al. (1977). They measured the retroreflectivity of shoulders and pavements of various types at different distances in front of the car in an extensive survey in different parts of the country. The results are given in Figures 4.2 and 4.3. The interesting thing is that the retroreflectivity results from both areas were low and very similar, although the retroreflectivity of shoulders tended to be slightly higher than that of pavements. Most shoulders were between 5 and 10%, most pavements were between 2.5 and 10% at all distances measured.

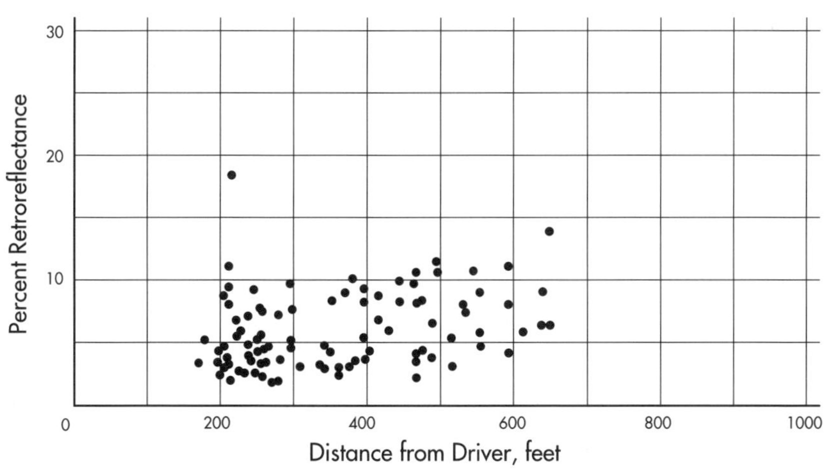

Figure 4.2 *Results of a survey of pavement reflectivity. Reprinted with permission from 770238 ©1977, Society of Automotive Engineers, Inc.*

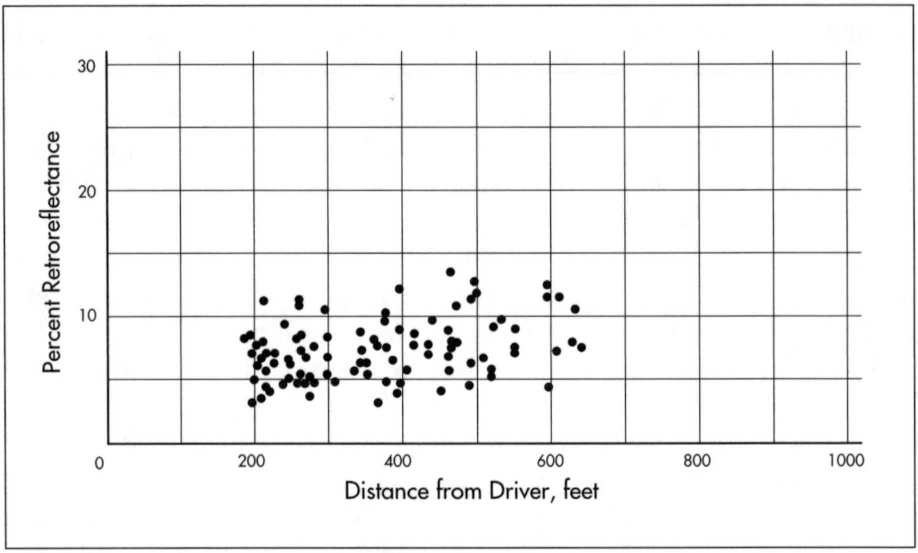

Figure 4.3 *Results of a survey of shoulder reflectivity. Reprinted with permission from 770238 ©1977, Society of Automotive Engineers, Inc.*

A study was also conducted to assess the effect of the road being wet. In this case measures were taken of pavement luminance at various distances in front of the test vehicle. The road was then wetted. Luminance readings were taken as before, at various time intervals after the wetting. These data are reproduced in Figure 4.4. The shape of the functions in Figure 4.4 is different than in figures

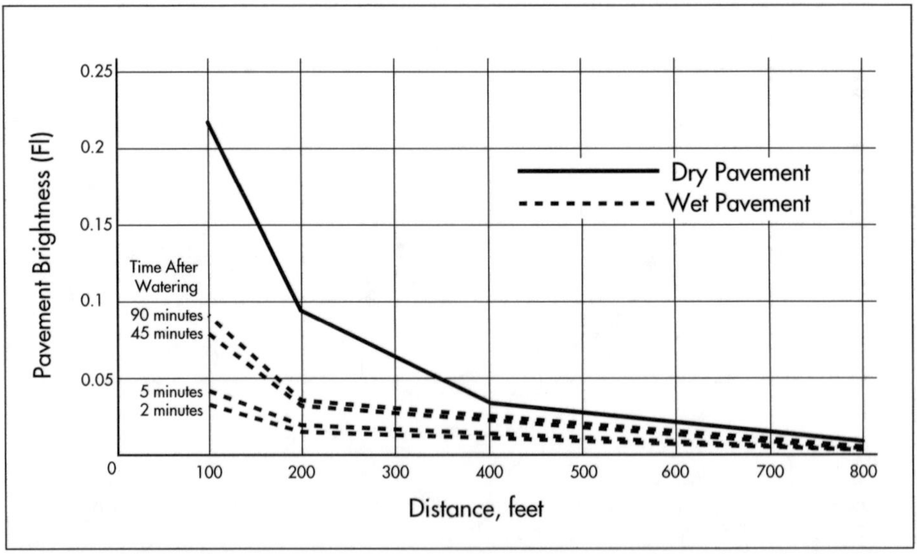

Figure 4.4 *Results of an investigation of the effect of moisture on pavement luminance. Reprinted with permission from 770238 ©1977, Society of Automotive Engineers, Inc.*

4.2 and 4.3 because the former are luminance readings and the latter shows percent retroreflectivity. Examining Figure 4.4 it is apparent that under dry conditions the road close to the test car is relatively bright, with the luminance decreasing as distance from the car increases, as would be expected. Immediately after the road was wetted the maximum luminance in front of the test car dropped to about 10% of the dry value. Even after 90 minutes the maximum pavement luminance was only about a third of the dry value. A cautionary note: the data on time after watering would not hold for all conditions. They would vary, depending on humidity, wind conditions and traffic.

The investigators also measured the reflectivity of clothing worn by 80 individuals at different times of the year. The results are reproduced in Figure 4.5 in the form of a cumulative frequency distribution. What these data show are that more than 40% of the garments measured had a reflectivity of 5% or less. More than 60% of the garments had a reflectivity of 10% or less.

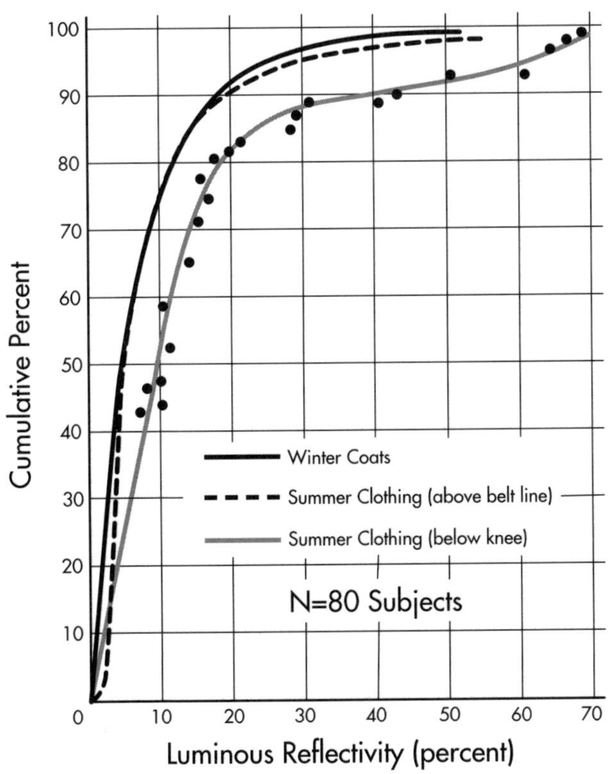

Figure 4.5 *Results of a survey of the reflectivity of clothing worn by pedestrians. Reprinted with permission from 770238 ©1977, Society of Automotive Engineers, Inc.*

These data make it clear that an object that interacts with automobiles on roads with some frequency (pedestrians) has about the same reflectivity as the road surface a large percentage of the time. This would seem to place the pedestrian at a substantial disadvantage. Data will be presented later in this chapter indicating just how much of a disadvantage it is. In addition, at the end of this chapter results will be provided of luminance and contrast measurements taken of pedestrian-sized targets in a field setting under various conditions.

Driver Visibility at Night

It's an all-too-familiar scenario. In the hours of darkness and in an area where there are no streetlights a pedestrian wearing dark clothing seeks to cross a two-lane road. The pedestrian looks left and sees nothing coming. There is a vehicle off to the right, but it looks far enough away. The pedestrian crosses the first lane, the center line, and steps in front of the vehicle previously seen. As is normally the case, the pedestrian's state of health does not benefit from the encounter. Also, as is often the case in the US, the pedestrian sues the driver of the car. At trial the driver of the car testifies that he saw the pedestrian just before impact and did not have sufficient time to stop or swerve out of the way. The plaintiff disputes this account through an expert who, quoting from a manual for drivers, says that visibility distance with low beams is 350 feet. With that kind of visibility the driver should have had plenty of time to detect the pedestrian and avoid the collision. Who is the jury to believe, the driver, who has an obvious reason for wanting the visibility distance to be as short as possible, or the (presumably) unbiased expert? This section is intended to provide a foundation of information that will enable the reader to address such questions with some authority.

Vehicle Lighting Systems

Virtually all vehicle headlighting systems offer two beams. The upper beam is designed for use when there are no other vehicles nearby in the forward field. Its design presents no serious problems. Of much greater concern is the low beam, which must provide adequate visibility while simultaneously protecting other drivers from excessive glare.

Based on this brief description of what the low-beam system must do, its design might be perceived as a relatively simple exercise. It is not. Figure 4.6 will help in understanding some of the trade offs that make the job difficult. The figure is a view of a straight, flat road seen from the center of the right lane at a height of about two feet (typical headlight mounting height on a passenger car). The numbers on the V axis give the distance, in feet, in front of the car. The dotted line in the upper left-hand quadrant shows the trajectory of the eyes of an

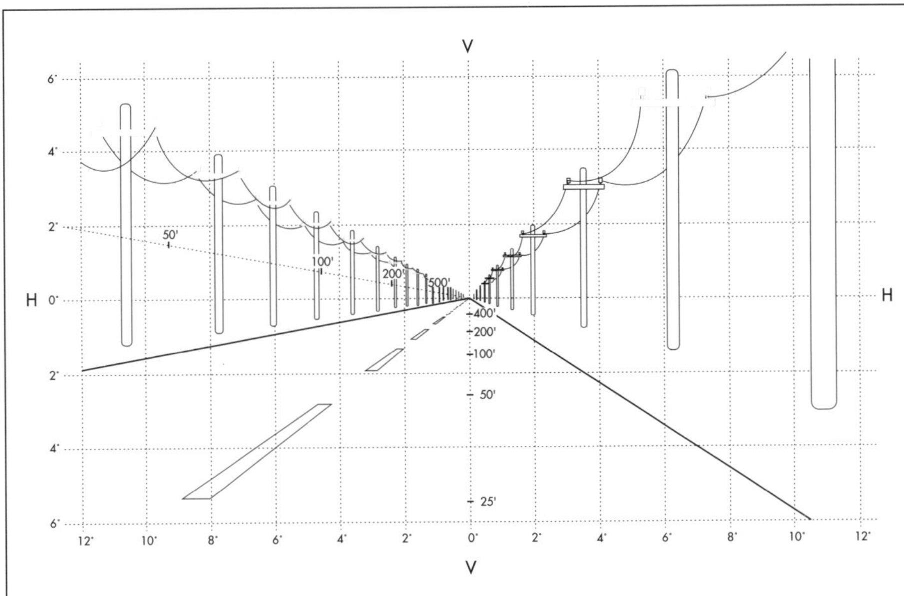

Figure 4.6 *A headlamp's view of a road.*

oncoming driver. The numbers on that line also represent distance, in feet, from the car in the right lane.

The trick in low-beam design is to get as much illumination below the H-axis as possible to help the driver see, while controlling illumination above the H-axis to reasonable levels, because it causes glare for other drivers. The illumination above the H-axis cannot be zero, because, for one important reason, virtually all signing is located there. Therefore, some illumination must be provided above the H-axis, raising the question of how much is appropriate given the conflicting criteria of sign visibility and glare protection.

A further complication arises from the extremely small angular separation between areas where illumination is helpful and where it is harmful. Headlights are attached to the sprung mass of a vehicle, and vertical aim is affected by passengers, baggage, and fuel levels. In addition, not all vehicles are given the best of care, and lamp aim can change for the worse over time for a variety of reasons. (Data on lamp aim and aim changes are presented in Chapter 5.) With these issues in mind it would be difficult enough to design a sound low-beam system if all the world's roads looked like the one shown in Figure 4.6. Of course, roads in the real world have vertical and horizontal curvature, which must also be considered in the beam design. The result of trying to deal with all of these sometimes-conflicting criteria is a compromise beam design that does not do anything really well. This is not to say that it is a poor design. A great deal of research (e.g., Bhise, et al., 1977) suggests that it is probably about the best that can be managed, at least for present-day technology.

Halogen vs. Non-halogen Sources

There is a great deal of misunderstanding concerning halogen headlamps. Many attorneys and experts seem to be under the impression that they are "better" than non-halogen lamps in that they are more powerful and/or provide better visibility. There would be merit in spending a few lines describing what halogen lamps are, and are not.

The usual light source, in automotive applications at least, is the tungsten-filament lamp. Heat the tungsten filament sufficiently by means of an electric current and it gives off light. It's simple and cheap, but does have a drawback or two. For one thing, it's less efficient in terms of lumens/watt than most other sources. This first became an issue during the fuel crisis days in the early to mid 1970s. Another concern comes from the fact that tungsten molecules boil off the filament when it is energized and redeposit on the nearest cooler surface. The result is a gradual blackening of the bulb over time and a consequent loss of output. You can see this effect in ordinary household light bulbs. In the smaller automotive lamps there is a significant loss of output as the bulb ages. Because of the large size of the envelope in the American sealed-beam headlamp, bulb blackening is not a problem. It was, however, a problem for European lamp makers, who utilized a separate-bulb system.

In a halogen lamp the tungsten filament is enclosed in a small bulb with an atmosphere containing some halogen gas. One of the features of the halogen atmosphere is that it sets up a reaction so that the tungsten molecules redeposit on the filament rather than the bulb, with the result that the latter stays clear. The filament is also operated at a much higher temperature, producing a whiter light and greater efficiency. The high temperatures would soften ordinary glass, so quartz was originally used to make the bulb in halogen lamps. Such lamps were often called "quartz-halogen" or "quartz-iodine" (iodine gas being one of the halogens used in this application) in the days after they were introduced on cars in this country. High-temperature glass is now used rather than quartz, and such sources are normally referred to simply as "halogen lamps" today.

Halogen sources were first used by European lighting manufacturers, largely because they solved the bulb-blackening problem. In the mid 1970s American auto makers petitioned the National Highway Traffic Safety Administration (NHTSA) for permission to increase the output of the high-beam system from 75,000 to 150,000 cp, to come closer to that allowed in Europe. After due consideration NHTSA agreed but, pointing to a concern for fuel economy, would not allow wattage to increase. Halogen technology offered a way to obtain more output from the same wattage, hence spurring the move to halogen in this country. The increases, however, apply only to high beams. There is one standard for low-beam systems, independent of the technology used to produce the light. It is simply not possible to improve seeing distance without putting more light on the target. Since both halogen and non-halogen lamps are controlled by the same regulations, the visibility distances provided by the two systems are the same on low beam.

European vs. US Headlamps

Starting in the 1970s there was a mini furor over European headlamps in the US. Car buff magazines seemed to vie with each other in presenting articles talking about the superior European headlights compared with the old, tired sealed-beam units used on US cars (and foreign-made cars imported to this country). Halogen technology was being used in European lamps at that time, but had not yet come into use in the US. European high beams were much more powerful than high beams on US cars (typically about twice the candlepower). European manufacturers also styled the headlamps into the sheet metal of the car. Purchasers of expensive European cars were often not happy with the cobbled look that the mandatory sealed beams sometimes gave their vehicles. The low-beam design of the European system is noticeably different. To the uninitiated it probably looks rather exotic. Terms such as "Z-Beam" and the names of major European manufacturers like Hella, Cibie and Bosch circulated among those who felt such things were important along with complaints about when American manufacturers were going to "get with it."

The sealed-beam headlamp has largely gone the way of the Dodo. Most passenger cars and many vans and trucks in the US have the headlamps styled into the body, the light source is in the form of a separate bulb, and halogen technology is standard. One rarely hears of the controversy any more. That's interesting because the main differences between the European system (known technically as CIE, which stands for Commission Internationale de L'eclairange) and that used in the US persist to this day. The European beam pattern is illegal for use in the US, but some vehicles may have such lamps, especially older cars originally equipped with sealed-beam lamps. European lamps are legal in Canada, and more likely to be found there.

The differences between US and European lamps are that the latter generally has a more powerful high beam and a low-beam that is less glaring. Iso-candela diagrams of typical US and European low beams are shown in Figure 4.7. (Iso-candela diagrams are intended to show the intensity and distribution of light from a source. The lines connect points of equal intensity.) Note the sharp transition from low- to high-intensity areas in the European lamp on top. The

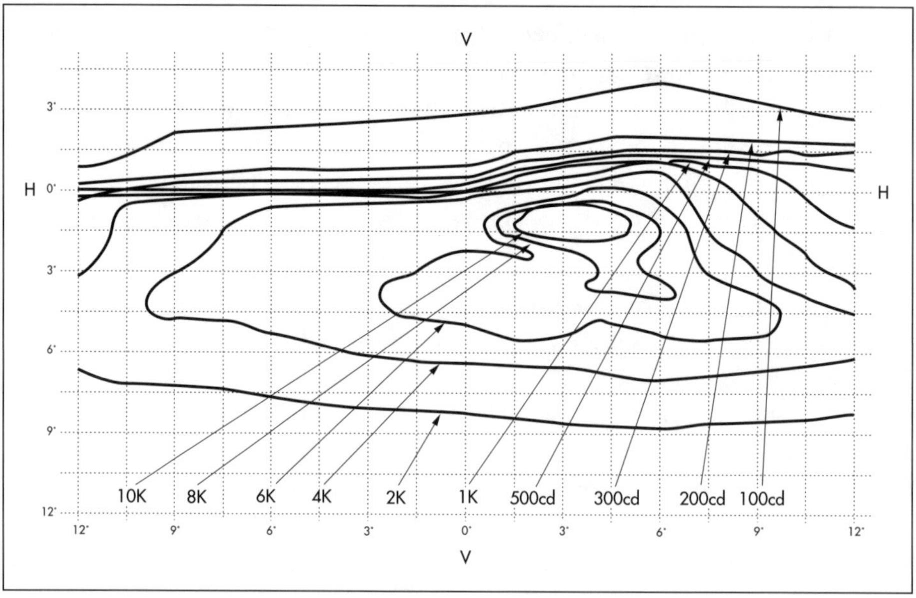

Figure 4.7 *Iso-candela diagrams of typical US and European low-beam patterns.*

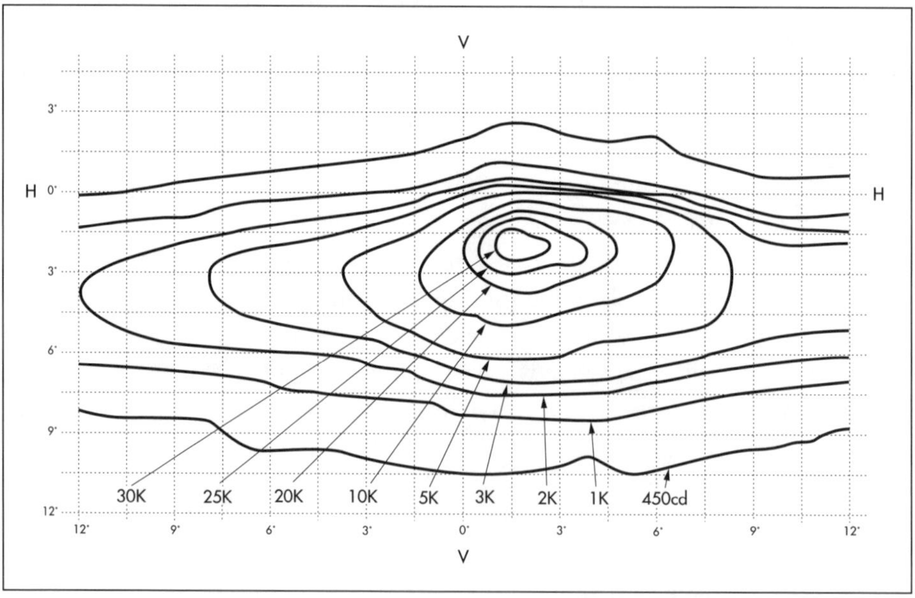

reasons for the differences are rooted in the historical development of the motor vehicle in the period between the two world wars. In Europe the automobile was much less a form of mass transportation than in the US in that era. Highways between cities were relatively empty and a driver could make good use of a very powerful high beam. On the other hand, European cities were generally much better lighted than US cities, reducing the need for a more powerful low beam. The fact that US cities were generally lighted to a much lower level than European cities, coupled with the more crowded rural highways, led to a different design philosophy on this side of the Atlantic.

In the late 1930s, American lighting manufacturers developed the sealed-beam headlamp. This is undoubtedly the most significant single development in the history of headlighting. It simultaneously solved two major problems: bulb blackening and the loss of output attributable to dirt and moisture entering the lamp enclosure over a period of time. The latter problem came about in large measure because unsealed lamps breathe, driving out air as they heat up and drawing air, together with dirt and moisture, back in again when they cool off. The sealed-beam lamp was inexpensive, available from a variety of sources, and maintained its output throughout its life.

Designers, however, grew increasingly unhappy with the restrictions posed by the sealed-beam lamp. The introduction of the rectangular sealed beam helped, but what they really wanted was to be able to style the lamp into the body, as the Europeans had been doing for years. In the early 1980s a proposal was advanced for a separate bulb system, such as the Europeans used. Use was made of O rings to seal the bulb and prevent dirt and moisture from entering the enclosure and contaminating the reflector and lens. It was argued that if the lamp were styled into the body it would improve air flow characteristics and enhance fuel economy. Thus was born the system used on virtually all vehicles sold in the US today.

A key issue confronting an expert who may discover that an involved automobile had European headlamps is that of the visibility distance they provide. Despite the fact that the beam patterns from the two systems look very different, a great deal of research has shown that the low-beam systems perform about the same (Olson, 1977).

Characteristics of US Headlamps

Safety regulations for new vehicles in the US are the province of the National Highway Traffic Safety Administration (NHTSA). These regulations are spelled out in the Federal Motor Vehicle Safety Standards (FMVSS). Regulations for lighting equipment are contained in FMVSS 108. In turn, FMVSS 108 references Society of Automotive Engineers (SAE) standards when it comes to the specifics of lamp output. For headlamps, photometric standards are listed in SAE J1383. The standards for headlamps are provided in table form, showing the maximum and/or minimum candlepower that can be projected into various portions of the forward field. The values for low beams are reproduced in Table 4.1 (from the 1995 SAE Ground Vehicle Lighting Standards Manual).

Table 4.1 SAE Photometric Standards for Low Beams

Dimensions (degrees)	Minimum (cd)	Maximum (cd)
10 U to 90U, 45R to 45L		125
8L to 8R, H to 4U	64	
4L to 4R, H to 2U	135	
1U-1 1/2L to L		700
1/2U-1 1/2L to L		1,000
1/2D-1 1/2L to L		3,000
1 1/2U-1R to R		1,400
1/2U-1R, 2R, 3R		2,700
1/2D-1 1/2R	8,000	20,000
1D-6L	750	
1 1/2D-2R	15,000	
1 1/2D-9L & 9R	750	
2D-15L & 15R	700	
4D-4R		8,000
H-2R	4,000	10,000
1D-V	6,000	15,000

The notation in Table 4.1 under "Dimensions" is somewhat cryptic. Refer to Figure 4.8. The letters U, D, R and L mean up, down, right and left, respectively. The reference points are the H and V axes in Figure 4.8. For example, 1/2D-1 1/2R means one half degree below the H axis and one and one half degrees to

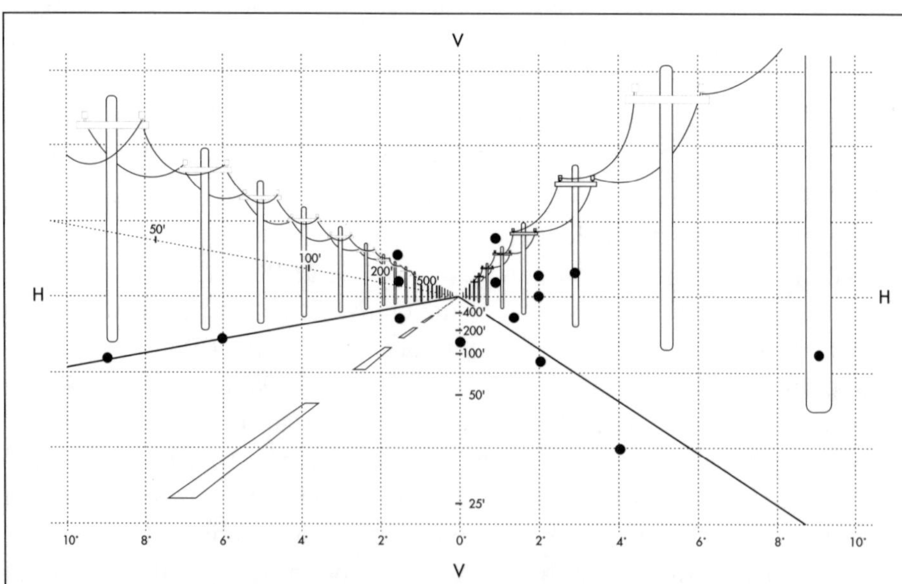

Figure 4.8 *SAE test points superimposed on a road scene.*

the right of the V axis. Figure 4.8 shows the road diagram of Figure 4.6 with most of the test points superimposed. Looking at the standards this way helps to make clear the logic behind their establishment.

The standards that govern the production of headlamps for automobiles sold in the United States are based on the distribution of candlepower. State laws, on the other hand, generally require that the headlighting system reveal a specific target at a certain distance. Many attorneys and some experts are aware of the statutes in their state and seem to assume that they are controlling. They are not. Regardless of what state legislators may have said about automotive lighting systems at some time in the past, federal regulations and SAE standards determine what headlights are, and these are silent as concerns the issue of visibility distance.

Figure 4.9 shows an iso-candela diagram of a typical low-beam lamp projected on the same road scene as Figure 4.6. Note how the main power of the beam is directed down and toward the right edge line of the road.

Motorcycle headlamps are covered by different regulations than those for automobiles and trucks (SAE J584). These regulations allow a broader range of beam patterns, including the European system. As a result, motorcycle headlamps have historically been available in a variety of patterns, sizes, wattages, and types of construction (Olson and Abrams, 1982). In recent years motorcycle headlamps

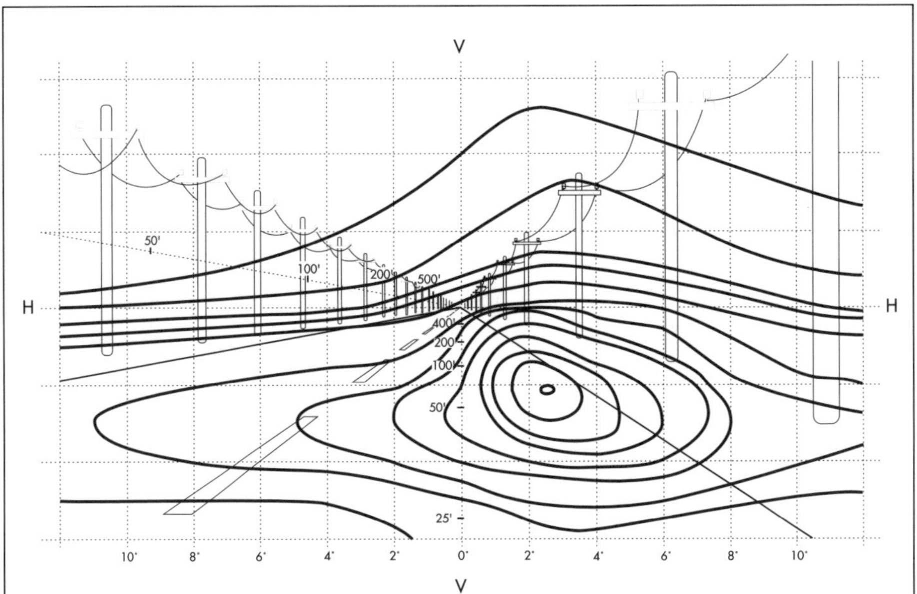

Figure 4.9 *Iso-candela diagram of a typical US low-beam pattern superimposed on a road scene.*

have become more like automotive lamps in construction, employing replaceable-bulb halogen technology. The best of these units are about equal in output to automotive headlamps, although the low-beam intensity distributions are more symmetrical about the V axis. Therefore, since most motorcycles have but one headlamp, they produce at best about half the illumination of an automobile. However, thanks to the intensity-visibility distance relationship discussed below and the fact that motorcycle headlamps are generally mounted higher than those on cars, visibility distances provided the operators of the two types of vehicle are roughly equal (Olson and Abrams, 1982).

The Intensity-Visibility Distance Relationship

As noted in Chapter 2, the illuminance on an object varies inversely as the square of the distance from the source of illumination. Thus, if the illuminance reaching an object is X at distance Y from a light source, the illuminance will be 0.25X at distance 2Y. On a basis of this relationship, doubling the output of a headlamp, as became possible several years ago with high beams when the maximum allowable output increased from 75,000 cd to 150,000 cd, should increase visibility distance by about 40%. Unfortunately, this is not the case. Figure 4.10, from Roper and Howard (1938), suggests that an increase of about 20% is all that can be expected.

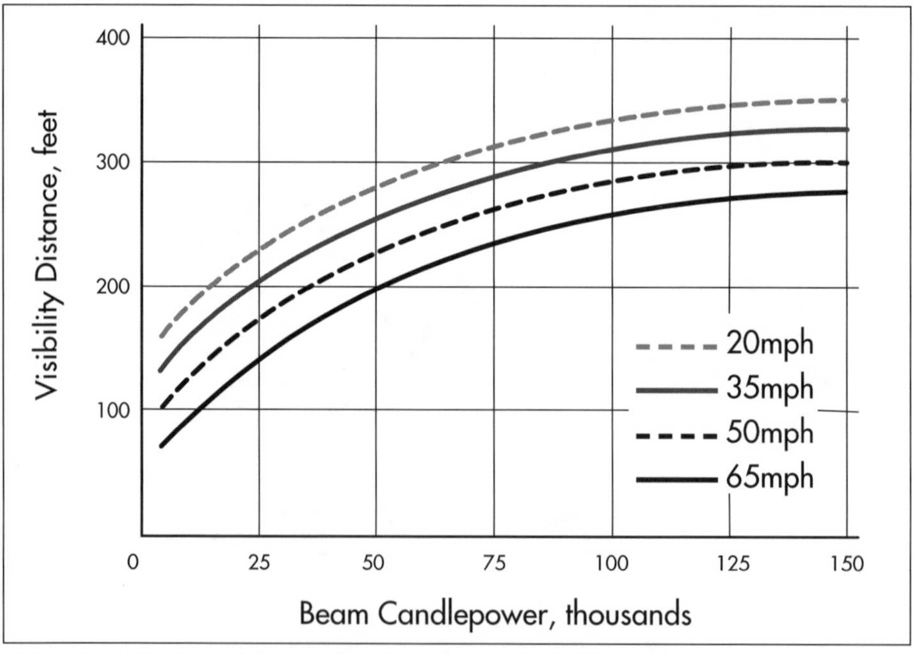

***Figure 4.10** The beam intensity-visibility distance relationship (Reproduced with permission from the* Transactions of the Illumination Engineering Society, *Vol. XXXIII, No. 5, published by the Illumination Engineering Society of North America).*

The reason that headlamp visibility distance does not increase as indicated by the distance squared law is partially due to factors such as atmospheric attenuation. The main reason, however, as discussed earlier, is that contrast is more important in determining whether something will be visible than is the illuminance reaching it. Increasing visibility distance is not a simple matter of increasing lamp output, even if the glare problems such an increase would cause could be ignored.

Implications

Present-day motor vehicle headlamps are the product of a long, evolutionary process. Low-beam headlamps in particular are asked to provide adequate illumination for safe vehicle operation at all legal speeds, allowing the driver to safely detect objects on the road and detect and read signs that can be placed on the right or left side of the road as well as overhead. In addition, the system should provide adequate illumination on hills and curves as well as straight-flat sections. All of this must be accomplished while holding glare for other roadway users to reasonable levels.

A person who suggested that headlamps are unlikely to successfully meet all these criteria would be correct. The existing system is a result of compromise that is weighted toward glare protection (not to suggest that this is a bad idea). The two major systems in use in the world today, the US and European, use rather different approaches to achieve the same general ends. Both are biased away from oncoming traffic (i.e., to the right side of the road in a right-hand-drive system). This makes sense in terms of seeing right-side delineation and the many key signs that are typically located there. It also pulls the main power of the beam away from the eyes of other drivers in the forward field under most driving conditions. In terms of the revealing power of the system, it clearly favors objects to the right. The differences in visibility distance to targets located to the right and left of the vehicle are substantial, as shall be described in some detail shortly. The decision to favor glare protection over revealing power also leads to marked limitations in the visibility distance that the system can be expected to provide. More about that later as well.

The Visibility Provided by Automotive Headlamps

Research Results

To return to the hypothetical mishap described at the start of this section, at what distance should a reasonably alert driver have been able to detect the pedestrian? To provide an answer, we will rely on data from a field test of different headlighting systems (Olson and Sivak, 1983).

There have been many investigations of the visibility provided by motor vehicle lighting systems, and the reader may question why the author is relying on his own work. The reason this study was chosen is that it is one of the most recent field investigations, and one of the most comprehensive. It also included pedestrian targets, which are often of direct interest in litigation.

The study was carried out as part of an effort to develop an improved low-beam lighting system. Six candidate systems were investigated. Two of these were standard US and European low beams, which were included as controls. The other four were different from the standard systems in one respect or another, incorporating features that it was hoped would yield an overall benefit.

In this investigation subjects drove or rode in a car that was operated on a private road in a rural area devoid of artificial illumination. The road was about a half-mile long, had two nine-foot lanes, was flat and straight, and was paved in asphalt that was worn and smooth. There were four possible targets. Three of these were clad in dark blue denim, were of about equal width, and differed in height. One was an experimental assistant (pedestrian). The other two were, respectively, 2.5 feet and 6 inches high. The fourth target was the pedestrian, wearing the blue denim trousers and a white vest. One or more of these targets could appear on each run through the course, at any point in the course, and on either the right or left of the test vehicle. The subjects had to detect the target, identify it by size and position, and press an appropriate button on a box in their lap. The distance from the target at which they pressed the button was recorded. Twenty-three young subjects participated in the study, providing a total of 60 measures on each target condition.

The results of this investigation, for US low-beam headlamps, are given in Figures 4.11 through 4.18. The figures are in the form of what is called "normal probability distributions," hence the rather strange-appearing vertical axis. This is a convenient plotting method for assessing performance by percentiles. A normal distribution such as described in Chapter 1 plotted this way appears as a straight line. Since most of the data fall nearly on a straight line in these plots, it means that the visibility distance performance measured in this test can be approximated by a normal distribution.

There are large differences evident in these plots as a function of target reflectivity, size and position right or left of the test vehicle. Response distances for the pedestrian wearing the white top ranged from 150 to 450 feet (5th to 95th percentile). The same target standing to the left of the test vehicle recorded response distances of 80 to 300 feet. Removing the white top reduced response distances substantially; from 50 to 250 on the right and 25 to 140 on the left.

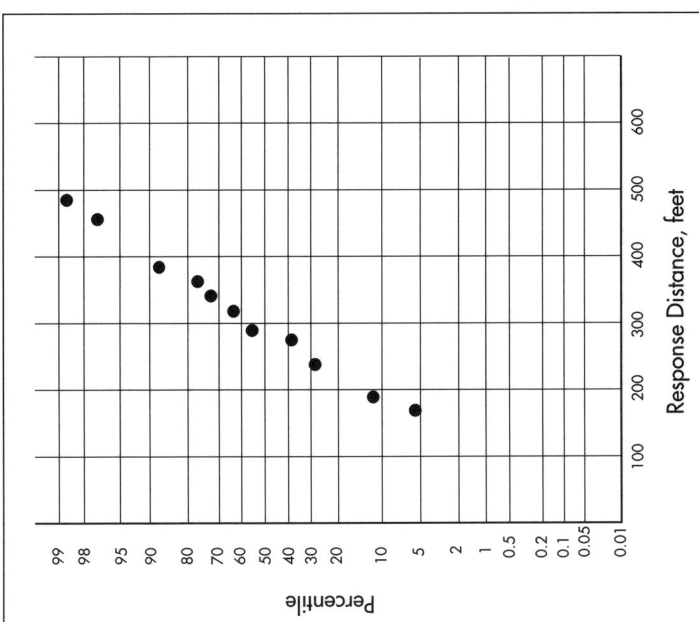

Figure 4.11 *Normal probability plot of response distances recorded to pedestrian target wearing white vest standing to right of test vehicle (from Olson and Sivak, 1983).*

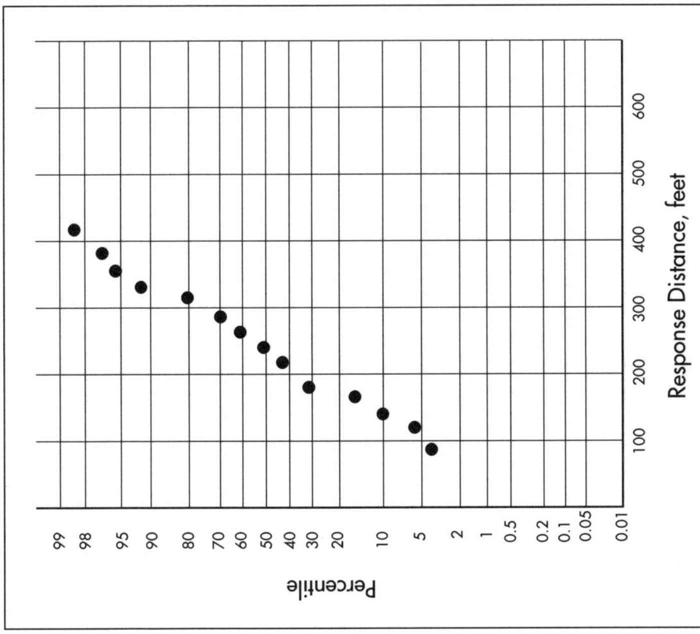

Figure 4.12 *Normal probability plot of response distances recorded to pedestrian target wearing white vest standing to left of test vehicle (from Olson and Sivak, 1983).*

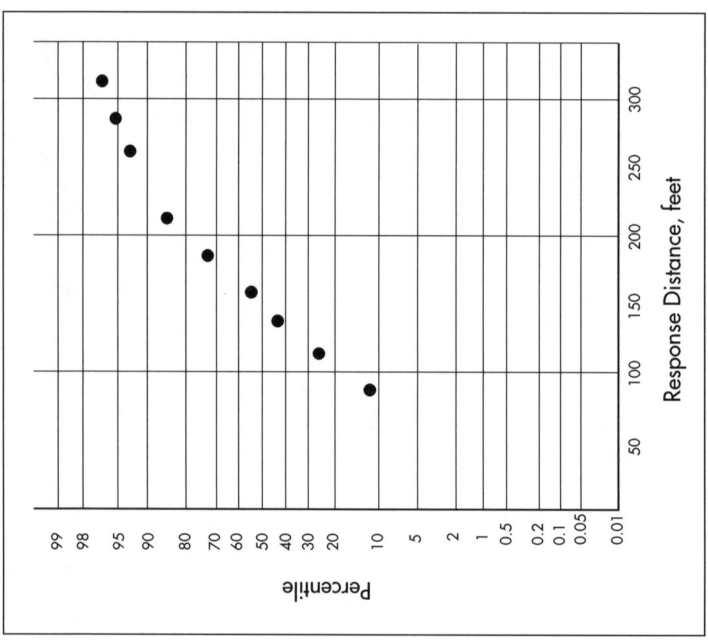

Figure 4.13 *Normal probability plot of response distances recorded to dark-clad pedestrian target standing to right of test vehicle (from Olson and Sivak, 1983).*

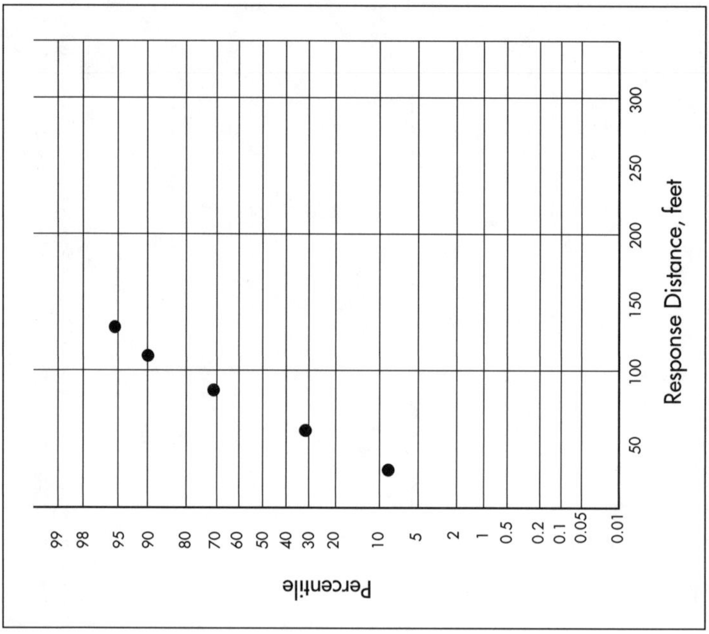

Figure 4.14 *Normal probability plot of response distances recorded to dark-clad pedestrian target standing to left of test vehicle (from Olson and Sivak, 1983).*

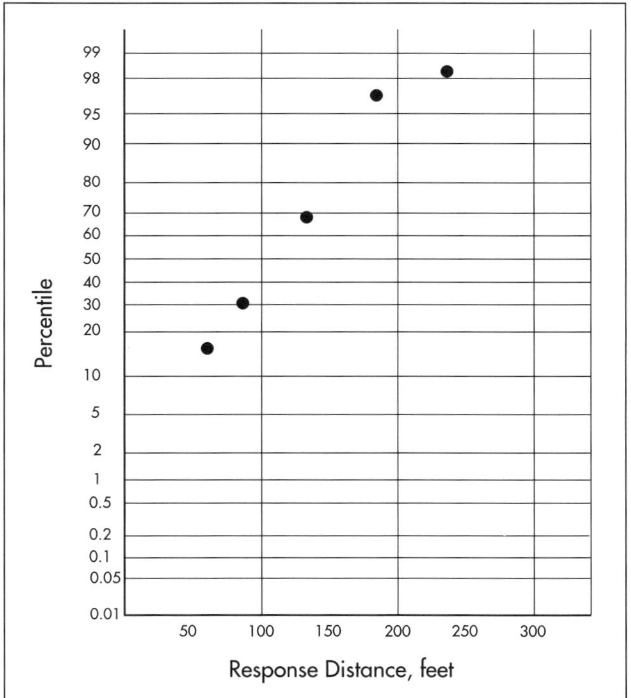

Figure 4.15 *Normal probability plot of response distances recorded to medium-size, low-reflectivity target positioned to right of test vehicle (from Olson and Sivak, 1983).*

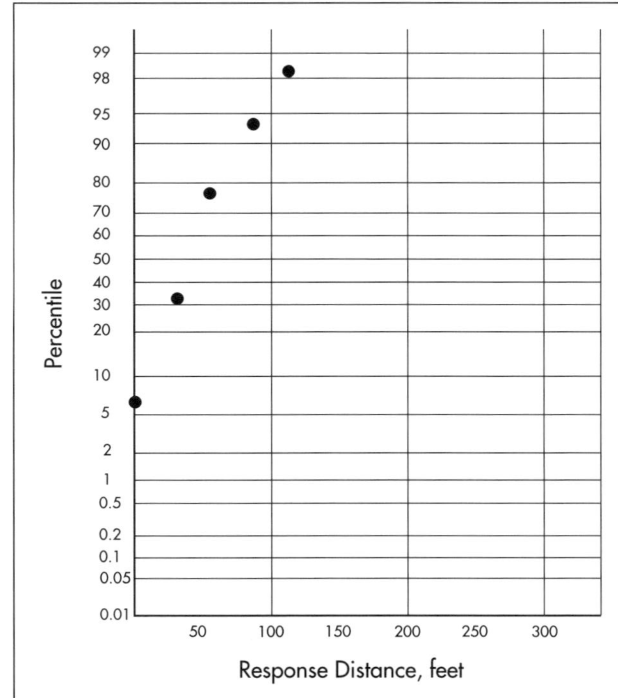

Figure 4.16 *Normal probability plot of response distances recorded to medium-size, low-reflectivity target positioned to left of test vehicle (from Olson and Sivak, 1983).*

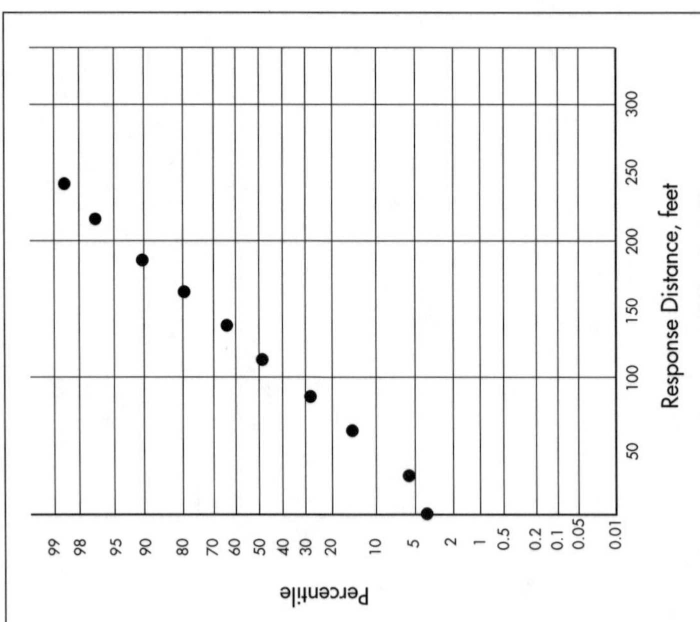

Figure 4.17 *Normal probability plot of response distances recorded to small, low-reflectivity target positioned to right of test vehicle (from Olson and Sivak, 1983).*

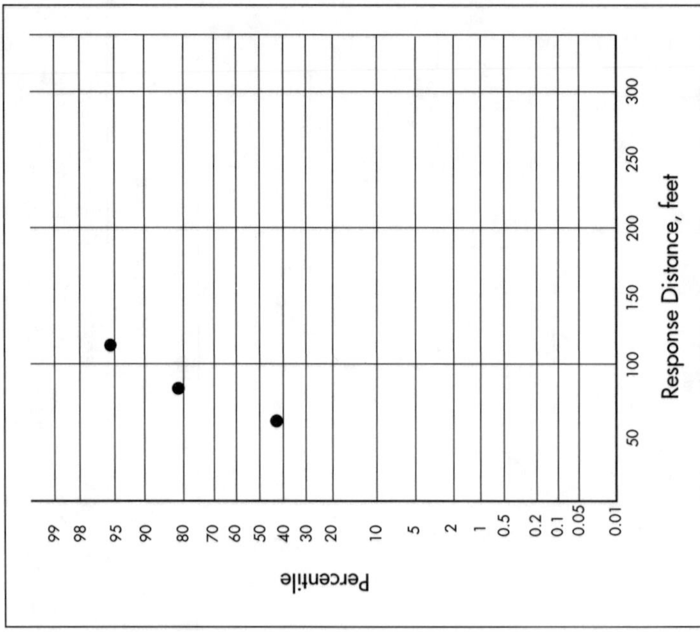

Figure 4.18 *Normal probability plot of response distances recorded to small, low-reflectivity target positioned to left of test vehicle (from Olson and Sivak, 1983).*

The response distances recorded to the smaller targets were somewhat less than in the case of the pedestrian targets when they were on the right side, but much less when positioned on the left side. The response distances to the medium-size target on the right side ranged from 40 to 175 feet, those to the smallest target ranged from 25 to 175 feet. On the left side, however, the response distances for these two targets ranged from 0 to about 100 feet.

The expression "response distances" is used in recognition of the fact that the distances recorded in this study were preceded by a perception-response interval. Research on choice reaction time (see Chapter 9) suggests that 0.5 second would be a reasonable estimate for this situation. The speed of the test car was 25 mph (36.7 ft/sec), meaning that about 18 feet should be added to the values in Figures 4.11 through 4.18 to arrive at an estimate for detection distance.

What do these data mean in terms of pedestrian safety? To illustrate, calculations were made to determine the percentage of trials in which the subjects would not have been able to stop short of the target pedestrian's position from various speeds. It was assumed that detection occurred 18 feet before the subject pressed the button in the test. In referring to a real-world scenario it was further assumed that perception-response time was one second and the car was brought to a stop at an average deceleration of 0.75 g. Table 4.2 lists the speeds selected, and the stopping distances that result, not including the distance covered during the perception-response interval.

Table 4.2 Speeds and Stopping Distances for Pedestrian Safety Exercise

Speed (mph)	Speed (ft/sec)	Stopping Dist. (ft)
25	36.7	28
35	51.3	55
45	66.0	90
55	80.7	135
65	95.3	188

To arrive at an overall stopping distance for each speed, including perception-response time, the 18 feet covered in the assumed perception-response time of 0.5 second in the test was added to the recorded response distances. Then the speed in ft/sec was added to the stopping distance to yield a total stopping distance from detection, including the assumed perception-response time of one second.

The results of this analysis are given in Table 4.3, for the pedestrian target in all blue denim (Dark Ped) and the pedestrian target with blue denim trousers and the white top (White Top Ped).

Table 4.3 Percentage of Trials in Which Subjects Would Have *Not* Been Able to Stop Short of the Pedestrian Position as a Function of Target Reflectivity, Speed, and Position Right or Left of the Test Vehicle

Speed (mph)	Dark Ped Right	Dark Ped Left	White Top Ped Right	White Top Ped Left
25	<1	5	<1	<1
35	12	70	<1	4
45	45	96	3	10
55	81	100	15	30
65	95	100	40	65

The results of this analysis indicate that even at speeds as low as 25 mph a dark-clad pedestrian approaching from the left of the vehicle would be at some risk. The risk increases rapidly with speed. Wearing a highly reflective top greatly increases visibility and reduces the probability that a driver will not see the pedestrian in time.

There are two very important points that must be kept in mind when considering the results in Table 4.3. The first is that they represent the performance of young drivers only. Older drivers (range of 60 to 75) in this and other tests detected identical targets at 67 to 75% of the distance of the young subjects. The probability of the subject being unable to stop short of the target position would have been substantially higher with older subjects.

The second important point is that the data in Table 4.3 have not been corrected for driver expectancy. The subject of expectancy and the difference it can make in visibility performance is discussed in a later section.

Target Reflectivity

Two levels of target reflectivity were employed for the pedestrian targets in the study just described. One was all dark blue denim, with a reflectivity of less than 5%. In the other a white vest was worn, retaining the dark lower garments. The reflectivity of the vest was about 70%. Clearly, there was a substantial difference in the average distance at which the subjects responded to each target.

An investigation by Mortimer and Olson (1974) provides a more comprehensive look at target reflectivity as a factor in visibility distance. They used a different target, which was about two and a half feet tall. In addition, glare was introduced from an approaching vehicle. Summary data on the effect of target reflectivity is provided in Figure 4.19.

The results are broken into three separation-distance categories, where separation distance refers to the distance between opposing vehicles. On the left side of the figure are average response distances when the separation between the

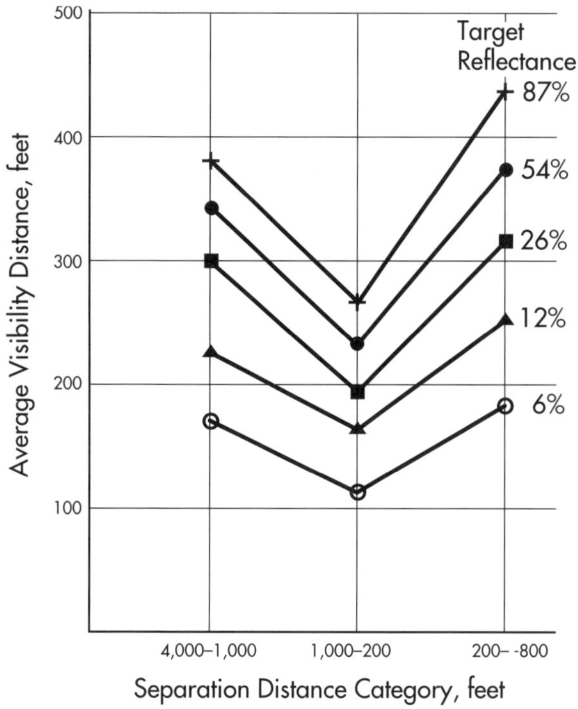

Figure 4.19 *Effect of target reflectivity on response distance as a function of separation between test vehicle and glare source (from Mortimer and Olson, 1974).*

two vehicles was from 4,000 to 1,000 feet. The middle category is for separation distances from 1,000 to 200 feet, the zone where glare effects would build to maximum. The category on the right is from 200 to 800 feet, with negative numbers meaning the vehicles have passed and there is no more glare. Under no-glare conditions in this study each increment of reflectivity increased the average response distance by 60 to 70 feet. A nine-fold increase in target reflectivity, from 6% to 54% resulted in the subjects' average response distance increasing by approximately 100% in all three separation-distance categories shown.

High Beam vs. Low Beam

The study by Olson and Sivak dealt only with low-beam systems. It is reasonable to ask what difference high beams would make in the results. The most comprehensive study comparing high beams to low beams has been reported by Mortimer and Olson (1974). This study included consideration of target reflectivity, target location, lateral separation between approaching vehicles, and a number of lighting systems, including standard US low and high beams. Representative findings are presented in Figures 4.20 and 4.21. These show that the differences between low and high beams depend in part on target reflectivity.

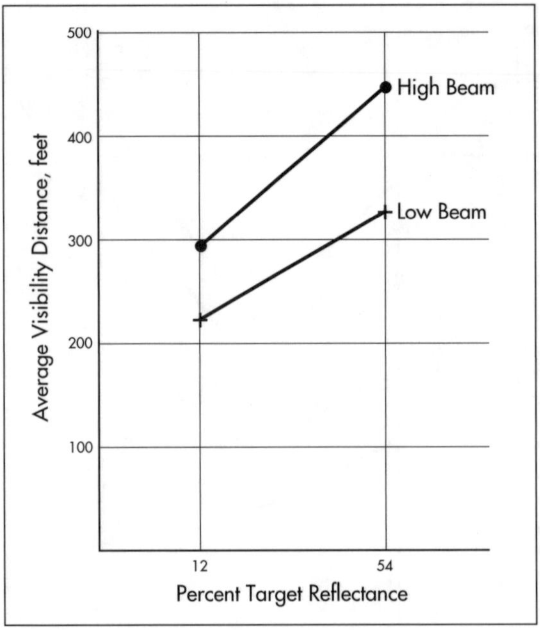

Figure 4.20 *Effect of target reflectivity and headlamp beam on response distance (from Mortimer and Olson, 1974).*

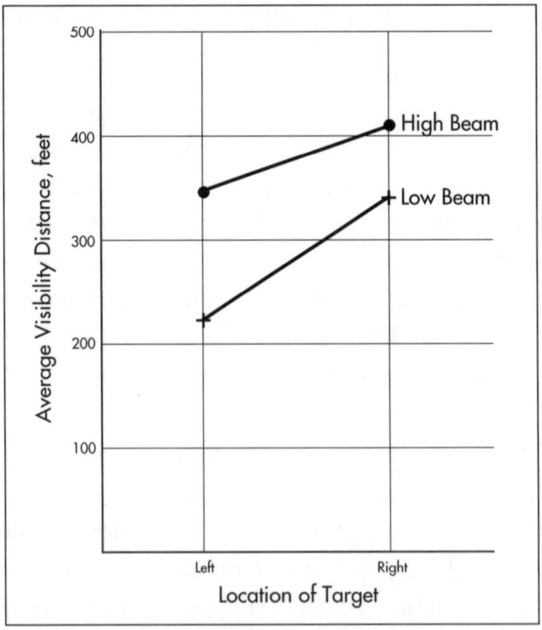

Figure 4.21 *Effect of target position and headlamp beam on response distance (from Mortimer and Olson, 1974).*

Summed over all conditions tested, visibility distance was an average of about 75 feet greater for high beams with a 12% reflectivity target, but about 100 feet greater for the 54% target. The major difference, however, was as a function of target location right or left of the vehicle (Figure 4.21). These data are averaged over all separation distances in a meeting situation, so the high beam response distances would be more affected by glare. Even so, performance on left-side targets was substantially better with the high beams. The difference on right-side targets is less pronounced. In a no-glare situation response distance would be the same for right- and left-side targets with high beams. In general, under no-glare conditions and using targets of relatively low reflectivity (i.e., 25% reflectivity or less), it was found that high beams improved visibility to target on the left side of the car by about 100%. They improved visibility to targets on the right side of the car by about 50%.

Expectancy

Definition

"Expectancy" is a predisposition of persons to believe that things will happen or be configured in certain ways. We all have expectancies that touch our lives every day in many ways. Consider the examples in Figure 4.22. Which way would you: turn the knob to move the dial to the right? Flip the switch to turn a

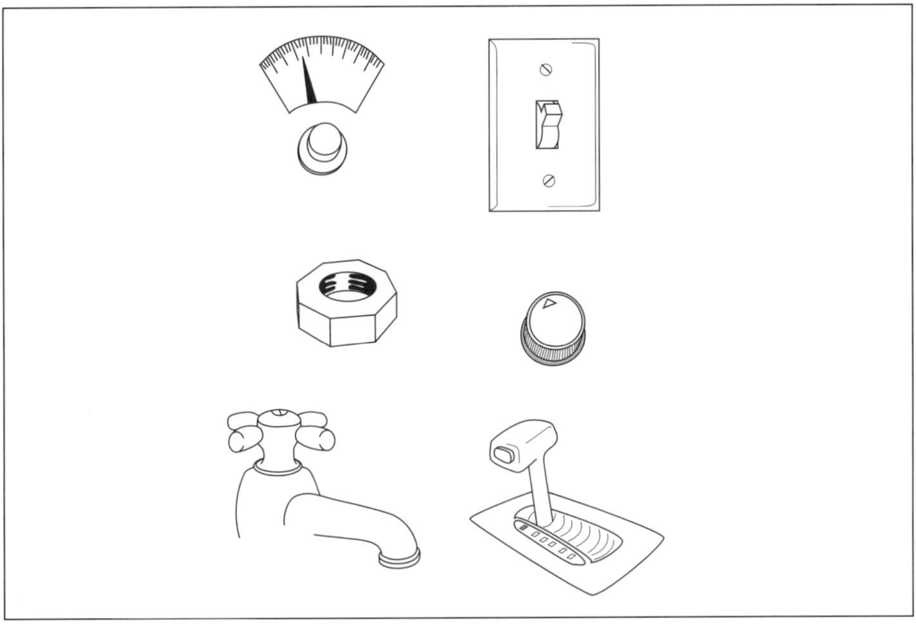

Figure 4.22 *Examples of everyday devices concerning which people have expectancies.*

light on? Turn the nut to tighten? Turn the knob to decrease the volume on a radio? Turn the handle to increase the flow of water? Move the lever to increase speed? If you are typical you would have answered clockwise, up, clockwise, counterclockwise, counterclockwise, and forward.

Some things make intuitive sense and design has, fortunately, generally followed that lead. For example, it seems logical to move a lever forward to make something go in that direction and to move the lever further forward to increase speed in that direction. Similarly, if speed is controlled by a pedal, it seems reasonable to increase speed by pressing harder on the pedal. Other things are probably arbitrary. The general convention of turning clockwise to tighten a threaded fastener or increase the volume on a radio or TV seems to have no logical basis; it could just as easily be the opposite. Being established, however, items that depart from that convention cause problems.

Driver Expectancy

All drivers have expectancies as well, which have developed from exposure to general practices in Civil and Traffic Engineering, as well as the behavior of other drivers. As Alexander and Lunenfeld (1986) point out, expectancy relates to a driver's readiness to respond to situations, events, and information in predictable and successful ways. Expectancy influences the speed and accuracy of driver information processing and is one of the most important considerations in the design and operation of highways and the presentation of information to drivers.

There has been a strong trend toward making road design, signing and signaling practices as uniform as possible. The result has been to develop driver expectancies in these areas. The advantage is that when expectancies are met smooth traffic flow, maximum throughput, and minimum conflicts result. When expectancies are violated quite the opposite conditions result, and it requires a more potent stimulus to reliably capture the driver's attention and more information to communicate the essential data than would otherwise be the case. The result is that perception-response time is normally increased, as is the probability of error.

Drivers have general expectancies, which can be altered by conditions. For example, a driver who encounters a series of sharp curves that require a speed change, unusually heavy traffic, concentrations of pedestrians, etc. will have his/her expectations temporarily altered (referred to by Alexander and Lunenfeld as "ad hoc" expectancies). A key function of signing is to set driver expectancies. This is particularly true of warning signs. Signs such as "School Zone, Children Playing," or "Construction Ahead" alert the driver to a potential problem and alter expectancies in ways that are helpful in reducing the probability of collisions.

When confronted with the issue of expectancy some attorneys will counter with a question such as: "shouldn't a prudent driver always be alert to the possibility that some emergency will occur?" The simple response is "yes," but the matter is a tad more complex than that. It is fair to say that a prudent driver should recognize the possibility that some emergency situation may develop at any time. On the other hand, it's also fair to say that drivers have a right to expect that other road users will behave rationally. In fact, experience teaches us that other drivers will virtually always respect stop signs and traffic signals, and will stay in their lane when movement out of their lane could cause problems for other drivers. Pedestrians will cooperate in this endeavor as well and not place themselves in the path of a car when the latter clearly has the right of way. It is certainly true that drivers and pedestrians will occasionally behave in ways that might be described as discourteous or simply stupid, forcing abrupt changes in speed or lane position on the part of some driver. It is generally safe to assume, however, that rational persons will not deliberately jeopardize their personal well being or risk damage to their vehicle. The movement of traffic would indeed be chaotic if drivers had to operate their vehicles in a way that would prepare them to respond to the possibility, however remote, that any vehicle or any pedestrian may violate their right of way at any time.

Correction for Expectancy

The data from the visibility tests presented earlier indicate that serious problems may result if a driver is confronted with a low-contrast object while operating a motor vehicle at medium and higher speeds at night. These results are based on a structured test in which the subjects were alert, free from drugs and alcohol, aware of the purpose of the test and the nature of the targets, and had no concerns with other traffic. Because of these conditions and the effect they would have on expectancy, the response distances measured in that or any other structured test are probably greater than could reasonably be expected in the real world. The question is by how much? A study directly applicable to this issue has been reported by Roper and Howard (1938). The subjects in Roper and Howard's study were recruited to conduct "subjective evaluations of headlighting systems." After a time they were told the test was complete and to drive back to the parking lot so they could go home. Without the knowledge of the subject, a dark-clad mannequin had been set up in the center of the lane they had to use. Measures were made of the distance from the mannequin at which the subject released the accelerator. With this "surprise" phase completed, the subjects were briefed on the true purpose of the study and then asked to approach the target again at the same speed, releasing the accelerator as soon as they could see it. Under the second, "alerted," condition response distances averaged twice those obtained in the surprise trial. The same approach was used in a more recent study, concerned with signing, with substantially the same results (Olson, 1990).

Roper and Howard's results may seem extreme. However, they appear reasonable when some of the differences between the surprise and alerted conditions are considered:

- In the alerted condition the subjects knew where the target would appear and could fixate that spot foveally. It is likely that detection in the surprise condition was accomplished peripherally.
- Knowing the nature of the target makes it possible to "detect" it using subtle cues that may not be adequate in the absence of such special knowledge.

With full knowledge of the nature of the test, and no need to be concerned with the demands of normal driving the subjects' expectancies are much different than they would be in normal driving. Under test conditions they can focus their attention on the target detection task and are less likely to be distracted by other things that might be going on.

In accident reconstruction, an investigator is sometimes interested in estimating the distance at which a driver should have been able to detect the target of interest. Such tests are often set up much like the alerted portion of the Roper and Howard study. It is possible to obtain useful information by such an exercise. For the reasons listed above, however, it is essential that the investigator understand that the likelihood of something being detected at all, as well as the distance at which it would have been detected, will probably be substantially overestimated. Suggestions for the way in which such investigations should be conducted in order to arrive at a more accurate estimate of the range of visibility distances to be expected from reasonably alert drivers will be offered in Chapter 8.

To return to the question posed to the jury by the hypothetical case described at the start of this section, the information presented here suggest that the version related by the defendant driver is more believable than that provided by the "expert." Individuals who walk in traffic at night, relying on drivers to see them, are placing themselves in some danger. Unfortunately, this situation is unlikely to be resolved by improvements in vehicle lighting anytime in the near future. It would be helpful to improve the understanding of both drivers and pedestrians concerning the limitations in nighttime visibility, and encourage those who do mingle with traffic at night to wear light-colored garments or (even better) retroreflective materials.

Why Do People Not Adjust Their Driving at Night?

Given the evidence that visibility at night when using motor vehicle headlamps is severely limited, it would be reasonable to expect that traffic would move more slowly at night. Clearly, that does not seem to be the case. The question is why?

There is evidence that people overestimate the visibility provided by vehicle lighting systems. For example, Allen et al. (1970) had subjects stand along the side of a road and estimate the distance at which an approaching driver could see them. At the same time the driver indicated the distance at which he/she could see each pedestrian. On average, the pedestrians' estimates were about twice the distance at which they actually could be seen. Of course, given the expectancies of the drivers in the test, they probably detected the pedestrians at an average of about twice the distance they would under real world conditions. This investigation was extended and confirmed by Shinar (1984). There are no comparable data for drivers, but the behavior of most of them while operating a vehicle at night suggests that they think they can see a good deal better than they really can. If this is true, we have an unfortunate combination of errors, with both drivers and pedestrians thinking visibility is better than it is.

Leibowitz et al. (1982) have advanced a theory to account for the fact that people often drive well in excess of speeds that would allow them to stop short of an unexpected, low-contrast object. The theory is based on the fact that there are two independent modes of processing visual information. One of these is called the "focal" mode, which is concerned with object discrimination and identification. Focal functions are optimal in the foveal area, and are much affected by level of illumination and refractive error. The other mode is called "ambient," which is concerned with spatial orientation. Spatial orientation can be accomplished in the foveal area, but, unlike the focal functions, it is adequate in the peripheral areas as well. In addition, ambient functions are much less sensitive to illumination levels and refractive error than focal functions. Under night driving conditions there is a selective degradation of these two modes, with focal vision being much more affected. This means that we suffer relatively little loss of ambient vision, which is useful for basic functions such as maintaining lateral position on the road. The fact that focal vision is greatly reduced is less appreciated because the demands on it are intermittent. Thus, since the driver can carry out routine control function about as well at night as during the day, overconfidence concerning the whole driving task may be generated.

Overdriving of Headlamps: The Assured Clear Distance Ahead (ACDA) Rule

The law generally holds that the safe operation of a vehicle is the responsibility of the operator, an idea that certainly accords with common sense. Clearly, willfully negligent behavior that endangers other persons should not be tolerated. One manifestation of this point of view is the assured clear distance ahead (ACDA) rule. Most if not all states have some version of the ACDA rule in their statutes. Basically the ACDA rule says that no driver shall operate a vehicle at a speed in excess of that which will allow it to be brought to a stop within the assured clear distance ahead.

The ACDA rule seems like a sensible extension of the general concept that places responsibility for the safe operation of a vehicle on the shoulders of the operator. It says the operator must be aware of the characteristics of the vehicle, and its operating environment, and always drive at a speed that will allow the vehicle to be brought to a stop short of any hazards that may appear in its path. The rule has some flexibility. Courts have held that there are limits to the ability of an operator to deal with certain types of hazards, the classic pedestrian-dart-out collision being one example.

The ACDA rule may be invoked as a counter to testimony concerning limitations in driver visibility at night. Relying on research data such as presented earlier in this chapter, an expert may offer the opinion that a driver had little or no chance to avoid a collision under the circumstances. The opposition attorney may come back with a question something like: "What you're saying is that Mr. so and so was overdriving his headlamps?" The short, honest answer is "yes." The problem is that this response may be very damaging, even leading to a jury instruction equating overdriving one's headlamps with negligence.

An excellent example of how the ACDA rule can work against scientific testimony concerning limitations in night visibility is cited by Leibowitz, et al. (1993). The case involved a fatal nighttime collision between a snowmobile and a flatbed rail car, which was across a grade crossing (Sharp vs. Norfolk & Western RR, Sandusky, Ohio). Testimony was offered that the rail car was first visible at a distance that would not permit the snowmobile operator to brake in time to avoid the collision. The trial judge instructed the jury that as a matter of law, the railroad should not be held liable because the snowmobile operator was in violation of the ACDA rule. When the jury awarded compensation to the estate of the operator anyway the judge overturned the decision. This ruling was upheld by the appeals court on the basis of the ACDA rule. Subsequently the decision was overturned by the Ohio Supreme Court. The opinion reads, in part:

> "Violation of the statute and a finding of negligence per se depend on whether there is evidence that the driver collided with an object which was, inter alia, reasonably discernible."

The expression "overdriving one's headlamps" can be taken to imply that the driver is operating at such a speed as to be unable to cope with anything that may happen to be in the roadway. That is hardly the case. Whether one is overdriving the headlamps is very much dependent on the contrast characteristics of the object that is encountered. Recall the data presented in Table 4.4. It is clear from that analysis that a dark-clad pedestrian is at some risk from a car going as slowly as 25 mph, even when the driver is expecting an encounter. Smaller objects, the presence of glare, and other factors can still further reduce the maximum "safe" speed. For some types of targets and driving conditions, the fact is that we begin to overdrive our headlamps almost from the moment the car starts to move forward.

The answer to the ACDA argument is that the limitations of vehicle lighting systems and human vision make it impossible to reliably reveal all possible, significant objects at anything other than very low speeds. The price we would pay for literally conforming to the ACDA rule is severely limiting nighttime speeds, perhaps to something in the range of 20 mph, and possibly prohibiting anyone over the age of 60 from driving at night. It's highly unlikely that the public would accept such restrictions, even if legislators could be induced to enact them. Individuals who took it upon themselves to drive at such speeds would pose a threat to their own well being as well as that of other roadway users by creating large speed differentials, and numerous conflicts with others driving at or near posted limits.

Leibowitz, et al. recommend several approaches to this problem. Most of them come down to educating the public, both those on wheels and those on foot, about the problem and what they can do to help. They also recommend differential speed limits. Lower speed limits at night might seem to have little practical effect, since the lower limits would still be well above those required to literally meet the ACDA criterion. They would, however, at least represent acknowledgment on the part of lawmakers that night driving is more demanding than day driving, hence lower speeds are desirable.

Measurements of Target Luminance and Contrast With Illumination from Automotive Headlamps

The information presented in this chapter up to this point should have made it clear that vehicle headlighting systems may not provide illumination adequate to reliably reveal some objects or conditions in time for the driver to avoid a collision, except at very low speeds. It was also pointed out that contrast is the key to visibility. If headlights have limited revealing power, that is tantamount to saying they are not generating sufficient target contrast except at relatively short distances. It would be useful at this point to present actual measures of target luminance and contrast to provide some indication of what levels are required to render an object such as a pedestrian adequately visible.

Method

The data to be presented were collected as part of a lighting investigation (Olson, et al., 1990), and were intended to show the levels of luminance and contrast provided by typical low- and high-beam systems on a pedestrian-sized object in a dark environment. The work was done to provide reference data for a computer visibility model then under development. Measures were taken of the luminance of two targets and their backgrounds on the same road facility used in the visibility distance test described earlier in this chapter. The two targets were each six feet tall and one foot wide. Each was painted a uniform gray. Paint was prepared to make the reflectivity of the darker of the two about 6%, the other 25%. The 6% target appeared dark gray. Its reflectivity approximated that of dark clothing typically worn by pedestrians in cold weather.

The targets were placed one foot from either the right or left edge of the test road. There were no sources of artificial illumination nearby or visible in the background of the targets. As viewed from the test car, the target appeared against a background of road surface across the bottom and part way up the side closest to the road center, and against a background of distant trees, shrubs and sky across the top and along the side away from the road center. Figure 4.23 consists of two photographs of a person standing at the test site to provide some idea of the background situation. These photographs were taken with the pedestrian at a distance of 100 feet from the camera.

The targets were illuminated by non-halogen, sealed-beam headlamps at a mounting height of 30 inches on a large station wagon. The headlamps had been checked to ensure that they conformed to SAE standards and had been carefully aimed. They were powered by a precision control system at 12.8 volts.

The test car was positioned in the middle of the road and aligned with the center line using reference marks on the front and rear windows. The instrument used to take the measurements is commonly referred to as a spot photometer.

Figure 4.23 Photographs of a person standing at test site.

It takes luminance readings only in one spot, the size of which can be varied. The point being measured is seen as a black dot in the instrument's viewfinder. The photometer was positioned behind the test car on a tripod, viewing through the open rear window, over the steering wheel and through the windshield, achieving a perspective essentially the same as that of a person driving the car.

Photometric measurements were taken at five distances (100, 150, 200, 300, and 400 feet) measured from the target to the headlamps. They were taken on both targets, on both the right and left of the test car, using high and low beams. For each combination of viewing distance, headlamp beam, target reflectivity, and target position 17 readings were taken. The locations of these readings are illustrated in Figure 4.24. Imagine that the rectangle in Figure 4.24 represents the six-foot-tall target. A luminance reading was taken at each of the points in and around the target represented by an X. Specifically, a reading was taken on the target at about the level of the face, chest, waist, knees and feet. Background readings were taken at the same levels as those on the target, to the right and left, as well as just above the target and just below it on the road surface.

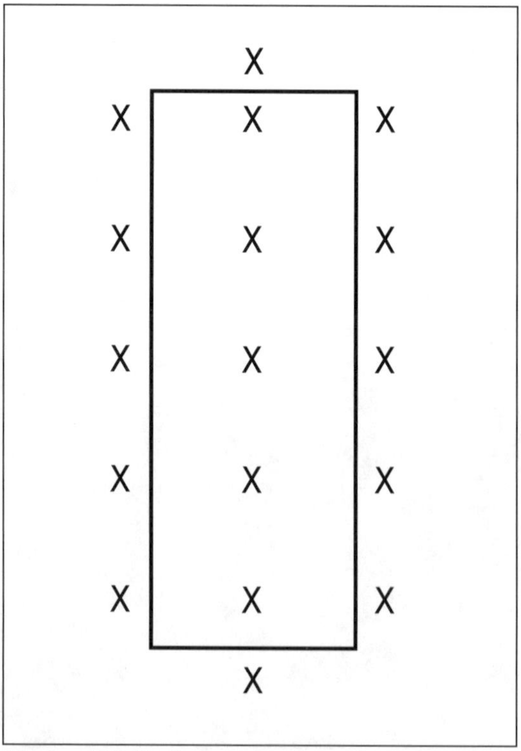

Figure 4.24 *Illustration showing points where photometric measurements were taken on and around test target.*

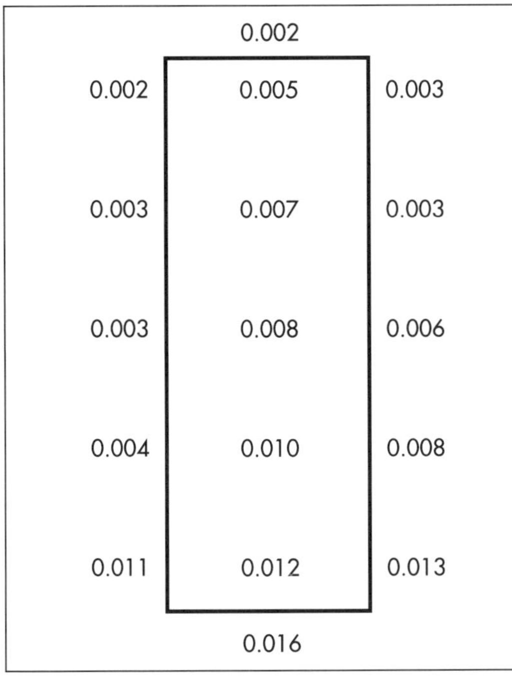

Figure 4.25 *Results of photometric measurements (in ft-L) on 6% pedestrian target, 300 feet, low beams, target positioned to right of test vehicle.*

Results

Figure 4.25 is an example of the results. This is for the 6% target, positioned to the right of the test car, viewed at 300 feet with low beams. Each of the numbers within and around the rectangle corresponds to a single reading (i.e., one of the Xs in Figure 4.24). The values are in foot-Lamberts (ft-L). As the reader will recall from Chapter 2, one foot-Lambert can be roughly approximated as the luminance of a piece of white paper illuminated at a distance of one foot by an ordinary dinner candle.

Figure 4.25 shows that the highest luminance measured for this combination of variables was 0.016 ft-L, which was on the pavement in front of the target. The highest luminance measured on the target itself was 0.012 ft-L, at the level of the feet. Note that the measures made on the background at the level of the feet are similar, meaning that there was very little contrast. Contrast improves a bit as one moves up the target to the levels of the knees and waist, but is still marginal. It is true that the target was visible to the investigators, or the measurements could not have been taken. However, experience derived from the visibility tests described earlier (specifically, see Figure 4.13) makes it clear that the probability of it being reported as detected would be very low at such a distance even under test conditions.

Table 4.4 *Results (in ft. Lamberts) of Luminance Measurements Made on Pedestrian-Size Targets and Their Backgrounds as a Function of Viewing Distance, Headlight Beam and Target Reflectivity.*

Target Positioned to Right of Test Vehicle

Target	Beam	Position	100 Ft Left	100 Ft TARGET	100 Ft Right	150 Ft Left	150 Ft TARGET	150 Ft Right
6% Large Target	Low Beam	Sky		0.002			0.004	
		Top	0.003	0.005	0.003	0.004	0.008	0.004
		Top Center	0.005	0.008	0.004	0.005	0.011	0.003
		Middle	0.011	0.026	0.007	0.008	0.020	0.007
		Lower Center	0.039	0.053	0.018	0.012	0.036	0.012
		Bottom	0.082	0.084	0.048	0.051	0.054	0.042
		Ground		0.127			0.069	
	High Beam	Sky		0.015			0.018	
		Top	0.015	0.078	0.016	0.012	0.059	0.016
		Top Center	0.018	0.097	0.021	0.015	0.067	0.012
		Middle	0.025	0.105	0.024	0.015	0.058	0.027
		Lower Center	0.044	0.088	0.035	0.018	0.048	0.016
		Bottom	0.027	0.057	0.046	0.021	0.040	0.025
		Ground		0.072			0.046	
25% Large Target	Low Beam	Sky		0.003			0.006	
		Top	0.004	0.018	0.005	0.004	0.028	0.004
		Top Center	0.008	0.034	0.005	0.006	0.048	0.006
		Middle	0.018	0.126	0.012	0.014	0.087	0.009
		Lower Center	0.045	0.246	0.017	0.018	0.144	0.009
		Bottom	0.082	0.378	0.066	0.048	0.210	0.039
		Ground		0.123			0.076	
	High Beam	Sky		0.022			0.010	
		Top	0.019	0.422	0.015	0.010	0.266	0.008
		Top Center	0.025	0.485	0.025	0.010	0.266	0.014
		Middle	0.022	0.481	0.020	0.027	0.269	0.032
		Lower Center	0.046	0.384	0.030	0.022	0.209	0.027
		Bottom	0.029	0.255	0.059	0.031	0.155	0.040
		Ground		0.069			0.047	

Table 4.4 *Results (in ft. Lamberts) of Luminance Measurements Made on Pedestrian-Size Targets and Their Backgrounds as a Function of Viewing Distance, Headlight Beam and Target Reflectivity.*

Target Positioned to Right of Test Vehicle

200 Ft			300 Ft			400 Ft		
Left	TARGET	Right	Left	TARGET	Right	Left	TARGET	Right
	0.004			0.002			0.004	
0.004	0.007	0.004	0.002	0.005	0.003	0.003	0.004	0.003
0.006	0.011	0.004	0.003	0.007	0.003	0.004	0.005	0.004
0.005	0.016	0.006	0.003	0.008	0.006	0.004	0.006	0.006
0.011	0.023	0.008	0.004	0.010	0.008	0.005	0.006	0.006
0.027	0.031	0.031	0.011	0.012	0.013	0.007	0.008	0.008
	0.040			0.016			0.009	
	0.008			0.009			0.006	
0.007	0.039	0.007	0.006	0.019	0.007	0.006	0.013	0.005
0.009	0.041	0.006	0.006	0.018	0.011	0.006	0.013	0.007
0.012	0.038	0.014	0.005	0.017	0.012	0.005	0.011	0.009
0.013	0.031	0.010	0.007	0.017	0.013	0.005	0.011	0.008
0.015	0.028	0.020	0.014	0.016	0.017	0.011	0.011	0.011
	0.029			0.018			0.014	
	0.004			0.003			0.004	
0.005	0.023	0.005	0.004	0.020	0.003	0.004	0.011	0.004
0.006	0.034	0.008	0.007	0.022	0.004	0.004	0.012	0.004
0.010	0.051	0.008	0.004	0.027	0.009	0.004	0.015	0.006
0.009	0.080	0.011	0.009	0.036	0.007	0.005	0.017	0.006
0.018	0.107	0.026	0.013	0.045	0.018	0.008	0.021	0.009
	0.039			0.019			0.010	
	0.013			0.013			0.006	
0.009	0.196	0.009	0.011	0.084	0.008	0.006	0.046	0.007
0.013	0.205	0.007	0.008	0.080	0.008	0.007	0.043	0.008
0.015	0.223	0.026	0.005	0.075	0.013	0.006	0.043	0.010
0.019	0.224	0.021	0.011	0.069	0.014	0.006	0.043	0.009
0.045	0.218	0.051	0.017	0.059	0.023	0.012	0.038	0.013
	0.067			0.021			0.015	

Table 4.5 *Results (in ft. Lamberts) of Luminance Measurements Made on Pedestrian-Size Targets and Their Backgrounds as a Function of Viewing Distance, Headlight Beam and Target Reflectivity.*

Target Positioned to Left of Test Vehicle

			100 Ft			150 Ft		
			Left	TARGET	Right	Left	TARGET	Right
6% Large Target	Low Beam	Sky		0.001			0.001	
		Top	0.001	0.003	0.002	0.002	0.004	0.002
		Top Center	0.004	0.008	0.003	0.003	0.007	0.002
		Middle	0.005	0.020	0.007	0.003	0.018	0.005
		Lower Center	0.017	0.036	0.009	0.013	0.020	0.004
		Bottom	0.036	0.056	0.069	0.023	0.030	0.032
		Ground		0.107			0.046	
	High Beam	Sky		0.002			0.003	
		Top	0.008	0.036	0.007	0.010	0.036	0.011
		Top Center	0.020	0.093	0.015	0.020	0.039	0.013
		Middle	0.014	0.087	0.012	0.011	0.041	0.013
		Lower Center	0.034	0.071	0.019	0.023	0.031	0.010
		Bottom	0.040	0.052	0.051	0.023	0.032	0.028
		Ground		0.056			0.038	
25% Large Target	Low Beam	Sky		0.001			0.002	
		Top	0.001	0.007	0.002	0.004	0.016	0.005
		Top Center	0.008	0.032	0.003	0.004	0.028	0.002
		Middle	0.005	0.092	0.010	0.002	0.063	0.007
		Lower Center	0.020	0.179	0.013	0.014	0.102	0.003
		Bottom	0.058	0.162	0.070	0.022	0.123	0.036
		Ground		0.109			0.045	
	High Beam	Sky		0.002			0.006	
		Top	0.005	0.171	0.010	0.009	0.179	0.015
		Top Center	0.019	0.461	0.014	0.024	0.200	0.010
		Middle	0.014	0.464	0.010	0.011	0.174	0.015
		Lower Center	0.025	0.337	0.016	0.030	0.147	0.009
		Bottom	0.034	0.235	0.035	0.026	0.121	0.036
		Ground		0.058			0.038	

Table 4.5 *Results (in ft. Lamberts) of Luminance Measurements Made on Pedestrian-Size Targets and Their Backgrounds as a Function of Viewing Distance, Headlight Beam and Target Reflectivity.*

Target Positioned to Left of Test Vehicle

200 Ft			300 Ft			400 Ft		
Left	TARGET	Right	Left	TARGET	Right	Left	TARGET	Right
	0.001			0.002				
0.003	0.004	0.002	0.004	0.006	0.003			
0.002	0.004	0.001	0.003	0.007	0.002			
0.002	0.009	0.003	0.003	0.007	0.003			
0.007	0.012	0.002	0.005	0.009	0.004			
0.014	0.016	0.016	0.010	0.010	0.010			
	0.025			0.016				
	0.004			0.005			0.003	
0.006	0.022	0.011	0.005	0.011	0.006	0.004	0.010	0.004
0.011	0.022	0.006	0.006	0.013	0.005	0.006	0.010	0.004
0.008	0.025	0.011	0.006	0.012	0.007	0.005	0.011	0.004
0.016	0.022	0.009	0.008	0.012	0.006	0.013	0.010	0.005
0.018	0.023	0.023	0.012	0.013	0.013	0.009	0.010	0.011
	0.028			0.016			0.010	
	0.003			0.002			0.002	
0.004	0.015	0.006	0.003	0.020	0.005	0.003	0.007	0.003
0.007	0.025	0.002	0.006	0.022	0.002	0.004	0.008	0.003
0.002	0.037	0.008	0.004	0.026	0.007	0.011	0.011	0.004
0.014	0.053	0.004	0.010	0.030	0.005	0.009	0.012	0.006
0.014	0.067	0.024	0.010	0.035	0.015	0.006	0.013	0.008
	0.026			0.015			0.007	
	0.007			0.007			0.006	
0.013	0.097	0.013	0.013	0.057	0.007	0.004	0.039	0.004
0.017	0.118	0.007	0.012	0.050	0.006	0.007	0.038	0.004
0.008	0.112	0.016	0.009	0.045	0.012	0.009	0.036	0.008
0.018	0.097	0.007	0.011	0.045	0.007	0.016	0.035	0.007
0.020	0.084	0.026	0.013	0.042	0.016	0.010	0.034	0.014
	0.029			0.017			0.013	

The complete photometric data are contained in Tables 4.4 and 4.5. Each table consists of a series of cells in which the test data are summarized. Each individual cell has the same format as Figure 4.25. There are no data in the 400-foot, 6%, left-side cell because the luminance levels fell below what the photometer could measure.

In reviewing the data in Tables 4.4 and 4.5 note that the luminance values and contrast tend to be much lower for left-side targets on low beam. This is a natural consequence of the candlepower distribution of the low-beam system described earlier. There should be no difference between right and left sides on high beam, however. The right-side targets in this test tend to have higher luminance levels than the left-side targets, suggesting that the car and/or headlamps were biased slightly to the right side. In addition, there should be about a 4:1 luminance difference between the 6% and 25% targets. The difference tends to be greater than that, which indicates that the reflectance of one or both was off somewhat.

The trends noted in the discussion of Figure 4.25 are evident throughout the low-beam data for the 6% target. As the distance grows shorter the luminance values on both the target and background increase, and contrast improves, particularly for the leg area. Still, referencing the test data reported in Figures 4.13 and 4.14, the probability of these targets being responded to at the shortest distance measured is less than 100%, even under test conditions.

Comparing low- and high-beam data on the 6% target, one difference that is immediately apparent is the greater homogeneity of target luminance values top to bottom on high beams. There is still little contrast at the foot level of the target on high beams, but there is much greater contrast at the face and chest levels. This, and not beam candlepower, is why high beams are more effective in revealing a taller target such as a pedestrian. On the other hand, a low target such as a small animal, or a pedestrian lying on the road, may be no more visible with high beams than with low beams.

The data from the 25% target show the dramatic improvements in contrast that come from increases in target reflectivity. Clearly, this "pedestrian" would be detected at a substantially greater distance than would the less reflective one.

Relationship to Visibility Distance

Interpreting the luminance and contrast data in terms of probability of detection requires referring back to Figures and 4.13 and 4.14. Using low beams, and with the target on the right, there were no reported detections at distances as great as 400 feet. Only about 3% of detections had occurred at 300 feet. About 50% had responded by 150 feet, and 80% by 100 feet. With the target on the left side the maximum response distance was about 150 feet.

Once again, it is necessary to recall that the test data need a correction for expectancy. Doing so by using data such as that from Roper and Howard (1938), would substantially reduce the probability of detection at any distance.

Implications and Limitations

The luminance and contrast data in this section, combined with the visibility distance data from an earlier section, should be useful as a means for understanding the limitations of motor vehicle headlamps in revealing objects when driving at night. The luminance and contrast data may also be of assistance in assessing visibility in situations where lighting provided by a motor vehicle is not at issue (e.g., scenes illuminated by fixed sources). This point will be discussed further in Chapter 6.

The reader must bear in mind that these photometric measurements were collected under a particular set of conditions. While the driving condition they represent is not unusual, it is certainly not representative of all driving conditions. The uncritical use of these data for driving conditions differing significantly from that described here could lead to recommendations that are seriously in error.

Chapter Overview

This chapter has been concerned with visibility while driving at night, using motor vehicle headlamps. It discussed the headlamps themselves, their capabilities as illuminating systems, and certain related topics. The chapter closed with a description of target luminance and contrast data collected under field conditions. Key point covered were:

- Contrast is defined as those characteristics of an object or condition that allow it to be differentiated from its background. Sufficient contrast is a prerequisite for visibility.
- There are many forms of contrast, but at night visibility is primarily determined by brightness contrast.
- The primary function of motor vehicle headlamps is to generate sufficient luminance contrast so that relevant objects and conditions can be detected and identified in time to allow the driver to take appropriate action.
- All motor vehicle lighting systems offer two beams. The low beam is designed for use when other drivers are nearby in the forward field. Its design must take into consideration a number of criteria, some of which are in conflict. As a result, the low-beam system represents a compromise that is biased toward glare protection and offers limited revealing power for low-contrast objects.

- Halogen technology offers more light output per watt and does away with the bulb-blackening problem. This makes it a good choice for automotive use.
- On low beam, the revealing power of halogen lamps is no different from that of non-halogen lamps.
- Lamps built to European (CIE) specifications have a low-beam system that appears quite different from that produced by lamps built to US (SAE) standards. Both accomplish the same general ends, however, and the revealing power of each system is comparable.
- Research on the ability of low-beam headlighting systems to reveal relatively low-contrast targets makes it clear that their capability is very limited.
- Targets to the left of the vehicle will, on average, be detected at about half the distance of targets to the right.
- High-beam systems will, on average, reveal the same target on the left side at about double the distance as will low beams. The average difference for targets located on the right side is about 50%.
- Driver expectancy is a key factor in visibility. On average, when an observer knows what's ahead and about where it will be encountered, it will be detected at twice the distance that it will when the observer does not have those advantages.
- Measurements are presented of target luminance and contrast taken under field conditions as a means of illustrating the levels required to achieve various probabilities of detection.

References

Allen, M. J., Hazlett, R. D., Tacker, H. L. and Graham, B. V. (1970). Actual Pedestrian Visibility and the Pedestrians' Estimate of His Visibility. *American Journal of Optometry and Archives of the American Academy of Optometry, 47,* 44-49.

Bhise, V. D., Farber, E. I., Saunby, C. S., Troell, G. M., Walunas, J. B. and Bernstein, A. (1977). Modeling Vision with Headlights in a Systems Context. Dearborn, Michigan. Society of Automotive Engineers Report No 770238.

Leibowitz, H. W., Owens, D. A. and Tyrrell, R. A. (1993). The Assured Clear Distance Ahead Rule: Implications for Traffic Safety and the Law. Unpublished manuscript.

Mortimer, R. G. and Olson, P. L. (1974). Development and Use of Driving Tests to Evaluate Headlamp Beams. Ann Arbor. The Highway Safety Research Institute. Report No. UM-HSRI-HF-74-14.

Olson, P. L. (1977). The Relative Merits of Different Low-Beam Headlighting Systems - A Review of the Literature. Ann Arbor. The Highway Safety Research Institute. Report No. UM-HSRI-77-55.

Olson, P. L. (1990). Minimum Photometric Properties of Retroreflective Signing Materials. *Transportation Research Record, 1247,* 56-68.

Olson, P. L. and Abrams, R. A. (1982). Improved Motorcycle and Moped Headlamps. Ann Arbor. The Highway Safety Research Institute. Report No. UM-HSRI-82-18.

Olson, P. L. and Sivak, M. (1983). Improved Low-Beam Photometrics. Ann Arbor. The University of Michigan Transportation Research Institute. Report No. UMTRI-83-9.

Olson, P. L., Aoki, T., Battle, D. and Flannagan, M. (1990). Development of a Headlight System Performance Evaluation Tool. Ann Arbor. The University of Michigan Transportation Research Institute. Report No. UMTRI-90-41.

Roper, V. J. and Howard, E. A. (1938). Seeing With Motorcar Headlamps. *Illumination Engineering, 33,* 412-438.

Shinar, D. (1984). Actual vs. Estimated Nighttime Pedestrian Visibility. *Ergonomics,*

Chapter 5

Factors That Degrade Visual Performance Under Night Driving Conditions

---

Introduction

The information on driver visibility offered in Chapter 4 is based on tests run under ideal conditions. Conditions in the real world are not always ideal. In this chapter a number of conditions having negative impact on driver visibility will be discussed. These fall under three general headings, based on whether they arise from the environment, the vehicle, or the driver.

Problems Arising from the Environment

Environmental problems can take two forms. One is anything in the atmosphere (e.g., rain, snow, fog) that interferes with vision. The other is characteristics of the background that affect target conspicuity. Both will be discussed in this section.

Precipitation and Other Atmospheric Problems

At night conditions such as precipitation, fog, smoke, haze and dust have in common the characteristic that they absorb and scatter light to some degree. This absorption and scattering has two effects. First, less light from the vehicle's headlamps reaches a target object, and less of the light reflected by the object is returned to the driver's eyes. Second, some of the scattered illumination is reflected back into the driver's eyes, causing the atmosphere to appear to light up. This reduces the target object's contrast, making it more difficult to detect.

"Wet" conditions such as rain, and sometimes snow and fog, create other problems as well. The most immediately noticeable is the fact that the windshield becomes wet, and requires wiping in order to maintain reasonable visibility. Even under the best of conditions visibility is reduced when the windshield is wet. If the wipers are worn, if the windshield is badly pitted or scratched, if the car is moving at high speed, or if the rainfall is very heavy visibility may be reduced a great deal (Bhise, et al., 1981; Ivey, et al., 1975; Kurahashi, et al., 1985; Morris, et al., 1977).

A film of water on the road can greatly increase the driver's problems in determining his/her lateral position as well as where the road is going. There are two reasons for this. As noted in Chapter 2, normally the road surface acts as a diffuse reflector, reflecting some of the illumination from the vehicle's headlamps back into the eyes of the driver, and causing the roadway near the car to appear relatively bright. Water fills in the small voids in the pavement surface, creating a smooth film much like a mirror. As a result headlamp illumination normally scattered by the road surface is reflected forward, causing the road to appear relatively dark and increasing glare for oncoming motorists. This effect was discussed in Chapter 4 and documented in Figure 4.4. The fact that headlight illumination is reflected forward when the pavement is wet can increase the luminance of objects in the forward field, compensating to some degree for the loss in visibility due to other causes (Woltman and Youngblood, 1977).

The reduction in pavement luminance in the wet makes delineation all the more important to the driver. Unfortunately, many forms of delineation also degrade when wet. Painted lane lines are the most common form of delineation. These are reflectorized by coating them with glass beads before the paint dries. When the layer of water on the road is deep enough to cover the beads they cease to function as retroreflectors. As a result, painted lane lines seem to disappear when the pavement is wet. This loss of delineation is evident in the wet-dry photographs in Figure 2.2.

The effect of water on the visibility of delineation has been a matter of concern for some time. Raised pavement markers are the best solution so far, and have been used extensively in the south and far west parts of the US for years. Unfortunately, the type of marker employed is vulnerable to snowplows, thus they were not suitable for states in the snow belt. With the development of raised pavement markers that are not affected by snow plows, they are coming into widespread use in northern states as well. A great deal of research has been carried out (e.g., Blaauw and Padmos, 1982) to find other satisfactory and economical solutions to this problem.

Problems arising from the environment are difficult to evaluate. It's one thing to say there was fog at the time, for example. But, fog varies from wispy stuff that has no practical effect on driver visibility to pea soupers that bring traffic to a halt. It's also often non homogeneous, its density varying greatly in place and time. Adding to the general confusion, witnesses often disagree about the degree to which visibility was affected at the time of a specific event, and this is one case where eyewitnesses are about the only source of information available concerning environmental effects on visibility. Lacking precise information about weather conditions, and given the general uncooperativeness of nature even if conditions are known, it is typically not possible to recreate them with any precision. Some thoughts on how this matter can be handled by the investigator are offered in Chapter 8.

Background Effects on Target Conspicuity

The visibility distance data presented in Chapter 4 were collected under conditions best approximated by rural two-lane highways. There were no lights, signs, or other similar items in the background to compete with the target object. These kinds of distractions, often characterized as "visual clutter," are common in real-world driving situations. The question is what effect do they have, if any, on target detection distance?

It should be intuitively clear that an object imbedded in cluttered surroundings is more difficult to detect and identify than one whose immediate surroundings are empty. For example, the letter "O" in the space below stands out clearly:

O

While the same letter imbedded in a matrix of other letters presents more of a challenge:

TYXGLMQP
LURXCNWB
BVUKAPKC
RCOEYATQI
EIPJDABXW

Figures 5.1 and 5.2 are photographs taken in areas that represent extremes in visual clutter. Other factors being equal, the scene represented by Figure 5.2 presents far more of a challenge to a driver in detecting an identifying an unexpected hazard.

While the loss in conspicuity and consequent reduction in detection distance in a visually cluttered setting seems obvious, there are no data on low-contrast targets to assist in estimating how much of a loss is to be expected. There are data on the effect of background clutter on the detection of retroreflective signs, however (Olson, 1990). The degree to which results obtained using these high-contrast targets can be inferred to low-contrast targets is unclear. The data will be described here to provide some indication of the effect of background clutter in the absence of anything else.

The study in question was conducted to provide guidance in establishing minimum levels of retroreflectivity for signs. A number of variables were examined, including background complexity. There were three levels of background

Figure 5.1 *Photograph of an area lacking in visual clutter.*

Figure 5.2 *Photograph of an area having a great deal of visual clutter.*

complexity, the lowest and highest of which are approximated by Figures 5.1 and 5.2. There was an intermediate level as well, which was an urban street with street lights and some signs. Comparisons were made of the level of sign retroreflectivity required to achieve the same response distances in the different settings. It was found that the sign had to have about ten times the level of retroreflectivity (i.e., ten times the luminance) in the high-complexity area to match the average performance of a sign in the low-complexity area. Signs in the medium-complexity areas had to have about three times the luminance of signs in the low-complexity areas to match their average response distances.

In all probability a significant portion of the differences in detection performance associated with area complexity was actually attributable to changes in adaptation level. That is, the subjects were adapted to a higher level of luminance in the more complex settings, so higher target luminance levels would be required to compensate for the loss in retinal sensitivity. Independent of that, it is clear that higher target luminance levels are required as area complexity increases. This can only be achieved by the car getting closer to the target to increase illuminance at the target. Strictly speaking, to achieve a ten-fold increase in target luminance would require reducing target-to-source separation by a factor of slightly more than three. Does this correction hold for low-contrast targets? In the opinion of the author, probably not. The response distances measured in the sign study were very long compared to the pedestrian visibility data described earlier. At closer distances the background may not matter as much. In any event, it is clear that background complexity, or clutter, plays a significant role in target conspicuity. If the analysis of a particular collision making use of data such as described in Chapter 4 indicates that a reasonably alert driver should have detected the target in time, but the event occurred in an area where there was much visual clutter, the opinion may have to be revised.

Problems Arising from the Vehicle

Windshields

One of the most critical components in the vehicle from a standpoint of driver visibility is the windshield. Windshields must meet a number of criteria, some of which are specialized (e.g., protection in crash situations). What a windshield does most is keep the wind, airborne objects and the elements out of the driver's eyes while simultaneously allowing that person to view the road. Hence, good optical quality is very important.

Unfortunately, windshields lead a hard life. They are subject to continuous bombardment by tiny airborne particles, occasional encounters with larger objects, and abrasive action from the wipers and careless efforts at cleaning. In addition, films can build up on both sides of the glass. As a result of all this many windshields, including some on relatively new vehicles, have optical characteristics that significantly degrade driver vision, particularly at night. Contaminants, surface pitting and scratches scatter light passing through the glass, reducing visibility in general and increasing the effects of glare. Rompe and Engel (1984), as one example, showed that the probability of detecting targets of varying contrast decreased from 91% with a clear windshield to 73% with a windshield having a moderate level of haze. Performance was greatly degraded when glare sources were introduced.

Heat-absorbing (tinted) windshields have been an object of some controversy for a number of years. The purpose of the tinting is to reduce the sun load on the vehicle's occupants and interior, thus improving comfort as well as the efficiency of air-conditioning systems on hot days. While it helps in this respect, the tinting also reduces visible light transmitted through the glass. Because of this, some have argued (e.g., Allen, 1970) that tinting the entire windshield should not be permitted, due to loss of visibility at night.

The loss in transmitted light due to windshield tinting is significant. A clear windshield, installed at an angle of 60 degrees from vertical, will transmit about 80% of light passing through parallel to the ground. A tinted windshield will transmit about 68% under identical conditions. This translates to an effective loss of illumination on objects in the forward field, and a consequent loss in visibility. Given the sometimes poor nighttime visibility drivers have, as discussed in Chapter 4, placing a piece of glass in front of them that further reduces visibility may seem difficult to justify.

The argument concerning heat-absorbing windshields comes down to balancing advantages and disadvantages. There have been a number of studies of visibility distance at night comparing clear and tinted glass (e.g., Bernstein, 1976, Doane and Rassweiler, 1955, and Dunipace, et al., 1974). Generally, these have shown losses in visibility distance associated with tinted glass ranging up to about 6%, depending on the target and test conditions. Whether this loss in visibility under night driving conditions is worth the gain in comfort under warm, sunlit conditions is something that will apparently continue to be debated.

Headlamps

Glare

Glare is an adverse effect on driver visibility and/or comfort caused by light source(s) within the visual field that are sufficiently brighter than the luminance to which the eyes are adapted. These effects are generally referred to as disability and discomfort glare respectively, although sometimes the latter is called psychological glare.

The term "disability glare" refers to a diminished visual capability associated with one or more light sources in the visual field. Disability glare arises from the fact that light entering the eye is scattered somewhat by the optic media, so that some of it ends up on other portions of the retina. This stray radiation reduces the contrast of objects imaged on the retina, and makes them more difficult to detect (Fry, 1955). The effect is much like trying to look through a veil. Visibility is good until the veil is illuminated by some source. When that happens the veil becomes relatively bright, diminishing the contrast of objects in the forward field. For this reason disabling glare is often called veiling glare. The effect becomes more pronounced with age (Fozard, et al., 1977), compounding the problems older drivers face.

Disability glare is affected by the luminance level to which the eye is adapted, the luminous intensity of the glare source(s), and their angular relationship to the direction in which the individual is looking. The fact that headlamp glare generally originates from a point very close to where the driver is (or should be) looking is one of the main reasons it is such a problem.

The effect of headlamp glare on target visibility in a simulated meeting situation on a two-lane rural road has been reported by Mortimer and Olson (1974). The results are reproduced in Figure 5.3. The data show average response distances for these 12% reflectivity targets as a function of the separation distance between the two vehicles and target position to the right or left of the car. With the target on the left (bottom figure) visibility distance averaged nearly 200 feet under no-glare conditions, but dropped to almost 100 feet at the maximum glare point shortly before the vehicles passed. No-glare performance was nearly 275 feet with the target on the right (top figure) and dropped to about 225 feet at the maximum glare point. The differences right to left without glare are attributable to the beam distribution characteristics discussed in Chapter 4. The much greater effect of glare in the case of the left-side target comes about from the necessity of looking more directly toward the glare source in order to see the target.

Exposure to very bright light can cause obvious discomfort. Why this happens is not clear, but work by Fry and King (1955) suggests that it may be due to minute fluctuations in pupil size. Discomfort glare may be no more than an annoyance, although there is the possibility of increased fatigue if the levels are high enough and persist long enough. Keeping discomfort attributable to glare to a reasonable level is a major criterion in low beam design.

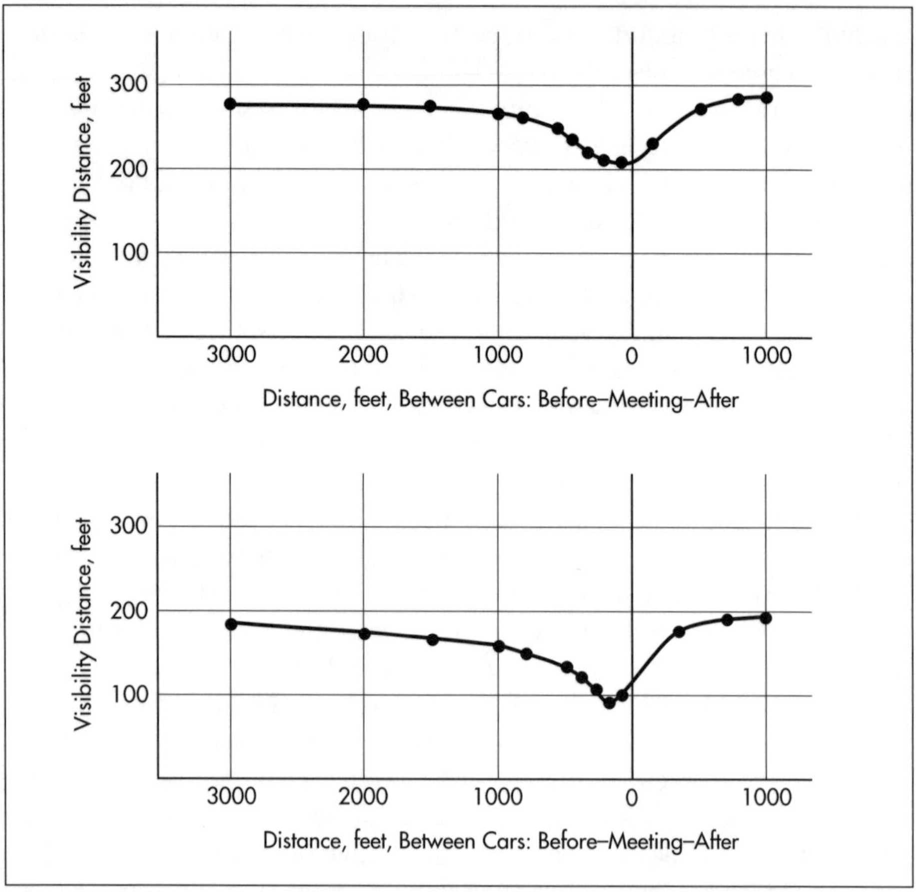

Figure 5.3 *Response distances of subjects showing effects of glare with target located on the right (top) and left (bottom) of the test vehicle (from Mortimer and Olson, 1974).*

Headlamp Aim

To a very significant degree, headlamp performance depends on the units being properly aimed. Hull, et al. (1972) ran tests to estimate how much difference in visibility relatively small aim changes can make. They found that if headlamps are misaimed up by one degree, as might happen if several full suitcases were placed in the trunk of a vehicle, visibility distance increased by 60 to 75%. Unfortunately, glare for other drivers increases greatly as well. Misaim down by a degree certainly poses no glare problems, but they found it reduces visibility distance by 24 to 45%.

Maintaining proper aim is difficult, for two reasons. First, as noted in Chapter 4, the angular separation between areas of the forward field where illumination is desirable and areas where it is not is very small. As a result minor deviations from proper aim can be very significant as measured by changes in visibility distance and glare. Second, there are many sources of aim error, some of which are difficult to control (Olson and Mortimer, 1974).

Misaim can arise from the lamp itself (e.g., improper filament position), by the lamp being incorrectly oriented in its mounting, and from the vehicle. Limited research also suggests that obtaining accurate aim through service outlets is a chancy business (Olson and Mortimer, 1974). Thus, inept service can itself be a source of aim variance.

In an effort to assess the quality of aim and other factors relating to automotive lighting in the US, a nationwide survey was conducted (Olson, 1985). It was found that headlamps were commonly aimed outside the limits given in SAE standard J599. That standard allows ± 4 inches at 25 feet (about ± 0.7 degree) for both horizontal and vertical dimensions. On vehicles four or more years old in the survey, less than 30% had both low-beam units aimed within SAE limits. On the other hand, nearly 60% of vehicles less than one year old had both low-beam units within SAE specifications. It was found that such things as headlamp aim and the frequency of non-functioning lamps were better in states that had mandatory inspection programs, but not by much.

Bearing in mind that headlamps are attached to the sprung mass of a vehicle, vertical aim changes as a function of loading are to be expected. Two studies were carried out in the early 1970s to estimate this effect (Hull, et al., 1971, and Olson and Mortimer, 1974). In each case the investigators selected a small sample of vehicles and loaded them systematically, checking the effect on pitch angle at each stage. It was found that the vertical aim of headlamps might increase by as much as 1.5 degrees, going from driver-only to a full-load condition. Filling the gas tank would increase vertical aim by 0.25 to 0.50 degree, compared to an empty state.

In recognition of the fact that there have been significant changes in automobiles since the early 1970s, another investigation of this type was conducted by Olson and Winkler (1985). Indeed, things seem to have improved appreciably. The change from driver-only to full-load condition was only about one degree on average in the sample of vehicles tested. Going from driver-only to full-passenger condition (i.e., no baggage) raised aim about 0.5 degree. Filling the fuel tank raised the aim an average of 0.25 degree, compared to an empty state, regardless of vehicle size.

Recognizing that aim is a major limitation to the effectiveness of headlamps, considerable thought has gone into means for improving it (e.g., Hull, et al., 1972). Comparing data on the aim of headlamps of vehicles in use taken in the 1970s with the 1985 survey just described suggests that appreciable progress was made in that era. However, aim is still a source of difficulty and will likely continue to be for the foreseeable future.

Beam Usage

From the discussion in Chapter 4, it is clear that drivers can significantly improve their forward visibility by using the high-beam system whenever possible. Yet it is equally clear that many drivers make much less use of high beams than they could. Some drivers confess to never using their high beams. The reasons given vary, but typically mention will be made of the nuisance of having to change whenever another car comes into view, or forgetting and having other drivers flash their lights to request dimming. While the data fall short of being scientific, informal conversations the author has had with large numbers of test subjects over the years suggests that they generally recognize that high beams provide greater visibility distance, but many of them think they can see adequately with low beams. Where that is the case, drivers may see no great need to use high beams.

How effectively do drivers use their high beams? A nationwide survey was conducted some years ago to address this question (Hare and Hemion, 1968). A number of sites were visited during the study. These included two- and four-lane unlighted roads with varying traffic levels as well as roads with fixed lighting. Overall, the investigators found that over 75% of the drivers observed used low beams when they could have used high beams without affecting other drivers. Beam usage depended on a number of factors, but mainly on traffic volume. Interestingly, the probability that high beams would be used varied with the part of the country, being higher overall in the southeast. Whether these differences are real or an artifact of the sampling technique is not clear.

Key results of the survey are reproduced in Figure 5.4. At traffic densities of 200 per hour or more, high beam use was rare, although it was about twice as likely in the southeastern part of the country. As densities decreased below 200 per hour the probability of high beam usage increased rapidly. In the study sample the probability reached 50% at about 100 vehicles per hour in the southeast. In the northeast the probability reached 50% at about 50 vehicles per hour. In the other two regions it barely reached 50% at the lowest volumes measured.

It is clear from the results of this investigation that high beam usage was well below optimum at the time of this survey. The question is whether things have changed significantly in the nearly 30 years that have passed since then. Driver education is more common today, so perhaps drivers are more aware of the differences in visibility produced by the two systems and more inclined to use high beams when possible. On the other hand, in many areas traffic densities have increased greatly since the late 1960s, reducing the opportunity to use high

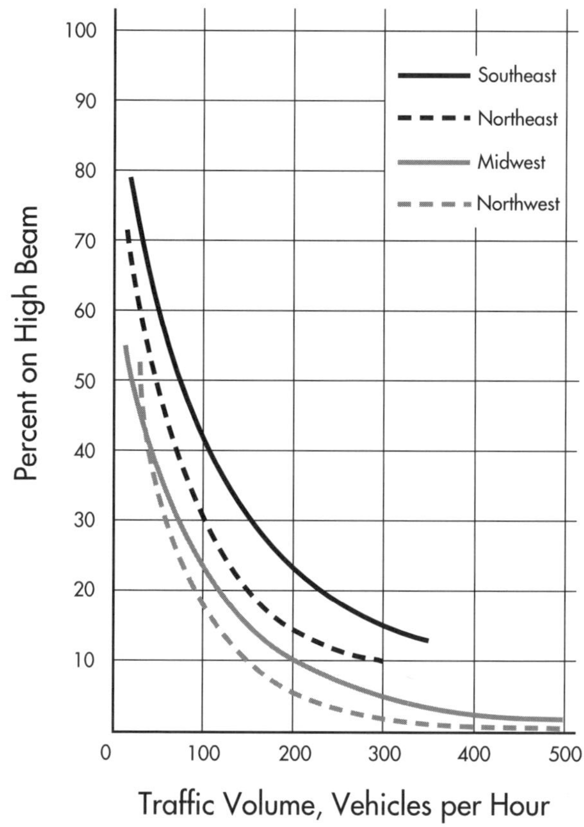

Figure 5.4 *High beam usage as a function of traffic volume and area of the country (from Hare and Hemion, 1974).*

beams. Since one of the implications of this investigation is that drivers are less likely to use high beams as the need for frequent dimming increases, this may argue for less high beam usage today. The question, however, remains open.

Occasionally in civil litigation an attorney will seek to score points by claiming that one party was negligent because he/she was using low beams under conditions where it appears high beams could have been used. To the extent that normal practice is a defense it appears that failure to use high beams when it is possible to do so is quite common.

Effects of Dirt

Headlamps can become very dirty very quickly, particularly in wet weather. Figure 5.5, from Rumar (1970), shows the results of measurements made on samples of vehicles under various driving conditions. Under wet and slushy conditions most cars had useful illumination reduced by more than half.

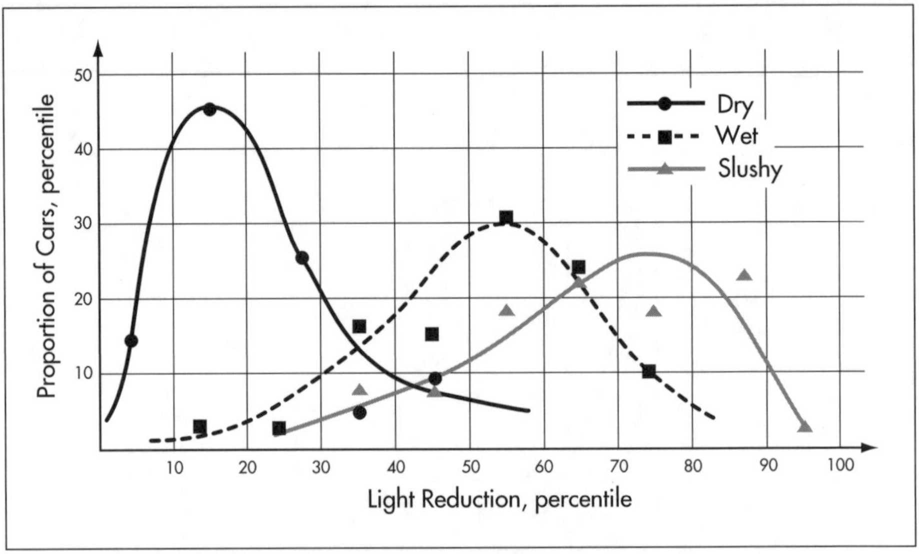

***Figure 5.5** Effect of dirt on useful illumination from headlamps. Copyright ©1986 by Matthew Bender & Co., Inc. Reprinted with permission from* Attorney's Guide to Engineering. *All rights reserved.*

Even moderate amounts of dirt on the headlamps causes light to be absorbed and scattered, reducing "useful" illumination (i.e., that projected below horizontal) and, surprisingly, often increasing glare to oncoming drivers. Olson and Sivak (1981) collected three headlamps from vehicles in a parking lot. The lamps ranged from fairly clean to moderately dirty. Each was photometered first as received and then again after cleaning. The dirtiest lamp exhibited reduced illumination at all test points compared to the clean condition. The other two lamps had lower candlepower in most areas below the H axis and higher candlepower in most areas above it compared to the clean condition. Thus, it appears that moderate dirt levels provide a double whammy, reducing useful output, but increasing output in the glare areas.

Due to the intensity-visibility distance relationship discussed in Chapter 4, the loss in forward visibility due to dirt on the headlamps is not as great as might be expected. Figure 5.6, also from Rumar (1970), shows percentage visibility reduction as a function of percentage light reduction for both high and low beams. Note that a 50% reduction in light output translates to about a 10% reduction in forward visibility for low beams, and about 15% for high beams. When light reduction is 20% or less there is actually a slight gain in forward visibility with low beams. This is probably due to the scattering effect just noted.

In an effort to reduce the detrimental effects of dirt on headlamps, cleaning systems have been developed. The most common are wiper-washer systems like those used on windshields.. High-pressure spray devices have also been tested.

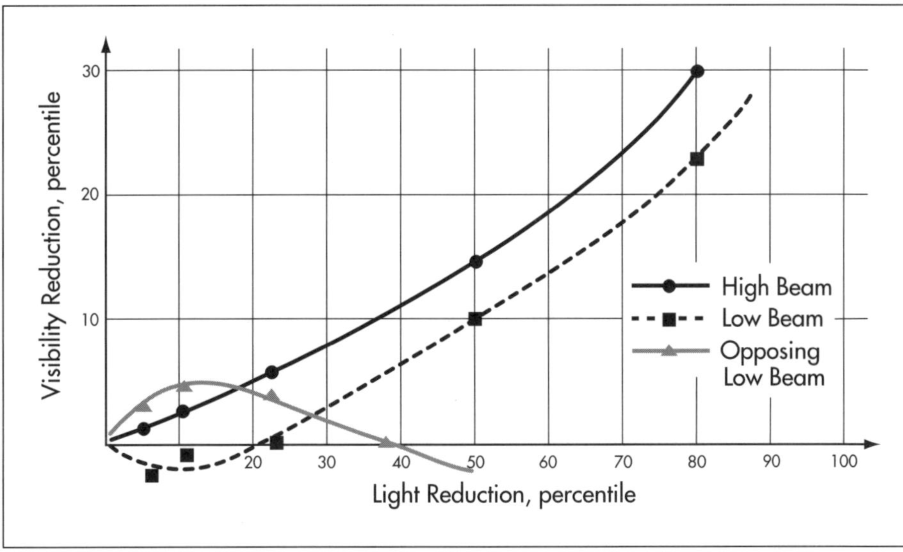

***Figure 5.6** Visibility reduction as a function of percent light reduction (from Rumar, 1970).*

Headlamp cleaning systems are common in some parts of the world, but have not yet come into use in this country, except on some European cars imported to the US.

Dirt on other lamps (i.e., marker and brake lamps) reduces their output and, hence, their conspicuity. This seems to rarely be a serious problem in the case of passenger cars, vans and pickup trucks, and in most cases, large trucks as well. Some trucks, such as dump bodies, have the lamps mounted low, between the wheels. In this position they are especially likely to become dirty and are less likely to be cleaned with any regularity. Where information is available, say through police photographs, the condition of marker and signal lights at the time of the subject event should be checked.

Dirt has a marked effect on retroreflectors because the light has to pass through the dirt layer twice. As part of an effort to set standards for the performance of retroreflective materials used on trucks, Olson, et al. (1992) measured losses in reflectivity of test samples of reflective material mounted on a number of large trailers in normal service over a period of one year. Samples mounted on the rear were especially affected, losses of 75-90% being common, especially in winter months. The investigators found that even when the trailer appeared reasonably clean the test patches might be performing at 50% or less of the installed values.

Problems Arising from the Operator

Problems with the operator that may affect visibility can be temporary or permanent. Temporary problems include fatigue, psychological states such as stress that may reduce attention to the driving task, and the effects of drugs and alcohol. Although these are significant factors in driving performance, this section will deal with certain problems that are permanent in nature.

Aging

One of the more important effects associated with aging as it affects the safe operation of a motor vehicle is a loss of acuity. As noted earlier, visual acuity involves the ability to resolve fine detail. Hence, acuity affects one's ability to read signs along the road, as well as the ease with which various conditions can be detected and identified. There is a clear relationship between acuity and age. On average, acuity peaks at about age 15, and declines steadily thereafter, reaching about one-third of peak value at age 80 (Verriest, 1971).

The most critical condition is at night. In general, acuity and other visual functions decline as the level of illumination decreases. However, the effects are more marked in the elderly. It is not completely clear why these losses in visual capability come about. It has been known for some time that the minimum level of illumination to which the eye can adapt, as well as the time to adapt from one level to another, increases with age (McFarland, et al., 1960). Two factors mentioned in Chapter 2 that certainly have a role are the reduction of the maximum opening of the pupil and yellowing of the lens. In addition, it is known that the oxygen supply to the retina is reduced with aging (Fozard, et al., 1977). In any event, as illustrated by the data presented in Chapter 4, older persons tend to do less well than younger persons on visual tasks at low levels of illumination. Indeed, even when matched in daytime acuity, Sivak et al. (1981) found that older subjects were able to read highway signs at only about two-thirds the distance of young subjects at night.

The disabling effects of glare are also more pronounced in older persons. Not only are older subjects more affected by glare, it takes them longer to recover when the glare source is removed. Figure 5.7 (Olson and Sivak, 1981) shows the results of a test of glare recovery. Subjects were required to continuously adjust the luminance of a disc target starting when a glare source was extinguished and continuing until stability was reached. The older subjects were much more affected by the glare when it was on, and it took them about 50% longer to adapt to the ambient level. Note too that the target disc had to have about twice the luminance to be visible to the older subjects at the ambient level.

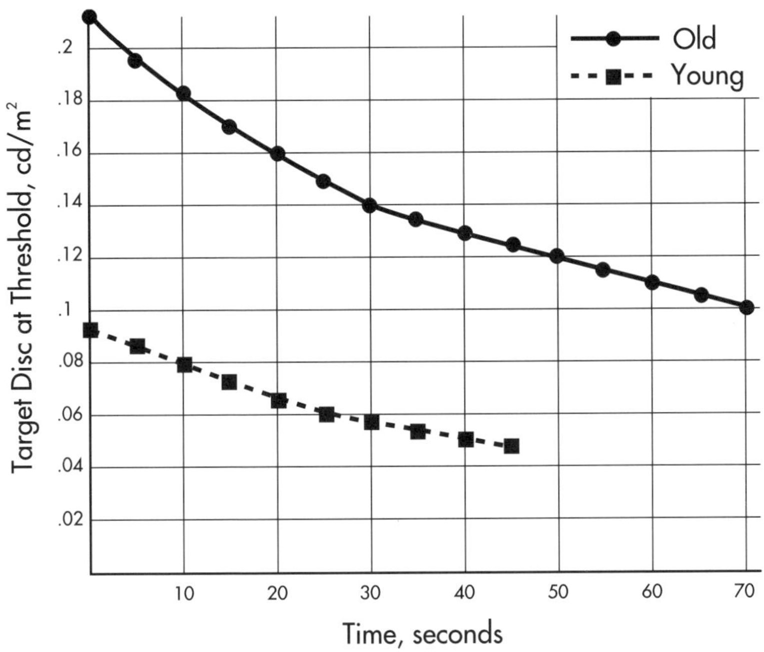

Figure 5.7 *Effects of glare and time for recovery from glare as a function of age (from Olson and Sivak, 1981).*

Night Myopia

Myopia is commonly referred to as near-sightedness. As noted in Chapter 2, it results when the distance from the lens to the retina in the eye is too great. With this condition nearby objects can be brought into sharp focus on the retina, while more distant objects are brought to a focus in front of the retina, resulting in a blurred image.

In total darkness the eye accommodates to an intermediate state (dark focus) that varies from person to person. Owens and Leibowitz (1976) have shown that the eye tends to accommodate to distances between infinity and that represented by dark focus as illumination levels are reduced. The result is "night myopia." Because most events of consequence to a vehicle operator occur at visual infinity (i.e., beyond about 20 feet), an eye that is accommodated to an intermediate distance will see them less well.

Available data indicate that night myopia may be fairly common, although most people are minimally affected. In extreme cases, individuals may have a focus point only a few feet in front of the car, with objects in the far field seriously blurred. An obvious solution to the problem of night myopia is to measure individual accommodative changes and prescribe corrective lenses to be worn while driving at night for the more serious cases. There are two problems in doing this. First, a person can have significant night myopia and not be aware of the fact. Thus, affected individuals are not likely to seek assistance voluntarily unless the condition is serious. Second, it is difficult to carry out conventional refractive measures at low levels of illumination, and night myopia cannot be predicted from measures taken at high levels of illumination. So, even if an individual felt the need, an Ophthalmologist or Optometrist may not be able to conduct the necessary tests and write a prescription. There may be merit in screening for night myopia, with corrective lenses required for night driving where appropriate, just as we require corrective lenses for daytime operation. This would require the development of suitable testing techniques that could be made widely available as well as dissemination of the nature of the problem and means for correction.

Color Blindness

Color blindness is a general term used to refer to a variety of conditions. Traditional classifications indicate that about 8% of males and 0.5% of females have some form of color blindness. Three levels of color deficiency are recognized:

Anomalous trichromats are "color weak." That is, their perception of one or more colors is less than normal, but not so severe as to fall into a more serious classification.

Dichromats suffer from an inability to distinguish one of the primary colors. The two most common types are *Protanopia*, an inability to distinguish red, and *Deuteranopia*, an inability to distinguish green. These two conditions affect about 2% of the population.

Monochromats are unable to distinguish any colors, seeing only in shades of gray. This conditions is rare, affecting only about 0.003% of the population.

Color deficiencies are of concern in the design and operation of traffic systems because of the wide use made of color coding. Probably the most obvious example is traffic signals. Shifting the transmissivity characteristics of the green lens more into the blue end of the spectrum has been of some help to persons with Deuteranopia. Standardization of color position (i.e., red at the top) has also been of benefit. Signals are, however, not the only thing color coded. Signs use color as one indicator of the class of message. Persons with a color deficiency will see certain signs less well than color normals, and may experience more problems in reading the message. Color coding can be a powerful tool in information transmission. Care must be taken, however, to ensure that persons with color deficiencies are not severely disadvantaged, or the result may be a net loss in system efficiency.

Night Blindness

Night blindness is a term used to refer to a condition in which the individual has a greatly reduced capability for vision at low levels of illumination. It comes about as a consequence of a prolonged deficiency in vitamin A. Persons severely affected would probably not even attempt night driving. There are degrees of the condition, however, and those less affected may drive at night.

Cataract

Cataract is a general term used to refer to any opacification of the lens. It may be manifest as a highly localized spot or a general loss of transmissivity of the lens. Cataracts have many causes, e.g., senile change, trauma, metabolic or nutritional defects, exposure to certain types of radiation (Davson, 1963). Cataracts reduce vision in the affected eye(s), and often increase the disabling effects of glare. They can be treated surgically, using a relatively simple procedure in which the lens is removed and replaced with an artificial one. There will always be some vision loss before surgery is recommended, and some people wait far too long before seeking medical assistance, with the result that a serious loss in vision results.

Aniseikonia

Aniseikonia is a condition in which the retinal image in one eye is significantly larger than in the other eye. This can result in a variety of symptoms, including spatial distortions and double vision. Many persons with this affliction can get along well enough during the day, due to the abundance of spatial cues, but they may experience problems at night.

Anisocoria

In Anisocoria the pupils of each eye are of different size. The result is that the retina of one eye receives less illumination than the other. This can produce an illusion known as the Pulfrich effect. This interesting phenomenon can be demonstrated to a person with normal vision by placing a dark lens over one eye and looking at something like a pendulum. The apparent path of the pendulum will be seen as elliptical, with significant movement toward and away from the observer. When driving, the Pulfrich effect can cause distortions in the perceived speed, distance and trajectory of other vehicles.

Chapter Overview

The information concerning driver visual performance is generally based on investigations carried out under ideal conditions. For a number of reasons, the conditions associated with a particular event may be less than ideal. This chapter has discussed a number of factors that can alter driver visual performance. The main points covered are as follows:

- Environmental problems can arise from things in the atmosphere that alter its transmissivity. This most commonly means rain, snow, dust and fog. The result is that light from the headlamps is absorbed and scattered on the way to the target as well as on the way back to the observer's eyes. In addition, light scattered in the atmosphere is reflected back into the driver's eyes, causing the atmosphere to appear to light up, with the consequence that target contrast is reduced.
- Visual clutter in the form of lights, signs, storefronts, etc. diminish target conspicuity and consequently have a negative effect on target detection distance. There are no good data to allow the investigator to correct for this factor. If data collected under optimum viewing conditions indicate visibility for a situation under investigation was marginal, then background clutter would make it unacceptably poor.
- A wet pavement has different reflective properties than a dry pavement. A wet pavement appears relatively dark to the driver and painted delineation is much harder to see. In addition, the glare from oncoming headlights is increased. The fact that more light from the headlamps is reflected forward can sometimes help in making an object more visible.
- A number of problems can arise from the vehicle and its components. One component frequently neglected is the windshield, which can become badly scratched and pitted with use. Even the windshield of a relatively new car can acquire coatings that seriously interfere with vision, particularly when light (either from the sun or the headlamps of other vehicles) is impinging directly on it.
- Headlamps are a frequent source of problems in night visibility. An inevitable by product of illumination with headlights is glare. Glare reduces visibility distance and may cause discomfort. Headlamps often go out of aim over time. Relatively minor changes in aim, particularly vertical aim, can cause major changes in forward visibility. Dirt on headlamps also affects visibility by scattering and absorbing illumination.

- Problems arising from the operator may be permanent or temporary in nature. This chapter focused in permanent problems that affect driver visual capability. These include aging and a number of visual disorders.

References

Allen, M. J. (1970). Vision and Highway Safety. New York. Chilton Book Company.

Bernstein, A. (1976). Visibility Distance Through Heat Absorbing Glass. Ann Arbor. University of Michigan Highway Safety Research Institute. Report No. UM-HSRI-76-17.

Bhise, V. D., Meldrum, J. F., Forbes, L. M., Rockwell, T. H. and McDowell, E. D. (1981). Predicting Driver Seeing Distance in Natural Rainfall. *Human Factors, 23(6),* 667-682.

Blaauw, G. J. and Padmos, P. (1982). Nighttime Visibility of Various Types of Road Markings; a Study on Durability, Including Conditions of Rain, Fog and Dew. The Society of Automotive Engineers. SAE Report No. 820412.

Davson, H. (1963). *The Physiology of the Eye.* Boston. Little, Brown and Company.

Doane, H. and Rassweiler, G. M. (1955). Cooperative Road Test of Night Visibility Through Heat Absorbing Glass. Paper presented to the annual meeting of the Highway Research Board.

Dunipace, D. W., Strong, J., and Huizinga, M. (1974). Prediction of Nighttime Driving Visibility From Laboratory Data. *Applied Optics, 13*(11), 2723-2734.

Fry, G. A. (1955). *Physiological Bases of Disability Glare.* Columbus, Ohio. Ohio State University, School of Optometry.

Fry, G. A. and King, V. M. (1955). The Pupillary Response and Discomfort Glare. *Journal of the Illumination Engineering Society*, 307-324.

Fozard, J. L., Wolf, E., Bell, B., McFarland, R. A., and Podolsky, S. (1977). Visual Perception and Communication. In: Birren, J. E. and Schaie, K. W. (eds.). *Handbook of the Psychology of Aging*. New York, Van Nostrand Reinhold Company.

Hare, C. T. and Hemion, R. H. (1968). Headlamp Beam Usage on US Highways. San Antonio. Southwest Research Institute. Report No. AR-666.

Hull, R. W., Hemion, R. H., Cadena, D. G. and Dial, B. C. (1971). Vehicle Forward Lighting Performance and Inspection Requirements. San Antonio, Texas. Southwest Research Institute.

Hull, R. W., Hemion, R. H., and Cadena, D. G. (1972). Guidelines for Improving the Stability of Headlamp Aim. San Antonio, Texas. Southwest Research Institute. Report No. DOT/HS-800-739.

Ivey, D. L., Lehtipuu, E. K. and Button, J. W. (1975). Rainfall and Visibility - The View From Behind the Wheel. College Station. The Texas Transportation Institute, Texas A & M University. Research Report No. 135-3.

Kurahashi, T., Fukatsu, Y. and Matsui, K. (1985). Method of Evaluating Visibility Provided by Windshield Wipers in Rainy Conditions. The Society of Automotive Engineers Report No. 851636.

McFarland, R. A., Domey, R. G., Warren, A. G., and Ward, D. C. (1960). Dark Adaptation as a Function of Age: I. A Statistical Analysis. *Journal of Gerontology, 15*, 149-154.

Morris, R. S., Mounce, J. M., Button, J. W. and Walton, N. E. (1977). Field Study of Driver Visual Performance During Rainfall. College Station. The Texas Transportation Institute, Texas A & M University. Research Report No. DOT-HS-802-289.

Mortimer, R. G. and Olson, P. L. (1974). Evaluation of Meeting Beams by Field Tests and Computer Simulation. Ann Arbor. The Highway Safety Research Institute. Report No. UM-HSRI-HF-74-27.

Olson, P.L. and Winkler, C.B. (1985). Measurement of Crash-Avoidance Characteristics of Vehicles in Use. Ann Arbor: The University of Michigan Transportation Research Institute. Report No. UMTRI-85-20.

Olson, P. L. (1990). Minimum Photometric Properties of Retroreflective Signing Materials. *Transportation Research Record,* 1247, 56-68.

Olson, P. L. and Mortimer, R. G. (1974). Analysis of Sources of Error in Headlamp Aim. The Society of Automotive Engineers. Report No. 750312.

Olson, P. L. and Sivak, M. (1981). Improved Low-Beam Photometrics. Ann Arbor. The Highway Safety Research Institute. Report No. UM-HSRI-81-4.

Olson, P. L., Campbell, K, Massey, D., Aoki, T., Sato, T., Battle, D., Traube, E., and Pettis, L. (1992). Performance Requirements for Large Truck Conspicuity Enhancements. The University of Michigan Transportation Research Institute. Report No. UMTRI-92-8.

Owens, D. A. and Leibowitz, H. W. (1976). Night Myopia: Cause and a Possible Basis for Amelioration. *American Journal of Optometry and Physiological Optics, 53*(11), 709-717.

Rompe, K. and Engel, G. (1984). The Influence of Scattered Light in Windshields on Driver's Vision During Night Driving. The Society of Automotive Engineers. SAE Report 840385.

Rumar, K. (1970). Dirty Headlamps - Frequency and Visibility Distances. Uppsala University, Department of Psychology, Sweden.

Sivak, M., Olson, P. L., and Pastalan, L. A. (1981). The Effect of Driver's Age on Nighttime Legibility of Highway Signs. *Human Factors, 23*(1), 59-64.

Verriest, G. (1971). L'influence de L'age sur les Foncitions Visuelles de L'homme. *Bulletin de L'Academie Royale de Medecine Bellique, 11,* 527-578.

Woltman, H. L. and Youngblood, W. P. (1977). An Assessment of Indirect Factors Affecting Reflective Sign Brightness. St. Paul. 3M Company.

Chapter 6

Visibility with Fixed Lighting

Introduction

The term "fixed lighting" will be used to refer to any light source that does not move. Generally this means streetlamps, but other sources such as security lights, illuminated signs, storefront lighting, and lighting in parking lots can also come into play. Many accident scenes will have some fixed lighting in the near vicinity. Assessing what effect, if any, this lighting has on the visibility of the target object is an issue of some importance. Although it is not the purpose of this chapter to make street lighting experts out of the reader, it would be helpful to provide a brief introduction to these sources of illumination, as well as an overview of research on street lighting systems.

Fixed Lighting Sources

There are a number of types of sources used in street-lighting applications. Most of the time the investigator will encounter only two, mercury and high-pressure sodium.

Mercury

Mercury lamps were developed in the 1930s and enjoyed wide use for many years. They are easily recognized by their blue-white color. Although they are being replaced by more efficient sources, they are still in common use. Allowing for losses due to the ballast, mercury lamps yield 37-54 lumens/watt, compared to 11-18 lumens/watt for incandescent lamps and 20-22 lumens/watt for halogen lamps. The roughly threefold increase in efficiency for mercury lamps compared to incandescent lamps, combined with a much longer life, represented a major step forward in its day and made mercury lamps very popular.

High-Pressure Sodium

High-pressure sodium lamps are a relatively recent development, recognizable by their yellow color. When mercury lamps are replaced it is usually with high-pressure sodium. They are also the source most likely to be used in new installations. Allowing for losses due to the ballast, high-pressure sodium lamps yield 60-130 lumens/watt, roughly double that of mercury lamps. They have a life expectancy slightly less than mercury lamps.

Other Sources Used in Streetlighting

Fluorescent

Fluorescent lamps are commonly used for indoor lighting, especially in workplaces. They have good color, efficiency (58-69 lumens/watt, including losses due to the ballast) and fairly long life. Their use in streetlighting has been limited by their large size. The main use of fluorescent lamps in roadway applications has been in sign, underpass and tunnel lighting.

Metal Halide

One of the chief advantages of metal halide lamps is their good color. They have efficiencies comparable to high-pressure sodium (65-110 lumens/watt, including losses due to the ballast), but substantially shorter life expectancies. Their use in roadway illumination has been mainly in the high-mast installations sometimes seen at freeway interchanges and in parking areas.

Low-Pressure Sodium

Low-pressure sodium lamps have the highest efficiency of any sources in use at present (78-150 lumens/watt, including losses due to the ballast). The color is monochromatic, which some people find objectionable. Their large size is a disadvantage, much as it is for fluorescent lamps. They are used in applications where high efficiency is desired and the poor color is considered to be of less consequence.

The Distribution of Illuminance From Street Lamps

In recognition of their purpose and the nature of the surface they are designed to illuminate, the optics of street lamps seek to produce something approximating a rectangular pattern. Figures 6.1 and 6.2 (from Zimmer, 1991) show iso-footcandle diagrams for two high-pressure sodium lamps. The actual pattern and footcandle readings depend on the lamp manufacturer, light source, wattage, and mounting height. These figures show iso-footcandle diagrams for a 250-watt lamp at a mounting height of 50 feet (Figure 6.1) and a 400-watt lamp at a mounting height of 55 feet (Figure 6.2). In a street lighting system a series of lamps would be placed at intervals on one or both sides of the road in question. The spacing between sources determines the degree of overlap of the patterns, and the uniformity of pavement luminance.

As is evident from the figures, it is desirable that mounting height be adjusted for lamp output. Often this is not done because it adds significantly to the

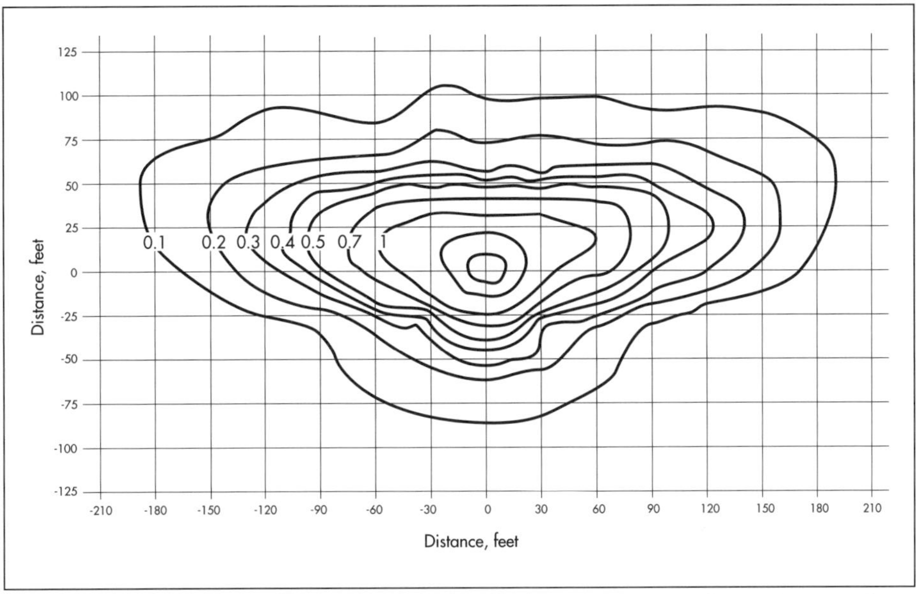

Figure 6.1 *Iso-footcandle diagram of a 250-watt high-pressure street lamp at a mounting height of 50 feet (from Zimmer, 1991).*

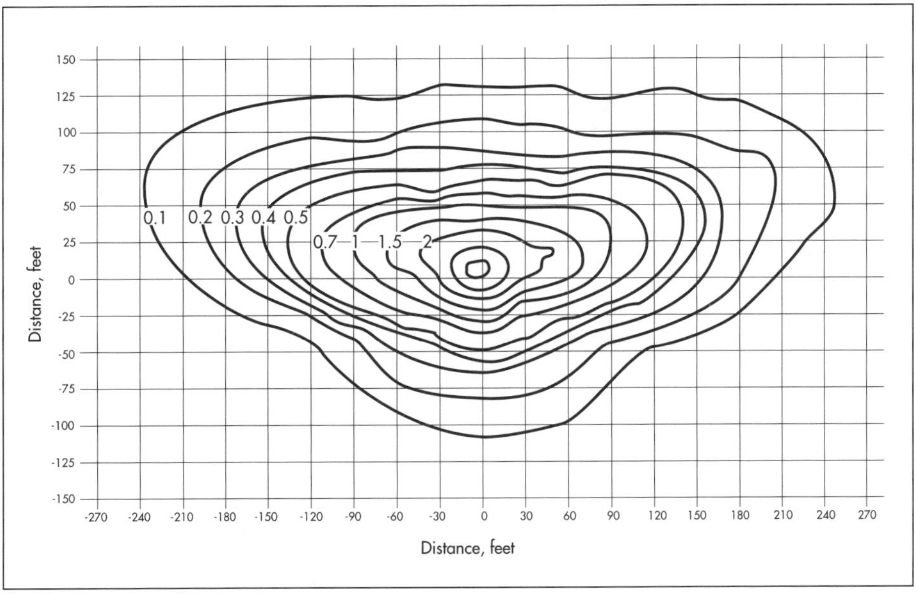

Figure 6.2 *Iso-footcandle diagram of a 400-watt high-pressure street lamp at a mounting height of 55 feet (from Zimmer, 1991).*

installation cost. The result of installing a higher-output source in the same fixture is to increase pavement luminance in the immediate area of the lamp. Pavement luminance uniformity may suffer, however.

Figures 6.1 and 6.2 are shown here to illustrate typical patterns from street lighting sources. The lamps used for these purposes come in a variety of wattages. The ones in Figures 6.1 and 6.2 are actually rather high-wattage units. Therefore, these data should not be taken as representative of all street lighting systems that the investigator may encounter, or even all high-pressure sodium systems.

The Scene When Illuminated by Fixed Sources

One of the most important characteristics of fixed lighting systems is a lack of uniformity in pavement luminance. This can have a major impact on the visibility of an object contained within an area having fixed illumination. Figure 6.3 is a photograph of a street with fairly ordinary lighting. The photograph, as is typical, exaggerates contrast, but the essential point is preserved. The road surface near the light source has relatively high luminance. The illuminance, and the pavement luminance, falls off as the distance from the source increases. In very

Figure 6.3 *Photograph of a street with fixed lighting.*

high quality systems the variation in pavement luminance is minimal. In most systems there is substantial variation in pavement luminance from point to point along the road.

The variation in luminance means that objects may be seen as a light object against a dark background, or a dark object against a light background. They may also appear as a dark object against a dark background, in which case the fixed lighting is of no help. All of these situations are depicted in Figure 6.4. The poorer the quality of the lighting system the larger the relatively dark areas become, as does the probability that one of them will form the background for the object of concern.

The apparent quality of illumination and its ability to reveal a target to an oncoming motorist can change markedly depending on the point of regard. Figure 6.5 is a view of a roadway in which a pedestrian collision occurred, taken from the sidewalk where the pedestrian entered the road. The immediate impression is that the area is very well lighted. The pedestrian may have thought so too. The area *is* well lighted in the immediate vicinity, so that the pedestrian is easily seen.

Figure 6.4 *Three photographs of a street scene showing different forms of contrast. (See next page)*

Figure 6.4 (continued) *Three photographs of a street scene showing different forms of contrast.*

Figure 6.5 *View of a roadway in which a pedestrian collision occurred, taken from the sidewalk from which the pedestrian departed.*

Figure 6.6 *View of the same roadway depicted in Figure 6.5 from the perspective of an approaching motorist.*

The same scene is shown in Figure 6.6, with the perspective shifted by 90 degrees to that of an approaching driver. Now the background for the pedestrian is a relatively dark area and there is glare from the headlamps of oncoming cars. As a result the pedestrian is much harder to see.

Research on the Performance of Fixed Lighting Systems

Research on fixed lighting systems has focused on the development of an index that could serve as a basis for specifications. A great deal of work has been carried out over a period of many years. A promising start toward a useful performance index was made by Gallagher and Janoff (e.g., 1972), who carried out an investigation measuring the response of passing motorists to an unexpected encounter with an obstacle in the road. The speed of the vehicle was measured, as was the distance at which the driver initiated an avoidance maneuver. Dividing distance by speed yielded time to target. Figure 6.7 shows average and 15th

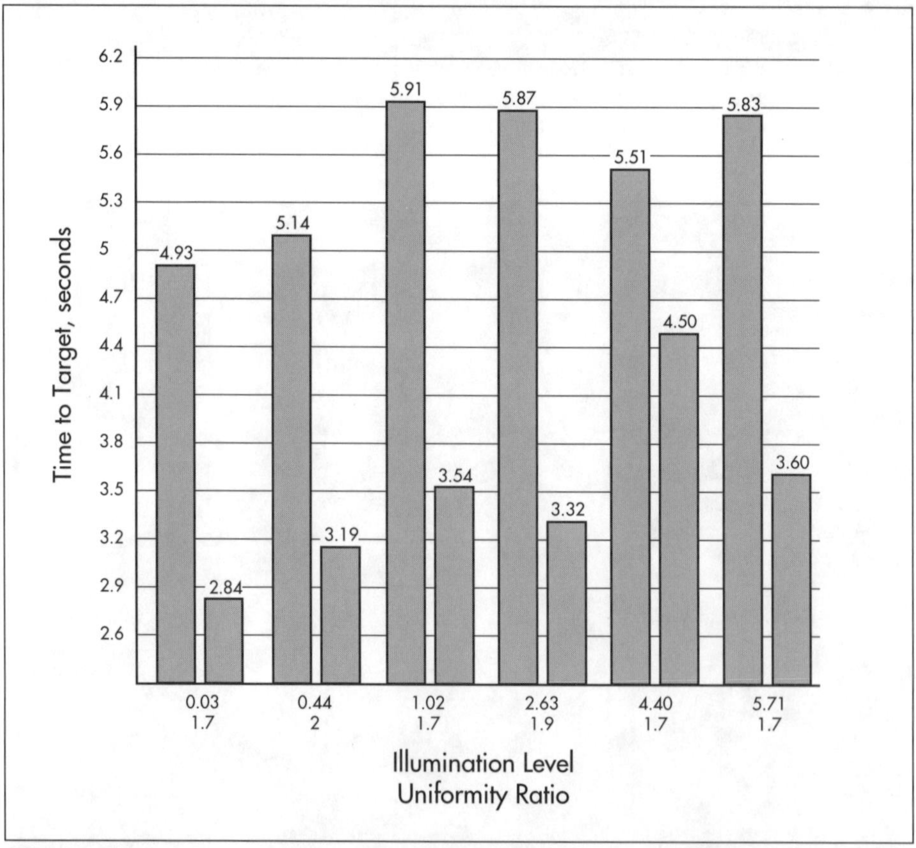

Figure 6.7 *Average and 15th percentile time-to-target scores for six illuminance levels in areas having relatively low uniformity ratios (from Gallagher and Janoff, 1972).*

percentile time-to-target scores at six illuminance levels (given in foot candles) in areas having relatively low uniformity ratios. The uniformity ratio shows the relationship of the areas of highest illuminance to the areas of lowest illuminance. For example a uniformity ratio of 1.7 means the areas of highest illuminance were 1.7 times greater than the areas of lowest illuminance. In this figure the illuminance level of 0.03 ft-c represents no fixed illumination, just vehicle headlamps. Increasing average illuminance to about one foot candle improved both average and 15th percentile time-to-target scores. Further increases in average illuminance provided no appreciable improvement in time-to-target performance.

Figure 6.8 shows time-to-target scores as a function of the uniformity ratio at two levels of illuminance. At an illuminance level of about one foot candle increasing the uniformity ratio reduced average time to target, although it had no consistent effect on 15th percentile performance. At a higher illuminance level

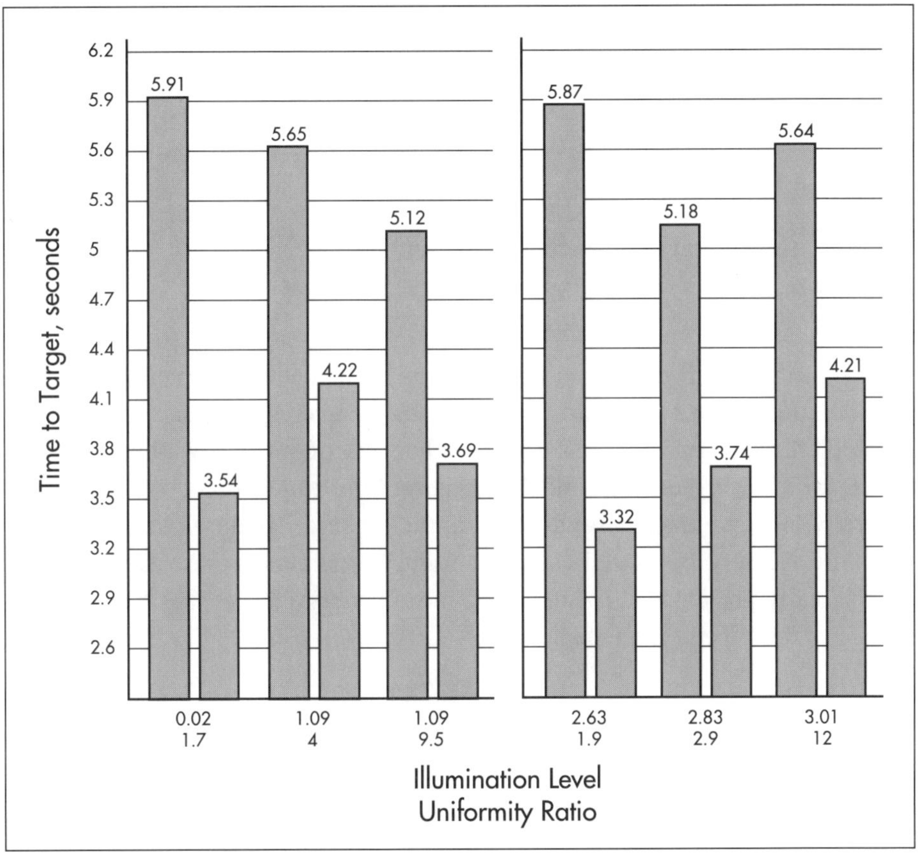

Figure 6.8 *Time-to-target scores as a function of the uniformity ratio at two levels of illuminance (from Gallagher and Janoff, 1972).*

increasing the uniformity ratio seemed to have little effect on average time to target, but actually seemed to improve 15th percentile performance.

This work was extended by Gallagher, et al. (1975). They carried out two studies, including a field investigation similar to that in the 1972 study, but with a different target. Central to their work was the development of what they called the visibility index. The visibility index is expressed as an equation as follows:

$$\text{VI} = C(RCS_{Lb})(DGF) \qquad 6.1$$

Where:

RCS_{Lb} = the Relative Contrast Sensitivity of observers adapted to a luminance condition equal to the background (L_b)

C = ΔL/L

Where:

ΔL = the luminance difference of the target and its background.

DGF = Disability Glare Factor

The disability glare factor, DGF is defined by the following equation:

$$\text{DGF} = \left(\frac{Lb}{Lb'}\right)\left(\frac{RCS_{Lb'}}{RCS_{Lb}}\right) \qquad 6.2$$

Where:

Lb = background luminance in foot-Lamberts

Lb' = (Lb + Lv)/1.074, a correction for sphere-base glare

Lv = veiling luminance in foot-Lamberts

The investigators compared time-to-target scores with the computed visibility index. Results are shown in Figure 6.9 for the average (mean), 15th and 5th percentile time-to-target scores. The visibility index compares well with time to target. Note also that 15th and lower percentile time-to-target scores were generally less than three seconds, even at the highest visibility index levels.

More recently Blackwell (1980) introduced the concept of visibility level. As originally presented it is intuitively more understandable that the visibility index just described. The equation is:

$$\text{VL} = \frac{\Delta L_{actual}}{\Delta L_{threshhold}} \qquad 6.3$$

Basically a "threshold" means a stimulus level that just barely allows detection. As a practical matter threshold is really a statistical concept. For example, suppose one wanted to measure the distance at which a pedestrian target could be detected under certain conditions. A study could be carried out. If this was

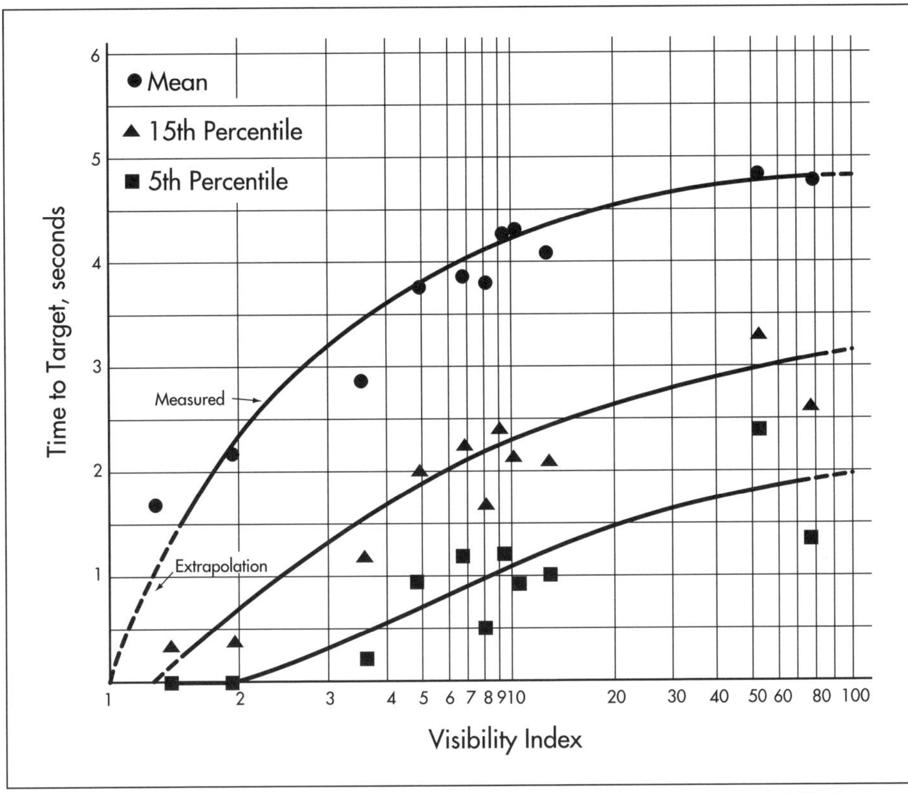

***Figure 6.9** Relationship between time-to-target scores and the computed visibility index (from Gallagher, et al., 1975).*

done the results would probably be approximated by a normal distribution such as described in Chapter 1. Given this dispersion of detection distances, where is the threshold? For convenience sake many investigators select the median as the threshold. In the case of the visibility level, however, a more stringent criterion is applied, and the threshold is taken as the level at which virtually all observers will have reported detection.

In the visibility level concept if the measured contrast of a target is equal to the threshold contrast VL = 1. Given the definition of visibility level, it would be expected that the probability of detection would be very high. The research on which the threshold data are derived, however, used informed subjects. A correction for expectancy is required when applying to real-world situations.

Janoff (1993) compared the three indices just described to determine their relationship. He found high correlations in each case. He also found a positive correlation between visibility level and safety. Interestingly, there was little or no correlation between safety measures and average level of illuminance and uniformity of illuminance.

Assessment of Visibility in a Field Investigation

Research such as that just described has great value in the design of street lighting systems that will improve safety for drivers and pedestrians both. Unfortunately, it is of little assistance to an investigator seeking to address the question of whether a given object in a specific location, characterized by certain lighting levels and distributions, should have assuredly captured the attention of a reasonably alert driver in time to take effective action.

Assessment of visibility in an area having fixed lighting is complicated by a number of factors. For a given situation there is no way to quantify these issues, but the investigator must be aware of them at least.

- The lighting will cause the driver to light adapt to some extent. In other words, the eyes will become less sensitive, meaning that contrast levels adequate to allow detection in a dark area will no longer suffice.
- Glare is normally not an important issue with fixed lighting sources, since they are typically far removed from the areas in which target objects occur. One exception is when the pavement is wet. Not only is pavement luminance greatly reduced, but reflections of the light off the pavement constitute significant glare sources close to the target.
- The light sources themselves provide visual clutter, even if there are no other visual elements such as signs and storefronts present. As discussed in Chapter 5, clutter affects target conspicuity adversely.
- With fixed lighting present an object may be marginally visible for some period of time as the vehicle approaches. The investigator may feel that the object's conspicuity is below a level that would assuredly capture the attention of a reasonably alert driver. The longer an object appears in the driver's field of view, however, the greater the likelihood that it will be detected. Thus, even though an object may be unlikely to be detected if exposed at a particular contrast level briefly, if it is present at that level for some period of time the probability of detection increases.
- Movement increases conspicuity. In a situation lacking fixed lighting object movement is of less consequence due to the limited visibility distance provided by the vehicle's headlamps. If the object is marginally visible for some time, as it might be with fixed lighting present, movement can significantly improve the probability that it will be detected.

For a driver operating in the absence of fixed lighting the illuminance reaching an object gradually increases as the car approaches. Eventually sufficient contrast will be generated to allow the object to be detected by the driver. With fixed lighting the illuminance reaching the target is at a higher level initially and remains relatively fixed until the car gets within several hundred feet, assuming low beams are in use.

If a field evaluation is conducted two things can happen. In the simplest case the object of concern will not be visible at a great distance, but will begin to become visible as the vehicle nears. This simply says that the fixed illumination by itself is not sufficient and additional illumination from the vehicle's headlamps is required. In this case the procedure is essentially that outlined in Chapter 8. In brief, the investigator should first determine the maximum detection distance. Due to the way such an investigation is conducted this distance represents about a 95th percentile measure were one to conduct a formal study with a number of subjects. For example, suppose the investigator determines that the maximum detection distance is 400 feet. On a basis of the data presented in Chapter 4, the expected scatter from the 5th to 95th percentile is 200-300 feet, with the longer value applying to more reflective targets. If 250 feet is selected for this case this says that the expected range of responses is from 150 to 400 feet in a controlled study, the median being about 275 feet. A correction for expectancy would reduce the median to about 140 feet, with scatter about that point at least equal to that experienced in the controlled study.

A more difficult case arises if the object is visible to the investigator at much greater distances than would be expected through the use of headlamps alone. The object may be seen as something dark against a light background (negative contrast) or the opposite. In the former case contrast will actually diminish as the vehicle nears and its headlights begin to provide significant illuminance. In either case, however, the question with which the investigator must wrestle is whether the object's conspicuity is such that a reasonably alert driver should detect it at a safe distance with either the fixed illumination or a combination of fixed illumination and the vehicle's headlamps. In considering this question the luminance and contrast data presented in Chapter 4 should be helpful.

The findings of the visibility research described in Chapter 4 for a dark-clad pedestrian standing to the right of the test vehicle were that response distances ranged from about 50 to 250 feet, with a median of about 150 feet. With a correction for subject perception-response time in the test the median becomes about 170 feet. A correction for expectancy requires that the median be reduced by 50%, in this case to 85 feet. Other research discussed in Chapter 5 suggests that the use of high beams will improve visibility to low-contrast targets to the right of the test vehicle by about 50%. Thus the high-beam data for the right-side, 6% target at 150 feet in Table 4.4 approximate the expected median unalerted detection distance for this target.

The relevant values for this target condition from Table 4.4 are reproduced in Figure 6.10, minus the background luminance readings. Investigators who have access to a luminance meter can measure the luminance of the target object to determine if it falls within this range. (Remember the values shown in Figure 6.10 are in foot-Lamberts. If the luminance meter reads in candelas/meter^2 multiply by 0.2919 to get foot-Lamberts.)

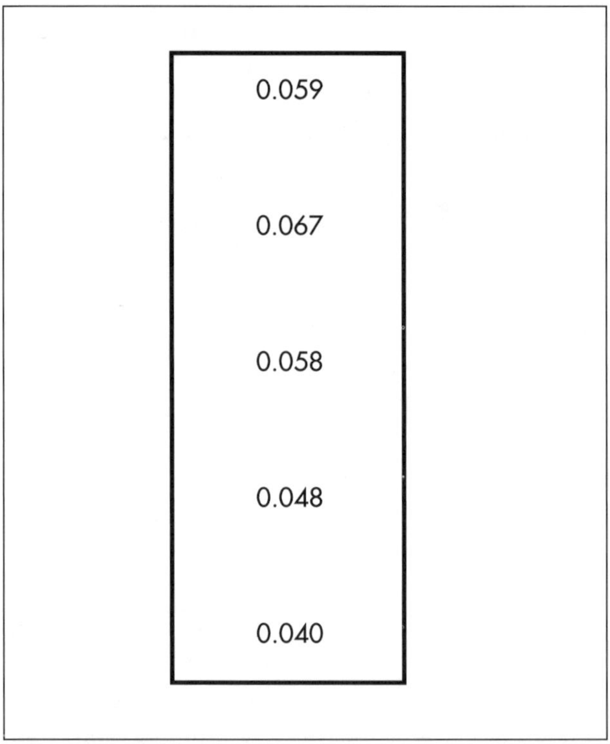

Figure 6.10 *Luminance readings taken on a 6% pedestrian target standing to right of vehicle, using high beams, at 150 feet.*

Lacking a luminance meter, the next best step is to use an illuminance meter. The illuminance reaching the target at this setting was approximately one foot candle (10.76 lux). So, assuming the reflectivity of the target object is about 6%, an illuminance of about one foot candle is required to achieve about 50% probability of detection. If the object's reflectivity is higher than 6%, the required illuminance is reduced proportionately.

If in either case the required values fall below those identified then a car should be introduced as a light source, bringing it in ever closer until the indicated values are obtained.

If the investigator is entirely lacking in light-measuring equipment the next best step is to look at the target with high beams at 150 feet in a dark area and compare the impression thus obtained with its appearance in the area with illumination.

Consideration must also be given to the issues discussed earlier, i.e., adaptation level, clutter, movement, and time in view, when arriving at an opinion. There is, unfortunately, a high degree of subjectivity involved, but at the present time there is no alternative.

Chapter Overview

Areas in which there is significant scene illumination provided by street lamps and other fixed sources present a difficult challenge for the investigator interested in assessing the visibility of an object or condition. This chapter has sought to provide some guidance to assist in the formation of reasonable opinions. The following are the principal points covered:

- There are a number of fixed lighting sources in use. For street lighting the most common are mercury and high-pressure sodium. Mercury lamps, which are blue-white in color, are being phased out. The most common replacement is high-pressure sodium, which is yellow in color. Other types that may be encountered are fluorescent, metal halide, and low-pressure sodium.
- The optics with which street lamps are equipped are designed to provide a rectangular pattern to maximize illumination in areas where it is most likely to be useful.
- Fixed lighting, whether from street lights or other sources is characterized by lack of homogeneity. There will be dark areas and light areas. The appearance of an object will depend on where it is located relative to the light sources. The apparent visibility of an object can also change greatly depending on the direction from which it is observed.
- Research on street lighting systems has sought to develop a metric that can be used as a basis for specifications. The measure most commonly used at present is visibility level (VL), which compares the contrast characteristics of the target object with the contrast required to assure detection.
- A field investigation may reveal that a target object is not visible from any significant distance with just the fixed lighting alone. In such a case the investigator should proceed as in the case of a scene where there is no fixed lighting.

- It often happens that the target object is visible for a considerable distance. If its conspicuity is below that judged adequate to assuredly capture the attention of a reasonably alert driver the investigator may use contrast data from Chapter 4 to guide in making an assessment of visibility.
- There are significant issues that the investigator must consider when dealing with an area in which there is fixed lighting. These are: the fact that the driver's adaptation level will be increased, the clutter created by the light sources, glare, the opportunity for prolonged viewing and appreciation of movement.

References

Blackwell, H. R. (1980). CIE Report 19.2 (draft). International Commission on Illumination. Vienna.

Gallagher, V. P. and Janoff, M. S. (1972). Interaction Between Fixed and Vehicular Illumination Systems. Philadelphia. The Franklin Institute Research Laboratories. Report No. FHWA-RD-72-51.

Gallagher, V. P., Koth, B. and Freedman, M. (1975). The Specification of Street Lighting Needs. Philadelphia. The Franklin Institute Research Laboratories. Report No. FHWA-RD-76-17.

Janoff, M. S. (1993). Investigations of Visual Performance Related to Visibility Level. Orlando. Proceedings of the 2nd International Symposium on Visibility and Luminance in Roadway Lighting.

Zimmer, R. A. (1991). Development of Iso-Footcandle Curves for Highway Lighting. College Station, Texas. Texas Transportation Institute. Texas A&M University. Research Report 1144-1F.

Chapter 7

Problems in the Use of Nighttime Photography as Evidence in Litigation

Introduction

It has been said that a picture is worth a thousand words. This is not true of all pictures, certainly, but it is an understatement with regard to some. Pictures in various forms (e.g., engineering drawings, artist's renderings, computer-generated displays, photographs) are commonly used in court. Their use will continue, and probably increase, because they can be very useful in helping jurors understand relatively complicated issues.

Photography is one of the most commonly used forms of visual presentation in court. It has great appeal for a number of reasons, not the least of which is that jurors tend to believe that what they see in a photograph is what they would have seen had they been there themselves at the time the photograph was taken. This belief is reinforced by their own experience, since most of them have probably taken photographs at one time or another. Unfortunately, most jurors have little technical knowledge about photography, hence little understanding of possible problems and limitations.

If the purpose of photographs offered into evidence is to show what something looks like under conditions approximating daytime levels of illumination, even an unskilled individual can produce acceptable images. These can assist jurors in a variety of ways, such as in understanding what an area or piece of equipment looks like, or in appreciating the injuries suffered by the plaintiff.

Many experts are offering into evidence nighttime photographs, videos, and even computer-generated displays purporting to show the visibility available to an individual in a particular situation. Relative to verbal explanations of the results of a reenactment, these displays are regarded as a great improvement by both lawyers and experts. This attitude is understandable, for the reasons mentioned earlier. There are a number of problems associated with this approach, however; problems that are seldom dealt with or even acknowledged by the individuals seeking to introduce this evidence. This chapter will review these problems. The intent is not to discourage the use of appropriate visual presentations, but rather to minimize the likelihood that they will be used in ways that will mislead the fact finder. The discussion to follow relates to all forms of pictorial representations purporting to represent the perception of a given individual.

It is reasonable to ask why, if it is helpful to show jurors photographs of what a scene looks like under daylight conditions, it is not equally helpful to show them photographs of what it looks like under nighttime conditions. After all, both types of photographs are intended to allow the jurors to see what they would have been able to see had they been there at the time the photographs were taken. The answer is that the criteria for adequacy are very different for the two situations. Generally, daytime photographs will serve their purpose if they are sufficiently clear to allow the jurors to see what they are supposed to see, and key elements are not distorted by inappropriate lenses, filters or the like. Within reason, exposure errors and distortions of contrast are of little or no consequence in daytime photographs. On the other hand, nighttime photographs are generally intended to depict with some precision the perceptions of a specific individual under defined circumstances. Therefore, they must meet not only the general criteria of daytime photographs but also depict with great accuracy the luminance levels and contrast present in the scene. In addition, in order for the pictorial representations to be effective tools, they must cause the perceptions of the jurors to reasonably duplicate that of the person or persons whose perceptions are at issue.

Suppose, for example, an expert takes nighttime photographs in an attempt to demonstrate the visibility of a pedestrian to a driver at one or more observation distances. If those photographs are shown to jurors two important assumptions are being made. The first is that the camera system can duplicate human vision with a high degree of precision. The second assumption is that the perceptions of the jurors to whom the photographs will be shown are a reasonable approximation of those of the individual whose perception is purportedly being represented. These are both weak assumptions, the second one especially. The remainder of this chapter will be devoted to a discussion of problems related to these two assumptions.

Limitations in the Camera-Film System

It is important to understand that a camera is not the same as the human eye, and film is not the same as the retina of the eye. The limitations of the camera-film system as a simulator of human vision are particularly acute under low-luminance conditions. William Hyzer has written extensively on this subject. It is not the purpose of this chapter to attempt to duplicate his excellent technical analysis. As Hyzer points out in one article (1993), a principal difficulty is the limited dynamic luminance range of photography as compared with that of the eye.

A typical result is distortions of contrast at one end or the other of the luminance spectrum. An example of the kind of difficulties often encountered is shown in Figure 7.1. Both of the photographs are of the same automobile viewed from the side under identical conditions. In the photograph at the top of Figure 7.1 the purpose was to depict the contrast of the vehicle body with its background. While that came out moderately well, the vehicle's side-marker lights appear much larger and more conspicuous than they did to the eye of the observer at the time the photograph was taken. They would also look that way to jurors, and may lead to a misperception on their part of the visibility of the vehicle. In the photograph at the bottom of Figure 7.1 an effort was made to duplicate the appearance of the side-marker lights. This is a much better approximation of their appearance to the observer, but now the contrast of the vehicle to its background is underrepresented.

There are instances where the dynamic luminance range limitation is of less importance. For example, if the intent is to depict the visibility of a relatively dark object in an unlighted environment, the required luminance range may be narrow enough to be accommodated on film. There are various approaches that can be used to make nighttime photography more accurate and to provide a fairer presentation to jurors. In one the photographer takes a series of Polaroid photographs of the scene, using different exposures. These are then viewed and compared with the scene itself to select one that most closely resembles what can be seen with the eye. The selected Polaroid exposure is then used as a reference when processing the conventional photographs. Other techniques have been developed and described in published papers, for example the efforts of Holohan, et al. (1989), and Harris and Harris (1992). These represent an improvement over what is often presented as "evidence" in court, and the individuals who use them are at least aware of some of the difficulties and have a sincere desire to minimize them.

The technical problems of rendering the scene accurately in the medium selected is often the least of the expert's worries. More significant in many cases, and far more difficult to resolve are the perceptual-cognitive issues to be discussed next.

Perceptual-Cognitive Issues

The greatest of care on the part of a skilled photographer can result in very misleading evidence if perceptual and cognitive issues are neglected. There are a number of ways to go astray. These will be listed and discussed below, in no particular order of importance.

Figure 7.1 Two photographs of the side of an automobile, showing distortions in contrast.

Field of View

The normal visual field for humans is close to 180 degrees in all directions, although in some applications certain dimensions are restricted. A camera can capture only a small portion of the visual field, normally much less than available to the individual whose vision is supposedly being represented. The result is that the jurors viewing the photograph cannot appreciate and need not be concerned with possible significant visual events outside that field. The inevitable result of the restricted field of view is to concentrate viewing by the observer and thus artificially enhance the visibility of the key object or condition being depicted.

Static Versus Dynamic Viewing

A photograph is a static representation of a slice in time. In most cases involving collisions in traffic the referenced situation was not static. The world looks different when everything is in motion, and the visual task is much more demanding. Movies, video or computer animations are an obvious solution to this problem. The person presenting them, however, must avoid the temptation to slow them down to ensure that the jurors do not miss the critical point they are supposed to depict.

Viewing Time

Jurors are often allowed to inspect visual materials at their leisure. Sometimes blowups are given to the jurors for their perusal, or a large photograph will be placed on an easel for an extended period of time during testimony. If the case relates to a dynamic event, such as a motor vehicle collision, it is blatantly unfair to allow prolonged viewing of a scene, since the involved party did not have that opportunity.

Adaptation Level

Differences in dark-adaptation level are rarely considered. If a nighttime photograph that accurately depicts the contrast between an object and its background is brought into court, it will typically be viewed at a much higher luminance level than existed in the field setting. As pointed out in Chapter 2, the human eye is designed for optimum performance at relatively high levels of illumination. If the jurors' eyes are adapted to a higher level of illumination than existed at the scene where the photograph was taken, they will be better able to see contrast differences on the image than they would have at the scene.

Harris and Harris (1992) describe a method in which the projected image of a scene is photometered to set the luminance of key elements equal to measurements made in the field, and the courtroom is darkened to bring the jurors' dark adaptation closer to the appropriate level. The downside is that some judges may not be thrilled by such a modification to their courtroom, and courtrooms having outside windows may not lend themselves to being darkened sufficiently during daylight hours. Granting those difficulties, the protocol described by Harris and Harris represents the kind of care that is required to minimize this problem.

Image Size

Figure 7.2 shows two photographs of the same pedestrian. The contrast levels in each photograph are about the same, but the larger figure is undoubtedly more conspicuous. The lesson here is that the investigator must take care to ensure that the angular size of all elements in the pictorial display is the same as they would be could the jurors view the scene directly from the represented distance. A six-foot tall pedestrian viewed at 200 feet, for example, subtends a vertical angle of about 1.7 degrees. If a photograph is taken of this pedestrian, with the intention that jurors be allowed to look at it using a viewing distance of 30 inches, the image size of the pedestrian should be 0.9 inch. As illustrated in Figure 7.2, if the image size is larger than that the pedestrian will be more conspicuous than he/she should be. This seems obvious enough, but it may be one of the most violated concepts of those being discussed.

Observer Expectancy

Observer expectancy, and the correction that must be made for expectancy when presenting the results of visibility studies applied to a real-world situation, is discussed in detail in Chapter 4. Briefly, expectancy relates to the mind set of an individual. We all have expectancies in everyday life as well as when operating a motor vehicle. In the latter context our expectancies go to matters such as roadway design, the placement and use of signs and signals and the behavior of other drivers. When expectancies are met drivers will respond sooner and are more likely to respond appropriately than when their expectancies are violated.

How does this relate to pictorial displays in the courtroom? The driver in question presumably did not expect to encounter the hazard that brought about the current litigation. The expectancies of the jurors, however, are quite different. The pictorial representation will typically be introduced with words like: "This is a photograph showing the visibility of the pedestrian at 200 feet." The jurors now know what they are looking for and where it is located (probably in the center of the photograph). If they have trouble seeing the object the expert will generally be pleased to point it out to them, all in a spirit of being helpful, of course.

It is clear from research on the subject that expectancy can have a profound effect on the distance at which a given object will be detected. It is naive for an expert to conduct a reenactment, determine the maximum distance at which

Figure 7.2 *Two photographs of a pedestrian showing effect of image size on conspicuity.*

he/she can see the object of concern, and then report that to a jury in a way that implies that everyone should have been able to see it at the same distance. Worse, it does a disservice to the system of justice because it provides misinformation to the jurors. Precisely the same criticism applies to pictorial displays when used as described. True, the concept of expectancy and the necessary corrections can be explained to jurors, but if they have been shown a pictorial representation depicting an object or condition that appears visible to them, a bias has been created that after-the-fact explanations may not be able to dispel.

Implications

There is a clear obligation on the part of any expert to provide the fact finder with information that is as accurate and complete as possible. The use of pictorial representations of various types attempting to depict the visibility of a given scene at night presents formidable difficulties to anyone who takes this obligation seriously. Many of the perceptual and cognitive problems discussed in this chapter play into the hands of the party in whose interest it is to want the object of concern to be as visible as possible. However honest the intentions of the individual presenting the materials, the result often is to misinform jurors and unfairly tilt the scales of justice.

This is a serious matter, which is apparently largely attributable to a lack of information on the part of attorneys, judges and experts concerning the issues outlined in this chapter. Until such time as a wider appreciation of these matters comes about, individuals involved in the litigation process will have to be very much on guard. There is, unfortunately, no easy solution to some of the problems raised in this chapter. Pictorial displays purporting to show what was available for someone to see at night must be carefully scrutinized. No attorney or expert should allow such evidence to be presented as part of his/her case if it suffers from one or more of the problems described. Any attorney or expert confronted with such evidence from the opposition must ensure that it meets all the criteria listed and be in a position to protest in an informed manner to keep it from the jury if it does not.

Chapter Overview

Pictorial evidence is commonly used in court and can be of great assistance to jurors in understanding relatively complex matters. Like any other kind of evidence, pictures must provide accurate information. A particular problem concerns nighttime photography, where the intent of the investigator is to provide a representation of what a particular individual could or should have seen. There are a number of issues to be considered. The following are the major points covered in this chapter.

- There are significant limitations to the film medium that make it very difficult to accurately capture the range of luminances found in a typical nighttime scene. A typical result is a distortion of contrast and consequent misrepresentation of contrast to the viewer.
- Perhaps of greater significance than the technical limitations of the medium are perceptual-cognitive issues. These also seem more likely to not be considered by investigators when presenting pictorial evidence. The points that follow relate to perceptual-cognitive issues.
- The field of view of a camera is significantly smaller than that of a motor vehicle operator. Persons viewing a photograph cannot appreciate and will not be concerned with visual events outside the field depicted.
- A photograph is static, unlike the typical traffic collision. Movies or video can depict a dynamic scene and are an obvious solution to this problem.
- Jurors are often allowed to view a photograph for a protracted period. This is not fair to the involved party, who typically did not have that luxury.
- Jurors will be adapted to relatively high levels of illumination in a courtroom. This will enable them to detect contrast differences in a photograph that they would not see if adapted to the level of illumination prevailing at the scene. Where possible, the courtroom should be darkened to a level approximating that at the scene where the photographs were taken.
- The image size of the object of concern in the photographs should be the same as it would have been had the viewer been at the scene when the photographs were taken.
- Jurors who view a photograph know what they are looking for and where it will be located. This puts them in a much better position to detect the represented object than the concerned party, who did not have those advantages.

References

Harris, J. L. Sr. and Harris, J. L. II. (1992). Forensic Photography and Nighttime Visibility Issues. *Journal of Forensic Sciences.* Vol. 37, Pp. 1084-1095.

Holohan, R. D., Billing, A. M. and Murray, S. D. (1989). Nighttime Photography - Show it Like it is. The Society of Automotive Engineers. Technical Report 890730.

Hyzer, W. G. (1993). The Eye, Brain, and Camera in Nighttime Accident Reconstruction. *PHOTO > Electronic Imaging.* Pp. 8-9.

Chapter 8

Evaluation of Visibility in the Field

Introduction

Investigators dealing with cases in which visibility is an issue will often set up and carry out a test, the purpose of which is to assess the visibility situation that confronted the subject driver. The test may take many forms but normally is a sort of mini experiment in which the investigators are the only subjects. These visibility tests are often carried out by recreating the accident scenario to at least a moderate degree of fidelity and having one or more observers determine the distance at which the hazard can be seen. This distance is then reported to the fact finder in a way implying that anyone could see it at the same distance "if they were paying attention." Someone who has read the material presented in the chapters preceding this one will realize that there are flaws in this approach, flaws that will probably lead to the visibility distance being greatly overestimated.

It is very important to understand that the task of the investigator is not merely to measure the distance at which something becomes visible. This is a trivial exercise, and only useful as a first step in the investigation. The true task of the investigator is to determine the level of target contrast at which it would assuredly be detected by a reasonably alert driver. This is a much more challenging job; one that requires knowledge of relevant data and the limitations of those data. In addition, unfortunately, there will be times when the situation is such that available data do not assist and reasoned judgment is necessary.

The purpose of this chapter is to provide guidance in planning, carrying out and interpreting the results of a field evaluation so that it will assist not only the investigators, but ultimately the fact finder in understanding the situation confronting a particular driver. To accomplish this the discussion will consider questions concerning facilities, equipment, procedures and interpretation of results. To assist the investigator in coping with an imperfect world, the discussion will also address the issue of which elements of the event in question should be reproduced with some fidelity and which are of lesser concern.

First Question: Why?

The first matter the investigator must deal with is why do a field evaluation? The question is not as dumb as it sounds. A field evaluation, if run properly, will take time to set up and carry out. That translates to a significant expense that must be borne by the client. If the situation in question fits that utilized in available research, then there is a very real question whether the expert can justify spending the client's resources in that way. The first step in the evaluation process therefore is to determine whether the situation under consideration conforms to that on which available data are based. If, for example, the case involves a dark-clad pedestrian in an unlighted area, this is a perfect fit to visibility data presented in Chapter 4. Even if there are differences the basic data may work well. In the case of the pedestrian collision cited as an example, investigation may reveal that the victim was wearing clothing that was more reflective than that employed in the referenced study. If the vehicle speeds were fairly high, however, a collision is probably going to happen anyway. The point is that research data were collected using equipment, procedures, and analyses more sophisticated than those normally available to an investigator for a specific case. In addition, the results are normally based on relatively large numbers of subjects, each of whom provided multiple responses to each condition under investigation. In fact, if the data collected in a field evaluation do not conform to those from a significant research effort using the same parameters the investigator has some explaining to do.

If there is a reasonable fit between a specific situation under investigation and available research data the client should be so advised. In the final analysis it should be the client's choice whether to go ahead with a field evaluation under those conditions. There may be good reasons for doing so, based on what the other side is doing, what the attorney believes will play well with the jury, etc., and the expert should be in a position to offer input to such a decision process.

Preparatory Phase

The preparatory stage is probably the most important part of a field evaluation. In it the investigator must acquire all the information necessary about the subject event, the status of all relevant elements at the time and at the present, and plan the investigation. Accordingly, there are a number of things to be considered.

In the ideal reenactment the investigator would have available the vehicle(s) involved, with all the relevant equipment in identical condition. All other factors involved, e.g., hazard elements, signs, lighting sources and weather would be identical.

All of the above could be accomplished if the investigator had access to a time machine. Lacking such a convenience certain concessions to reality are usually necessary. The process of litigation being what it is, often considerable time has passed since the event under investigation. The involved vehicle(s), even if driveable after the crash, may have disappeared. The road may have been re-paved or even undergone major renovation. Signs have aged, or been replaced. Signals or new or upgraded lighting systems may have been installed. The number of things that can happen to complicate the investigator's life are almost limitless. Still, one must go forward. It would be helpful for the investigator to understand what elements in the crash scenario are important to duplicate with some precision and what elements are not. Fortunately, many elements can be substituted without causing problems.

Having said that, it must be admitted that the substitution of elements, or an expressed attitude that such and such a detail doesn't matter to the accuracy of the investigation, opens the investigator to possible negative scrutiny by opposing counsel. It's one thing for the investigator to know that certain details of the investigation need not be duplicated exactly. The fact finder, however, probably doesn't know that, and it's safe to assume that astute attorneys will seek to exploit that ignorance to their own advantage. Therefore, the investigator must be prepared to discuss up front why certain items were not duplicated exactly. Failure to do so may put the expert in the position of hearing something like: "My expert used an exemplar of the same year, make and model, while the one you used was two years newer," accompanied by a suitable sneer. This forces the expert to explain that the differences are irrelevant and why, which may look like excuse making to the jury, even if one can get it in under cross examination. Thus, there are good reasons to be as faithful in the field investigation as possible, simply as a means of avoiding irrelevant criticism. There are, however, limits to what can be done in a given situation. The discussion to follow is intended to provide some guidance in this decision-making process.

Physical Facilities

By "physical facilities" is meant the roadway and relevant associated items such as lighting, signs and signals. Generally, these will not have changed all that much, which is fortunate. Where changes have occurred the investigator must be prepared to document those changes and accommodate the investigation to them, even if that means using another site.

For someone interested in visibility issues, normally the most important single item is lighting. The following is a list of suggested actions to be taken by the investigator:

- The investigator should inventory all lighting in the area, including that from security and parking lot lights, illuminated signs and storefronts. Recognizing the limitations of night photography (see Chapter 7), photo documentation may be helpful as a supplement to sketches or scale drawings. The purpose of such photographs is not to illustrate the capability of the sources but to show their relationship to the primary area of interest and to each other. The danger here, of course, is that the other side might seek to use the photographs to assist their argument. Therefore, the investigator must make it very clear that they are not intended to document the quality of illumination from these sources.

- Distances of light sources from the relevant areas should be measured. (By "relevant areas" is meant the area of collision certainly. For moving objects like pedestrians, it also includes their path during the time it would have been within the driver's field of view.)
- If the investigator has access to an illuminance meter it may be helpful to measure the contribution of sources such as store fronts, security lights and illuminated signs in the relevant area, if for no better reason than to demonstrate their irrelevance objectively.
- For sources other than street lights, make an effort to find out what changes, if any, may have occurred between the time of the subject event and the investigation. Businesses start up and go away with some regularity. Some light sources (e.g., signs, parking lot lights) may not be left on all night. Better to be able to say "I checked, and it was/was not on at the time of the collision" even if the source is judged irrelevant to the visibility issue.
- As part of the overall documentation, the investigator can take illuminance meter readings of the street lights in the area, but this is generally not worth the effort. Obtaining a reasonable grid of illuminance readings is time consuming. In addition it requires the assistance of at least one other person to write down the readings and watch for traffic to minimize the risk of the investigator's name being added to the list of victims. Once obtained, the readings by themselves generally do not allow the investigator to address the bottom-line question of the adequacy of conspicuity for the particular object or condition of concern. There are exceptions, as noted in Chapter 6. A single reading, or at most a few readings should suffice in such cases.

If street lighting has been added to a scene the investigator normally has no choice but to find another area without lights, unless local officials can be persuaded to turn the lights off for purposes of the test. Fortunately, one dark place is pretty much like another, and finding a suitable unlighted test area should not pose much difficulty. In the case of upgraded lighting there is more of a problem. Generally, the simplest strategy is to conduct the investigation anyway. Three things can happen.

1. If the resultant analysis shows that the object or condition of concern would likely not have been capable of assuredly capturing the attention of a reasonably alert driver at an adequate distance under the upgraded system, then it certainly would not have been capable of doing so under the previous system of illumination. An exception here may occur if the upgrading also involved relocating light sources relative to the area in which the event occurred. In this case one possible solution is to move the object position so that its location relative to the light source is the same as at the time of collision.
2. If the object or condition is found to be highly conspicuous with the upgraded system, then it probably would have been adequately conspicuous under the previous lighting system as well.
3. If the conspicuity of the object or condition is marginally adequate with the new lighting system, then the investigator has a problem. Here one solution, awkward as it may be, is to try to find an area where the lighting more nearly approximates that of the original area. Local officials should be able to supply information on the type of lamps installed in various areas. With luck, some areas will still have the older style lighting system. In some cases it may be possible to compensate for the higher source output by moving the target further from the lamp. This is only practical where the sources are relatively far apart, as when they are placed only at intersections. Clearly, it is necessary to know the relative output of the two systems. If isocandela diagrams are available for the two sources under consideration (see Chapter 6), these can be used to guide placement. Lacking such data, an illuminance meter will be required in order to determine how far the target object is to be moved. In this case the investigator will have to locate an older style source, take a reading at the appropriate distance, and then find a new position in the area of the collision based on that reading.

In areas where traffic volumes are high it may be very difficult to set up a test in safety. Unless local officials are willing to shut down the road, the only solution is to wait until traffic thins out, generally in the wee hours of the morning. This, however, may make it difficult to match key environmental issues. For example, if the collision occurred during the period of civil twilight, the time of the investigation must be controlled within a window of about five minutes. The investigator must use imagination and good sense to arrive at a workable solution when confronted with such a situation.

Vehicles

Having the exact vehicle is one of the least important items in the investigative process. A vehicle of the same general configuration is desirable, however. Headlamp mounting height is important, assuming visibility from that vehicle, with that vehicle's headlamps is at issue. The rule of thumb is that visibility distance increases or decreases by about ten feet for every inch change up or down in mounting height. This is probably only true for relatively modest changes in mounting height, but it does say that the exemplar should have the same mounting height as the involved vehicle. Seat position and driver eye height are other elements that should be controlled as closely as possible.

Vehicle Lighting and Marking Equipment

Type or Manufacturer of Lamps

As noted in Chapter 4, so long as low beams are under consideration, it is irrelevant whether the headlamps are halogen or non-halogen. An exception arises in the case of headlamps if high beams were involved. Halogen lamps will generally have more powerful high beams than non-halogen lamps, and the appropriate type should be used when evaluating visibility with high beams.

The manufacturer of any light source on a vehicle is not relevant since all must meet SAE standards. In the case of headlamps it is true that there are minor differences from one manufacturer to another, but the intensity-visibility distance relationship discussed in Chapter 5 ensures that the differences between makers of headlamps are inconsequential to performance.

Taillamps, brake lamps, reflex reflectors, and to some extent side marker lights differ greatly from vehicle to vehicle in the case of passenger cars. Where these sources are of significance to the investigation there is no substitute for using a vehicle having the same configuration. There is much less variability in the case of trucks, but the investigator must be careful. Particularly in the case of side markers, in recent years many trucking companies have added lights and reflective material to try to improve side visibility. It is important to find out precisely how the vehicle was fitted out and duplicate that to the degree practical.

Headlamp Aim

The most critical element in vehicle lighting is headlamp aim, which is discussed is some detail in Chapter 5. Aim is difficult to control accurately, tends to drift off with vehicle use, will be altered significantly by vehicle loading, and can have a major effect on the visibility that the lighting system will provide. It's nice to know all this but, unless the vehicle or at least the area in which the headlights are mounted is essentially undamaged and the investigator can lay hands on it shortly after the event in question, it is normally impossible to know the aim condition of a particular vehicle at a particular time.

In most cases all that can be done is ensure that the headlamps on the exemplar vehicle are reasonably well aimed when the test is carried out. This is not a trivial task. It is entirely possible that a vehicle taken to a service outlet will emerge with the headlights worse aimed than when it entered. The investigator should check the aim before resorting to a trip to a garage. Stand the vehicle on a level surface facing toward a wall at a distance of about 25 feet. Turn on the headlights. The hot spots should be clearly visible, about the same height, with their tops at a height equal to the distance from the ground to the center of the headlamps, as illustrated in Figure 8.1 from the SAE Ground Vehicle Lighting Standards Manual. In addition, the centers of the hot spots should be separated by the same horizontal distance as between the sources. On the road the hot spots should be visible in the vicinity of the right edge line, 125 feet or so ahead of the vehicle. If the system comes close in these tests, leave well enough alone. If the vehicle is sent to a service outlet for aiming, this check should be carried out anyway, to make sure the work was done correctly.

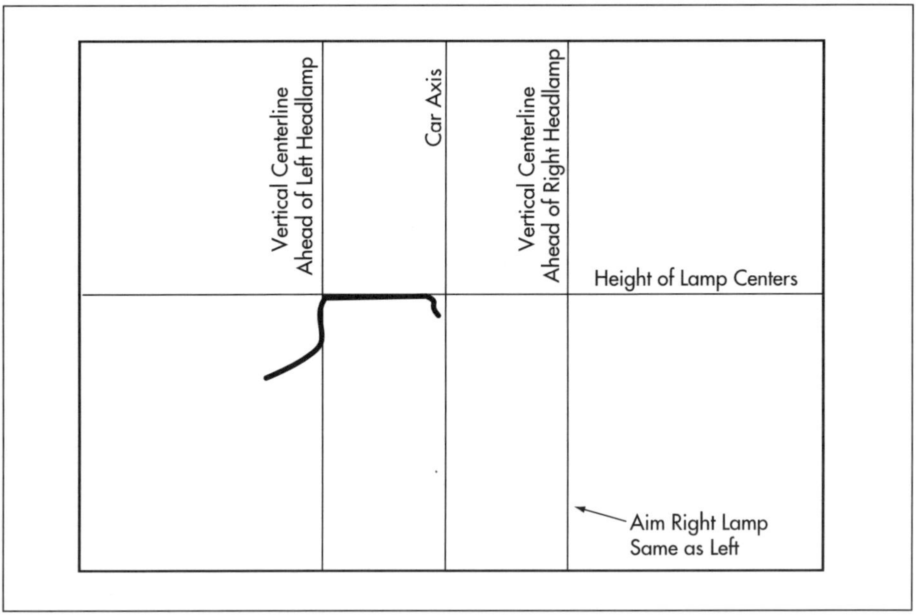

Figure 8.1 *Visual aiming illustration from SAE Standards. Credit line: Reprinted with permission from J599 ©1995, Society of Automotive Engineers, Inc.*

Vehicle loading is also an issue of consequence. As noted in Chapter 5, load has an effect on vertical aim. If an exemplar vehicle is loaded up with observers and/or equipment in the rear to reenact a collision in which there was only a driver, this may result in the aim being pulled upward and visibility distance being overestimated.

The investigator should attempt to determine how the involved vehicle was loaded at the time and try to duplicate that condition. Ordinarily, front seat passengers will have no effect on aim. Before loads are added that were not in the vehicle at the time of the event in question, the investigator must check to be certain that aim is not affected.

Lamp Output

The voltage delivered to the lamps, and their consequent output, varies with engine RPMs. With the engine off, the battery will supply about 12 volts. However, with the car being driven at reasonable speeds the electrical system will typically provide substantially more than 12 volts. The output of a lamp increases with voltage in a non-linear fashion. Figure 8.2 illustrates the relationship between voltage and output in lumens for a typical halogen bulb. The output is

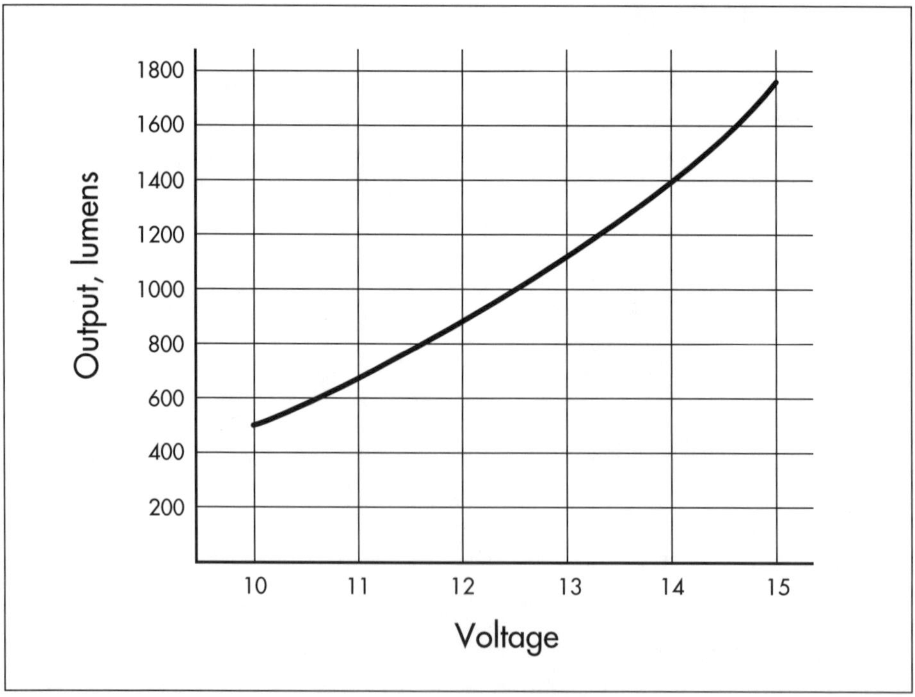

Figure 8.2 *Relationship between voltage and headlamp output.*

about 860 lumens at 12 volts, about 1100 lumens at the design voltage (12.8 volts), and about 1400 lumens at 14 volts. The equation that describes this relationship is:

$$Lm_2 = Lm_1 \left(\frac{V_2}{V_1}\right)^{3.5} \qquad 8.1$$

Where:

Lm_2 = desired lumen value
Lm_1 = known lumen value at a given voltage
V_1 and V_2 = voltages associated with lumen levels

For example, if it is known that 13 volts yields 1140 lumens, the equation can be used to determine the lumens at 12 volts (861), or any other voltage level in the general range of 12-15 volts.

The obvious moral of this story is that reenactments must be run under conditions where the lamps are being operated at realistic voltages. The intensity-visibility-distance relationship described in Chapter 4 means that the differences in visibility will not be major if this factor is ignored, but a careful investigator will account for it regardless.

Dirt on Glass Surfaces

As noted in Chapter 5, dirt on headlights can build up quickly and significantly reduce output. Once again, the intensity-visibility-distance relationship comes to the aid of the investigator, meaning that large losses in output may have only a modest effect on forward visibility. Dirt on marker and signal lamps is another matter, and the relationship between output and conspicuity is much more direct. Dirt on retroreflective surfaces is particularly serious. Also of consequence are dirt and other contaminants on the windshield, particularly when lights are shining on the windshield.

An investigator might occasionally get a case where he/she has access to the same vehicle and can be reasonably sure the lamp aim has not changed. The probability that glass surfaces will have the same level of contaminants, however, is essentially zero. Since the original condition cannot be duplicated the only reasonable recourse is to ensure that all glass surfaces are clean.

A problem arises if photographs taken of the vehicle post crash indicate that the lamp surfaces and/or windshield was dirty. It is probably not possible to duplicate the dirt level simply based on the photographs. The obvious strategy is to carry out the evaluation with everything clean. If the visibility of the target object still falls below levels predetermined as minimum for adequate response then the dirt does not matter. On the other hand, if visibility is well in excess of that minimum, then it would take horrendous dirt levels to make a difference. If the visibility falls between these extremes there may be some merit in trying to simulate dirt levels by spraying dirty water on the surfaces and letting it dry.

Environmental Conditions

Weather, other than "clear and dry," presents formidable problems to the investigator. As a practical matter, it is generally not possible to accurately duplicate precipitation in any form. Restrictions to visibility such as fog, smoke, and blowing dust or snow are probably worse. The most common weather problem the investigator is likely to encounter is rain. The issues here are restrictions to visibility associated with water droplets in the atmosphere and water on the windshield, as well as the change in pavement reflectivity. With luck and diligence an investigator who has some flexibility can probably manage to put a reenactment together in rainy conditions. If there is some understanding of how hard it was raining at the time, based on witness testimony or weather data, an effort should be made to duplicate this as well, further complicating matters for the investigator.

Other restrictions to visibility such as those mentioned earlier are more difficult to deal with and often there is no real solution in terms of an accurate reenactment. The investigator will have to use good sense and ingenuity in dealing with these situations.

Lighting Conditions

Artificial lighting was covered earlier in this chapter. If the collision occurred in the period of civil twilight (about one half hour before sunrise or after sunset) the investigation must be carried out at a time when the sun position is as close to that of the subject event as possible. This is particularly important if the subject driver was facing toward the setting or rising sun at the time.

The investigator may wish to check on moon phase and position and try to duplicate this as best as possible. Fortunately, there is no moon visible at night, in clear weather, about half the time. Add in those occasions where the sky is overcast and more than half the time it will turn out that there was no moon visible at the time of the event in question. This condition is easy to duplicate. Where there was a moon visible, its phase, altitude and azimuth can be approximated if the investigator has considerable flexibility in scheduling. Then it is necessary to hope that the weather cooperates. As noted in Chapter 2, moonlight generally is of no consequence in typical night visibility situations, but there is merit in trying to factor it in where practical, if only to address the obvious criticism from the other side if it is ignored.

Observer Age

Observer age is a factor that should not be overlooked. The effects of age on visual capability at night were discussed in Chapter 5. They can be very significant. If, for example, the subject driver was elderly but the investigator is relatively young probable detection distance may be overestimated by 25-50%. Admittedly, there are substantial differences in visual performance from one individual to the next, and it is not possible to know the precise capabilities of a particular person without appropriate testing. It is reasonable, however, to point out to the fact finder the differences in vision capability as a function of aging and offer an opinion concerning the probable effect in a specific instance. The involved driver may actually participate in the visibility testing, with his attorney's approval. The results, of course, are likely to be dismissed as self-serving by the opposing attorney if they do not support that individual's preconceptions.

Execution Stage

With the target object, exemplar vehicle, road and all other details taken care of, it is time to carry out the work. Assuming visibility distance is the issue, there are various methods that can be employed. These come under two headings, depending on whether the test vehicle or the target is moving.

In either condition the evaluation can be run with the distance between target and observer decreasing until detection occurs, or the opposite with the distance increasing until it is no longer visible. It is important to note that the methods will yield different results. The detection distance will be significantly less when the target is initially not visible. The difference is probably attributable to the slight uncertainty as to exactly where and when the target will appear. Since this method more nearly approximates the normal conditions of a collision it is recommended.

Some investigators prefer that the exemplar vehicle be stationary and the target moved, where it is practical to do so. Obviously, it is necessary to rev up the engine to some extent to be sure the voltage to the lamps is at normal operating level. The main problem with having the vehicle stationary is in attaining accurate horizontal alignment. In Chapter 4 a point was made concerning the small angles involved in the forward field, and the difficulties this causes in lamp design. Misalignment of as little as one degree can have a significant effect on the visibility of an object in the forward field. It is extremely difficult to align a car within one degree of a lane center line. When the car is moving forward there is some yawing from side to side, true enough. If the driver is conscious of this issue, it can be kept within reasonable bounds and the horizontal misalignment will be better, in all probability, than if the work is done with the vehicle stationary. It also requires much less effort.

When visibility assessments are done speed is of no consequence. The objective is to obtain a reasonably accurate estimate of maximum visibility distance. Distances can be pre marked, and the test vehicle driven slowly toward the target object until it is detected. Later tests can be conducted at speed, which may assist the investigator in appreciating the time-distance relationship. It is best, however, to start slow. If visibility is very poor, higher speeds may be dangerous, if nothing else.

Some investigators take readings of output from the vehicle's headlamps at various distances. As in the case of readings of output from fixed sources discussed earlier, this can be done if the individual feels it is important. There seems no reason to do it routinely, however. It is a time-consuming activity, there are the problems with the horizontal alignment of the vehicle, as discussed earlier, and the readings really do not assist the investigator in addressing the bottom-line issue of visibility distance.

Analysis and Interpretation

When a detection distance has been determined, what then? The following is a step-by-step outline in getting to a final opinion:

1. The distance obtained in the visibility analysis probably corresponds to about the 95th percentile of what would be obtained in a controlled test. That's because of the way it is done and the limited number of trials. Subjects in a normal study may be involved for one to two hours, giving them time to become bored and somewhat tired. Thus, their best performance would be about what an investigator would accomplish in a brief series of trials, but there would be considerable variability downward, as exemplified in the test results described in Chapter 4.
2. The next step is to estimate the probable range of response distances that would be obtained in a formal investigation as a means of approximating the median. Suppose a reenactment was carried out using a pedestrian target and the visibility distance was found to be 300 feet. The test data in Chapter 4 suggest that the probable range of response distances obtained in a test would be from about 100-300 feet, with a median of about 200 feet. A more reflective target, such as the pedestrian with the white shirt, may produce a range of response distances of about 300 feet. In general, the greater the maximum

distance at which something can be seen, the greater the probable range of response distances one would obtain in a formal study.

3. Now a correction for expectancy must be applied, as described in Chapter 4. In the example above, where the estimated median was 200 feet, a correction for expectancy would reduce the median to about 100 feet. There will still be considerable scatter about the median, probably more so than in the controlled study. The shape of the distribution is somewhat uncertain, however. In all probability it assumes a positively-skewed shape, in this case running from zero or near zero to a maximum of about 300 feet.
4. The final step is to apply what is known about the driver's response in the situation under investigation to determine if it fell within reasonable bounds. In the pedestrian collision used as an illustration, suppose there were 20 feet of pre-impact skids. If the pre-braking speed had been estimated at 60 ft/sec, the use of a perception-response time range of 0.60 to 1.25 seconds (see Chapter 10), or 36 to 75 feet, means that this driver probably had detected the pedestrian at a distance between 56 and 95 feet. The visibility distance analysis indicates that the driver's performance was within a range consistent with that of a reasonably alert driver.

Chapter Overview

This chapter is concerned with practical issues in carrying out a field visibility evaluation. The following are the principal points covered:

- The first visibility issue the investigator should address is whether the situation under evaluation fits available test data reasonably well. If it does, the question becomes whether a field evaluation is justifiable. The final decision will be based on several considerations, but the client should be advised of the relationship of existing test data to the case under consideration.
- In the preparatory phase the investigator determines what equipment and procedures are required and plans the test. While attention to every detail minimizes later criticism, it is normal that some compromise is required in terms of test elements. Some items (e.g., test vehicle, headlamps) can be substituted without concern, the condition of some (e.g., headlamp aim, dirt on glass surfaces) usually cannot be known. Assumptions are often necessary and the usual assumption is that everything was in near-perfect condition.

- In areas where there is fixed lighting the investigator may find it useful to prepare a diagram of the area showing the sources and distances from the area of the collision. A check should be made to determine if any changes have occurred since the event under investigation and what business-related lights, signs, etc. were on at the time. If lights that have the potential to affect the visibility of the target object have changed then the investigator must take steps to accommodate to this problem.
- The test is best carried out using a moving vehicle and stationary target. Other procedures present problems that can affect the test results. Speed of the test vehicle is not relevant. Low speeds allow greater accuracy in the measurement of distance and are safer.
- The visibility distances measured in a typical field evaluation correspond to about 95th percentile performance in a formal study. The investigator must allow for this fact in estimating the median and making a correction for expectancy.

Section II
Driver Perception–Response Time

Chapter 9

Driver Perception–Response Time

Introduction

Consider the following scenario: A driver comes around a curve and finds himself confronted with a stalled truck. The driver brakes, but does not stop before colliding with the truck. In the ensuing litigation the plaintiff driver testifies that he braked as soon as he saw the truck. Considering sight distance, skid marks and the speed claimed by the plaintiff, an expert engaged by the defense calculates that it took the driver nearly two seconds to begin braking after the truck entered his field of view. This, the expert contends, is an unreasonable perception-response time. The expert goes on to state that 0.75 second is a proper perception-response time for a reasonably alert driver under these conditions. Had this driver responded appropriately, it is argued, the severity of the collision would have been significantly reduced or it might have been avoided entirely. In this case the jury must decide whom to believe as concerns the time to respond to the hazard posed by the truck. Clearly, if they agree with the expert, the plaintiff's chance for a favorable verdict will be substantially reduced.

The time that it takes a driver to perceive and respond to an unexpected situation is of considerable interest to those who design the roadway system as well as in many instances of litigation resulting from motor vehicle crashes. In this chapter the subject of driver perception-response time is reviewed. It begins by describing the necessary steps in perception-response, then reviews the available literature on the subject. Various factors that can affect perception-response time are covered, and recommendations are offered. Chapter 10 deals further with the subject, describing some common situations in which adjustments to the basic perception-response time estimate are called for.

Perception-response time starts with a stimulus that may be applied to any of the sense organs. In the context of motor vehicle operation it is almost always a visual stimulus that is of consequence. Therefore, this chapter is written under the assumption that the perception-response interval is initiated by something that must be apprehended visually. It is recognized that a response may ultimately come from an auditory input, or the driver may have felt something hit his/her vehicle or feel as though something has been run over, as examples of other types of stimuli. In most cases such sensations result in visual search on the part of the driver prior to making a response, substantially prolonging what will shortly be described as the identification stage of perception-response.

A word of caution would be appropriate at this point. It will become evident while reading this chapter that meaningful work on perception-response time in the context of motor vehicle operation is difficult to carry out. That fact, combined with the realization that there are a virtually unlimited number of real-world scenarios that can call for a quick response on the part of a driver means that considerably less than 100% of cases are covered by directly relevant data. The available data can offer some general guidance for instances that are relatively straightforward. The data are less helpful in those cases characterized by one or more complicating elements. This state of affairs is not likely to be remedied in the foreseeable future. In every instance it is necessary that the investigator carefully consider the facts of a case to determine whether it fits within the constraints of available data, and use caution and informed judgment when rendering an opinion when it does not.

Background

Definition

Perception-response time is the interval between the appearance of some object or condition in the driver's field of view and the initiation of a response. Basic to the definition is that there must be a well-defined entry of the object into the individual's field of view, after which it becomes possible for it to be detected. The interval starts, for example, when a pedestrian steps out from behind a parked truck, and ends when the driver responds by starting to turn the steering wheel and/or hitting the brake pedal.

The time to complete the elected maneuver is normally not included in perception-response time. This is calculated separately, taking into account variables such as speed, drag factor, and type of vehicle. One case where maneuver time *is* included is a concept called decision sight distance. This is an engineering criterion applicable to conditions such as work zones with a lane closure. In the American Association of State Highway and Transportation Officials (AASHTO) design manual *A Policy on Geometric Design of Highways and Streets* (1984) decision sight distance is defined as the distance required for a driver to detect an unexpected or otherwise difficult-to-perceive information source or hazard in a roadway environment that may be visually cluttered, recognize the hazard or its threat potential, select an appropriate speed and path, and initiate and complete the required maneuver safely and efficiently. Decision sight distance is clearly applicable to certain crash scenarios, so the time recommendations will be discussed in this chapter as well.

Components of Perception-Response Time

During the perception-response interval the object or condition of concern has to capture the attention of the observer. In addition, a certain amount of mental processing has to take place before any response can occur. These steps in processing have been given various names and descriptions by different authors. What follows here is adapted from Perchonok and Pollack (1981).

- Detection. Perception-response time begins when some object or condition of concern enters the driver's visual field. This first step concludes when the driver develops a conscious awareness that "something" is present. The something may be within the field of view of the driver for some time before it is detected. This would be true particularly in cases where the object has poor contrast, is relatively small and/or appears in the far periphery of the eye. In such cases there is the potential for a significant delay between the presentation of the stimulus and its coming to the attention of the observer. Typically, once detection occurs the eyes will be moved to bring that which has been detected into focus on the foveal portion of the retina so that the next step can be undertaken.
- Identification. In this step sufficient information is acquired about the object or condition to be able to reach a decision as to what action, if any, is required. Identification need not be complete in detail. For example, it is not necessary to know if the object ahead is a truck or boulder, knowing that there is something ahead that the driver does not want to hit is more than adequate. If that which is being identified is moving, or capable of movement, it is also necessary to determine what it is doing. This may require estimates of speed and trajectory as part of an effort to predict its future position.
- Decision. At this point the operator must decide what action, if any, is appropriate. Assuming some action is decided upon, the choices generally come down to a change in speed and/or direction.
- Response. In this step commands are issued by the motor center of the brain to the appropriate muscle groups to carry out the required action(s).

It is useful to list the various steps in perception-response as a means of emphasizing the complexity of the event, the nature of the information that must be obtained and processed, and the various ways in which things can go wrong. An unfortunate side effect of such a listing is that it tends to create the impression that the steps follow each other in a regular and rigid process. Humans seldom operate in such a simple fashion. It is true that nothing else can be accomplished until detection is complete, but there is probably some degree of overlap in the other steps. One example is the driver who releases the accelerator and covers the brake with a foot while trying to identify something and decide what to do about it. The boundaries between the various steps are blurred at best. Since they are all internal, there is no way to separate them with any accuracy. Sometimes investigators talk about perception-response time as though it consisted of two sections that can be readily separated and timed. For example, it is not uncommon to hear someone speak of perception time as being a particular value and response time another value, adding them together to arrive at a total perception-response time. This needlessly complicates the issue and implies a state of knowledge that does not exist. What we do know something about is the time between the appearance of a stimulus and the initiation of a response. Hence, it is reasonable to deal only with the total perception-response time, not its components.

The Time to Respond

The Basics

When a potentially damaging stimulus is contacted by an individual a withdrawal response is initiated without conscious participation of the affected person. For example, if your hand touches a very hot surface you will jerk it away quickly. The time from touching the hot surface to initiation of withdrawal is typically about 0.10 second. This is called a reflex response. A reflex response is essentially preprogrammed. What happens in the case of a very intense stimulus such as a burn is that the signal travels via sensory nerves to the spinal cord, there causing appropriate motor nerves to be stimulated, leading to the withdrawal response. The stimulus also travels up the spinal cord to the brain so that the individual becomes consciously aware of the problem, but by that time the withdrawal response is already underway. By minimizing the amount of time the body is in contact with a potentially damaging stimulus, such reflexes have a clear protective function.

A reflex such as that described is accomplished in the time required for the nerve impulses to travel the distance from the stimulus site to the spinal cord, make the necessary connections (called synapses) and travel back again to the muscles. The perception-response time with which this paper is concerned takes longer, not only because the nerve impulses must travel further (i.e., to the brain and back), but because the information they represent must be processed in the brain before any action can be taken. The processing involved will have a significant effect on the time required for the individual to respond.

In the simplest kind of response-time investigation the subject will rest a finger on a telegrapher's key with the instruction to release it as quickly as possible when a stimulus such as a light is presented. Sometimes an alerting signal such as a buzzer is provided just before the stimulus is presented as part of a deliberate effort to minimize random error. In such a study detection, identification, and decision are accomplished in minimal time because the subject's attention is focused on the stimulus, the nature of the stimulus is known, and the response has been dictated by the experimenter. Response times of about 0.20 second will typically be obtained.

Even a simple study like that described can be affected by a variety of factors. In general, the larger or more intense the stimulus the shorter the response time (Postman and Egan, 1949). Responses will be faster with the preferred hand, and faster with either hand than with the feet (Huffman and Hummel,1967; Hoffman, 1991). Different sensory modalities yield different response times. For example response times are generally shorter to auditory than visual stimuli (Postman and Egan, 1949). Some investigators contend that this phenomenon is actually a function of stimulus intensity. The only way to settle the issue is to equate the intensity of different kinds of stimuli, then run an appropriate study. Unfortunately, equating stimuli in different sensory modalities is a significant challenge.

The subject's life can be complicated somewhat by changing the task. For example, if the alerting signal is not used, and the interval between trials is variable, the result will be an increase in response variability and in average response time. The *minimum* times will remain the same, but there will be more relatively long times, presumably because on those occasions the subject's attention was directed elsewhere when the stimulus was presented, thus lengthening the detection interval. In general, the longer the average interval between trials, the greater the response time variability (i.e., the greater the number of relatively long response times).

There is another whole class of perception-response studies that alter the subject's task in rather interesting ways. Suppose, for example, the subject is given an array of several lights and instructed to respond to only one of them. This would have no effect on detection, but it does require the subject to determine whether the relevant stimulus has been presented, an identification task. The test could be further modified by requiring a different response to each light, which introduces an element of decision. As might be expected, both of these approaches result in longer minimum response times and greater response variability than that associated with the simple response-time test. How much longer will depend on how much information must be processed before a response can be effected. Damon, et al. (1966) reviewed research on the relationship between response time and the number of choices available to the subject. They found that one choice yielded an average response time of 0.20 second, and two choices an average of 0.35 second. Additional choices added an average of about 0.05 second to response time, up to a total of nine choices, at an average of 0.65 second.

Response Time in the Operation of Motor Vehicles

What does the research summarized above say about the time required for a driver to respond to the emergency situation described at the beginning of this paper? Unfortunately, not much. True, the time taken to accomplish the various components can be altered by the nature of the task, but it is difficult to determine whether the amount of information being processed compares with that typical of driving situations in general, let alone a particular situation. For drivers, there is great variability in the conspicuity of the stimulus, in the amount of information being processed at the time, and where their attention is directed when the stimulus enters the field of view. In addition, while the response choices available to the driver may appear to be limited, the proper choice or balance of choices may not be all that obvious to someone in a rapidly changing situation. Given these facts, there has been a great deal of interest in research that would more adequately simulate the driving situation.

Given that there is a real need for information on driver perception-response time, a reasonable person might wonder why researchers don't get busy and obtain it. As often is the case, the job is a tad more complicated than it appears. In the interest of protecting the well being of persons who participate in such studies, there are stringent limits on what can be done to them. Certainly one cannot create circumstances that pose a real or perceived high level of risk to the subjects or to innocent bystanders without their prior informed consent. Since many of the situations of interest in accident investigation do pose a real or perceived risk, and going through the process of obtaining prior informed consent would alter the subjects' expectancies, there is a significant problem in designing an experiment that will yield data that one can use with confidence to generalize to real-world emergency events. Despite the difficulties, there has been no lack of imagination on the part of experimenters. The rest of the chapter will review a number of studies that have endeavored to collect realistic perception-response time data using a variety of approaches.

It is unfortunate that many of the earlier studies on perception-response time, and some of the more recent ones, do not report percentiles or even the range of times measured, typically providing only averages. The point was made in Chapter 1 that design must accommodate the widest practicable range of individuals and performances, and the average is an inadequate statistic for that purpose. In this chapter research results will be described in terms of percentiles, where appropriate data are available.

Many perception-response time studies have been run in simulators or in motor vehicles using subjects who were to some degree aware of the nature of the test. Perhaps the earliest of these was carried out at the Massachusetts Institute of Technology (1934). A number of variables were examined (e.g., various foot positions, whether the vehicle was moving or stationary, visual vs. auditory stimulus). Average perception-response times ranged from 0.24 to 1.65 seconds. DeSilva and Forbes (1937) and Lister (1950) have published reviews of many of these earlier studies. Averages were reported as ranging from 0.44 to 0.70 second.

Several studies have been conducted by having a subject drive a car equipped with a light signal someplace in the field of view of the driver, often mounted on the hood. The light would be switched on at random intervals, with the subject responding by tapping the brake pedal as quickly as possible. In one such study (Olson, et al., 1984) the response times ranged from about 0.45 to 0.85 second. The median value was about 0.60 second, the 85th percentile about 0.75 second. These results are close to those reported by Konz and Daccarett (1967) and Nagler and Nagler (1973), not to mention the estimate offered by the "expert" in the hypothetical case with which this chapter opened. The methodology used in these studies is clearly a poor approximation of situations with which a driver may be confronted in the real world. There is some uncertainty concerning when the stimulus will be presented, true enough. But the nature of the stimulus is known and the response has been dictated by the experimenter, making the identification and decision stages trivial.

A more realistic stimulus was used in a study carried out at the Road Research Laboratory in Great Britain (Grime, 1952). Subjects drove a car in an urban setting with instructions to apply the brakes whenever they saw a pedestrian step into the street. The time from when the pedestrian entered the road until the brakes were applied was recorded. The average time was 0.71 second, the 85th percentile time was about 1.2 seconds. Although the stimulus was realistic, the expectancies of the subjects were not, and the decision process was simplified by the instructions.

Barrett, et al. (1968) also studied a pedestrian encounter, using a simulator that the users could drive freely about a model landscape. The subjects were allowed to become familiar with the device and roads it contained before they were presented with the sudden appearance of a pedestrian in their path. Only 11 subjects participated in the study, and the data are not presented in a way that is helpful in estimating population performance. The subjects were divided into two groups on a basis of their response time. The faster-responding group (average of 0.83 second) would have missed the pedestrian, the slower group (average of 1.13 seconds) would not.

One of the more interesting and often-cited of the earlier studies was reported by Johansson and Rumar (1971). Drivers on a roadway were stopped and asked if they would be willing to participate in a study that required them to respond to a sound signal by tapping their brake pedal enough to turn on the brake lights. The nature of the sound was not specified, only that it would occur someplace in the next ten kilometers. Those who agreed then proceeded on about five kilometers to be greeted by a klaxon horn hidden in a rural mailbox. Their response time was measured by a hidden assistant. The median response time was 0.66 second, and the 85th percentile response time was about 1.0 second. Recognizing that the task rendered the identification and decision stages unrealistic, the experimenters tested a subsample of these individuals in a test having a reasonable level of surprise. It was found that their mean response times increased by about 35%. The investigators concluded that the response times recorded in their study should be increased by about 35%, to more adequately reflect normal conditions of alertness. On this basis the 85th percentile would increase to about 1.35 seconds.

The value of the data derived from the work of Johansson and Rumar is largely dependent on the accuracy of the 35% correction for expectancy. Clearly, there would be merit in conducting further research that would, hopefully, verify their findings.

In an effort to get closer to reality, a number of investigators have conducted field studies under one of two conditions:

1. Take experimental subjects who have been misled concerning the purpose of the study and arrange for them to have a surprise encounter with some apparent hazard.
2. Create some situation on a normal highway and measure the response of passing roadway users.

The problem with the first approach is that experimental subjects may be unduly alert because of the test situation, even if they do not actually expect the stimulus that is ultimately presented. The major limitation to the second approach was discussed earlier, i.e., an experimenter cannot jeopardize the safety of other people without their prior informed consent. Since obtaining consent would invalidate the hoped-for results, there are distinct limits to the kinds of situations an experimenter can create in an effort to obtain a braking response from a passing driver. A number of studies of the types described have been reported, and, despite the limitations just noted, they constitute the best body of data on driver perception-response time currently available.

A traffic situation that confronts drivers with some regularity is the change of a traffic signal from green to yellow. It is easily possible to measure times from the start of the yellow phase to the onset of the brake lights of cars whose drivers elect to stop. One of the earliest of these was carried out as a by-product of a study of driver response to the yellow phase of traffic signals (Gazis, et al., 1960). The investigators carried out measurements at six locations. Response times ranged from 0.6 to 2.4 seconds, with an average of 1.14 seconds.

Wortman and Matthias (1983) reported a similar study, on a somewhat larger scale. Their results are shown in Table 9.1. There were some differences from site to site, with the 85th percentile perception-response times ranging from 1.5 to 2.1 seconds.

Unquestionably, the work on driver response to yellow light onset provides valuable information for that specific situation. The extent to which it generalizes to other situations is open to debate. It seems reasonable that drivers approaching a traffic signal that has been green for some time anticipate the possibility of its changing, and are monitoring the signal fairly closely. If it does change the driver has to decide if he/she can clear the intersection safely or must stop. The possibility of attracting unwanted attention from law enforcement officials may also enter into the equation. Detection and identification are trivial in that setting, the only significant issue is decision.

What is sometimes referred to as the "trap" technique has been utilized for studying the response of motorists to unexpected brake signals. It is conducted as follows: While operating in normal, free-flowing traffic, one test vehicle merges in front of a potential subject, a second one merges behind, "trapping"

Table 9.1 Response Times of Approaching Drivers to the Onset of the Yellow Phase of Traffic Signals at Different Locations

Intersection Approach	Average Time (sec)	Standard Deviation (sec)	85% Time (sec)
University Drive	1.28	0.82	2.0
Southern Ave. (Day)	1.49	0.62	1.9
Southern Ave. (Night)	1.43	0.73	2.0
U.S. 60	1.38	0.60	2.1
First Ave.	1.24	0.51	1.8
Sixth Street	1.55	0.70	2.0
Broadway Blvd. (Day)	1.16	0.48	1.5
Broadway Blvd. (Night)	1.09	0.44	1.5
All Approaches	1.30	0.60	1.8

From: Wortman and Matthias (1983)

the subject between them. Hopefully, this can be accomplished without arousing the suspicions of the subject motorist. When all is ready the lead vehicle presents a brake signal for a brief period of time (without actually slowing), and experimenters in the trailing vehicle measure and record the response. Studies of this type have been reported by the Allen Corporation (1978) and Sivak et al. (1978, 1981). For conventional braking systems, Allen Corporation reported an average perception-response time of 1.45 seconds. In the 1978 paper Sivak et al. report an average of 1.38 seconds. The response times measured in the second study (1981) varied depending on the vehicle used and the driving conditions. In two of the three tests the average response time was about 1.25 seconds, with an 85th percentile value of about 1.90 seconds.

The "trap" technique was developed as a means for evaluating the effectiveness of brake signal systems and was used in several investigations during the development of the center-high-mounted brake light. It was thought to be an effective evaluation tool for that purpose. There is some question about the degree to which the results can be generalized to situations other than that. Unless one is following very closely (something that was avoided in the cited studies) the onset of brake lights on a lead car is not necessarily the sort of thing that would produce a panic response on the part of the following driver. Brief brake applications are not uncommon in traffic. Following drivers may pause momentarily to see if the lead car is actually decelerating prior to applying their own brakes. If so, this would produce a fairly long identification period and a high estimate of perception-response time for a true emergency situation.

Summala was interested in the time it would take drivers to respond to a stimulus requiring lateral movement. Two studies were carried out. In the first (1981a) the investigator turned on a light along the edge of the road, in the other (1981b) he briefly opened the door of a parked car to cause approaching cars to move to the left. The time history of this displacement was recorded. In each of the studies Summala found that the displacement commenced at an average of about 1.5 seconds after the stimulus had been presented, reached its half-way point at about 2.5 seconds, and reached a maximum at something between 3 and 4 seconds. On a basis of these results Summala recommends that at least three seconds should be allowed for drivers to perform steering avoidance maneuvers when changes occur in the roadway environment.

McGee et al. (1983) attempted to deduce perception-response time by listing its individual components, surveying the literature to find appropriate values for each, and summing these values to obtain totals. Their results are shown in Table 9.2. Using these data, if a situation was felt to call for all of the components listed (Total A), an 85th percentile perception-response time of 3.2 seconds is indicated. If no decision was felt necessary (Total C), the total time at the 85th percentile drops to 2.3 seconds.

These recommendations rest on two questionable assumptions. The first is that there is no overlap in the execution of these steps, so that their times can be simply summed. As was pointed out earlier, it is likely that there is some degree of overlap in the various steps, so summing the individual times may lead to an overestimation of the total. The second assumption is that an individual who has a perceptual latency at a given percentile will perform at about the same level for each of the other components. Results of studies that have made some effort to separate the steps in perception response (e.g., Olson, et al., 1984) suggest that this is not the case. If not, this assumption would result in reasonably accurate estimates of perception-response time at the median, but progressively greater overestimates at higher percentiles.

The most comprehensive investigation of perception-response time in a real-world setting is that of Triggs and Harris (1982). They created a number of situations on rural highways that they felt were likely to produce a braking response from passing drivers. Typically these were set up over hill crests, so the point at which the hazard first entered the driver's field of view would be clearly defined. The investigators measured the time from entry of the hazard into the driver's field of view until the brake lights came on. Included among the situations were such things as disabled vehicles, a warning of road repairs ahead, a parked police car, and amphometers (a speed-measuring device commonly used in Australia, consisting of two pneumatic tubes across the road). They were also

Table 9.2 Results of an Effort to Deduce Driver Perception-Response Time, Based on Summation of Assumed Components Taken From the Research Literature

	Percentile of Drivers					
Element	**50**	**75**	**85**	**90**	**95**	**99**
1. Perception						
a. Latency	0.24	0.27	0.31	0.33	0.35	0.45
b. Eye Movement	0.09	0.09	0.09	0.09	0.09	0.09
c. Fixation	0.20	0.20	0.20	0.20	0.20	0.20
d. Recognition	0.40	0.45	0.50	0.55	0.60	0.65
2. Decision	0.50	0.75	0.85	0.90	0.95	1.00
3. Brake Reaction	0.85	1.11	1.24	1.42	1.63	2.16
Total A (1a-d+2+3)	2.3	2.9	3.2	3.5	3.8	4.6
Total B (1c-d+2+3)	2.0	2.5	2.8	3.1	3.4	4.1
Total C (1a-d+3)	1.8	2.1	2.3	2.6	2.9	3.6

From: McGee et al. (1983)

able to turn on railroad crossing flashers in front of oncoming cars at a few sites. The 85th percentile perception-response times measured by Triggs and Harris for these various situations are shown in Table 9.3.

There is considerable variability, with the times ranging from 1.50 to 3.60 seconds. Some of the differences seem understandable. For example, the "Road-works Ahead" sign probably did not excite much sense of urgency in the absence of evidence of construction. The railway crossing signals will be less conspicuous during the day, and there is the possibility of scanning the area to determine if there is a train nearby. Other cases are somewhat surprising, particularly the police vehicle and amphometers, although they would be of primary interest to drivers who were going in excess of the posted speed limit.

Table 9.3 Perception-Response Times of Passing Motorists to a Variety of Roadway Situations

Roadway Situation	85% Response Time (seconds)
C.R.B. "Roadworks Ahead" sign	3.00
Protruding vehicle with tire change	1.50
Lighted vehicle under repair at night	1.50
Parked police vehicle	2.80
Amphometer: Dandenong North	3.40
Amphometer: Dandenong North	3.60
Amphometer: Tynong	3.60
Railway Crossing: Night (general population)	1.50
Railway Crossing: Night (rally drivers)	1.50
Railway Crossing: Day	2.53
Car following	1.26

From: Triggs and Harris (1982)

A study on the specific issue of stopping sight distance has been reported by Olson, et al. (1984). Subjects were told that they were driving a car for purposes of "familiarization" for a study to be conducted the following day. They drove a winding route for several miles, eventually cresting a hill in a rural area to find a 6-inch-high and 3-foot-wide obstacle (actually a piece of foam rubber) in the left portion of their lane. Time was measured from the entry of the obstacle into the field of view until the subject's foot contacted the brake pedal. With this "surprise" encounter completed the subjects were briefed on the true purpose of the investigation. They were then asked to drive over the hillcrest five more times at the same speed, releasing the accelerator and tapping the brake pedal when they detected the obstacle, which was moved up and down the slope between each trial. Finally, a red signal lamp was attached to the hood of the car in front of the driver. As they returned to the point of origin they were instructed to monitor the lamp, and release the accelerator and tap the brake pedal each time it came on. This was done five times during the approximately ten minutes it took to make the trip.

The results of this investigation are shown in Figure 9.1, based on 49 young subjects. This figure is in the form of a "normal probability distribution," which is a convenient way of plotting data where percentile performance is of interest. It is designed so that data from a true normal distribution, as described in Chapter 1, would form a straight line. The curved shape of the data in Figure 9.1 indicate positively-skewed distributions, which is to be expected with response-time data. The 85th percentile perception-response time for the surprise encounter was about 1.3 seconds, and the 95th percentile was about 1.6 seconds. The shortest times measured were about 0.8 second, and response times ranged up to about 1.8 seconds.

Perception-response times for an identical encounter, but with the subject expecting the obstacle, were about 0.4 second faster, except at the higher percentiles where the difference was about 0.5 second. Response times to the light on

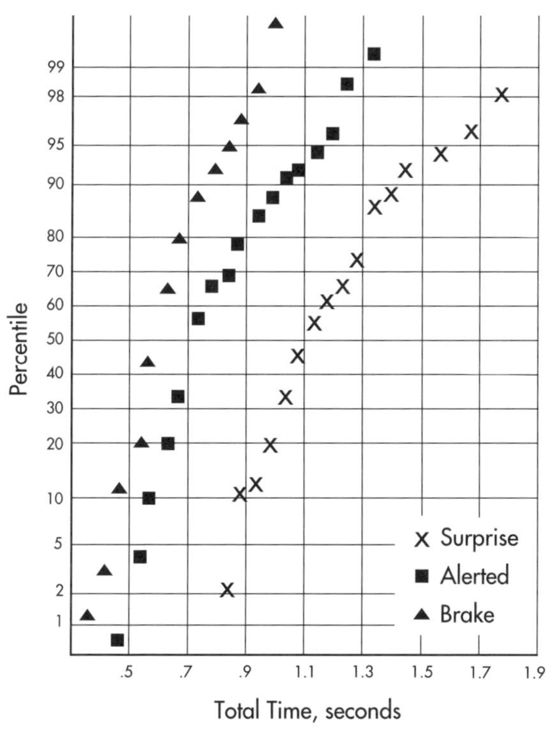

Figure 9.1 *Distribution of perception-response times recorded under three conditions. (Reprinted with permission from* Human Factors, *Vol. 28, No. 1, 1986. Copyright 1986 by the Human Factors and Ergonomics Society. All rights reserved.*

the hood were faster still, with the difference between these and the expected encounter with the roadway obstacle ranging from 0.1 second to about 0.3 second at the higher percentiles.

The Time to Change Lanes

The time for a driver to carry out the necessary preliminary activities and change lanes on a multi-lane road is not technically perception-response time, but it is an issue of consequence in litigation with some frequency. Therefore, the available information will be reviewed at this point.

Finnegan and Green (1990) reviewed five articles concerned with driver lane-changing behavior. The data indicate that, typically, drivers will make between 2 and 3 head movements (checking mirrors or looking to the side), which consume 1.0 to 1.5 seconds each. When glances to the road ahead are included the findings are that preparatory visual search would range from 3.7 seconds in the absence of traffic, up to 6.6 seconds when traffic is present. Another 1.5 seconds would be allowed for the lane change itself, making a rounded total of 8 seconds. The start point, presumably, is when the driver decides that such a maneuver is desirable or necessary, i.e., at the end of what would normally be considered the decision interval.

Finnegan and Green point out that the data have significant limitations, and should be interpreted with some caution. They do, however, provide an indication of the order of magnitude of time required to execute this common maneuver.

Decision Sight Distance

A discussion of the time to change lanes leads naturally to a discussion of decision sight distance. Decision sight distance was earlier defined as the distance required for a driver to detect an unexpected or otherwise difficult-to-perceive information source or hazard in a roadway environment that may be visually cluttered, recognize the hazard or its threat potential, select an appropriate speed and path, and initiate and complete the required maneuver safely and efficiently. It is appropriate to consider decision sight distance as a criterion any time a roadway situation requires a driver to carry out a relatively complex maneuver such as a lane change in traffic. It is certainly applicable to common situations such as construction zones with a lane closure. It may be applicable to certain crash-related scenarios as well.

The basic work to develop the guidelines for decision sight distance was carried out by McGee, et al. (1978). Their recommendations are given in Table 9.4. Note that the total response time is divided into three categories. The first of these they call detection and recognition. The second, called decision and response initiation, corresponds to the portion of the lane change time prior to the actual maneuver as described by Finnegan and Green. Finnegan and Green recommend 3.7 to 6.6 seconds for this period, which is very close to the 4.2 to 7.0 seconds from McGee, et al. The last time category in Table 9.5 is maneuver time, which McGee, et al. set at 4.5 seconds for all but the highest speed, three times the length given by Finnegan and Green.

The decision sight distance criteria are intended to be conservative in that they should be applicable to a variety of situations and allow the driver make the required maneuver in a reasonably comfortable way. In other words, it is intended to create warning distances that will avoid the necessity of emergency responses on the part of a driver. In this respect it differs from stopping sight distance, another civil engineering guideline.

Table 9.4 Recommended Time Values (in seconds) for Decision Sight Distance for Various Speeds.

Design Speed (mph)	Detection and Recognition	Decision & Response Initiation	Maneuver (Lane Change)	Summation
30	1.5-3.0	4.2-6.5	4.5	10.2-14.0
40	1.5-3.0	4.2-6.5	4.5	10.2-14.0
50	1.5-3.0	4.2-6.5	4.5	10.2-14.0
60	2.0-3.0	4.7-7.0	4.5	11.2-14.5
70	2.0-3.0	4.7-7.0	4.0	10.7-14.0

From: McGee, et al., 1978

Stopping sight distance is a criterion used to ensure that the roadway itself, or associated structures, will not hide some hazard from a driver until he/she is too close to deal with it effectively. For example, should something be spilled on a road surface just over a hillcrest, stopping sight distance is used to establish the radius of the crest vertical curve so that a driver going at a design speed will be able to detect the hazard and stop short of it. This is clearly an emergency situation. The estimate of perception-response time currently used in stopping sight distance is 2.5 seconds, which recent research has shown to be excessive when dealing with relatively straightforward situations and drivers who are reasonably alert (Olson, et al., 1984). It may be realistic, however, when allowance is made for drivers who are fatigued, or under the influence of alcohol or drugs to some extent.

Recommendations

If one thing is clear from the preceding discussion it is that "perception-response time" is a highly variable quantity. As an aid to understanding why, Table 9.5 has been prepared. The table breaks perception-response time into its four basic components and offers a qualitative assessment of the time required for various situations. For example, in the simplest of reaction-time studies the stimulus is known and expected, so detection and identification are accomplished in minimum time. In addition, the response is prescribed by the experimenter, so there is no decision, and the response is as simple as lifting one's finger from a key. So-called "choice" response studies result in longer times because they complicate the identification and sometimes the decision and response stages.

Moving the subjects to a car, having them drive and press the brake in response to something like a light on the hood will lengthen detection time (because the subject is occupied with things other than monitoring the light) and provide a "normal" response time because the foot must move from accelerator to brake. The identification and decision stages are specified as a condition of the study and are minimal. A study such as conducted by Johansson and Rumar (1971) will lengthen the identification phase as well (because the nature of the sound was not specified), but still leave the decision phase minimal. Finally, studies such as that of Triggs and Harris (1982) result in "longer" times in all three preliminary phases, as well as a "normal" response. The times in the first three phases may be "longer" or very much longer, depending on how much time it

Table 9.5. Analysis of the Time Taken in Various Components in Perception-Response Studies

Study Type	Components of Perception Response			
	Detection	Identification	Decision	Response
Simple Response Time	Minimal	Minimal	Minimal	Minimal
Choice Response Time With Multiple Stimuli	Minimal	Minimal	Longer	Minimal
Choice Response Time With Multiple Stimuli and Options	Minimal	Longer	Longer	Longer
Simple Field Studies	Longer	Minimal	Minimal	Normal
Semi-Alerted Field Studies	Longer	Longer	Minimal	Normal
Passing Driver Studies	Longer	Longer	Longer	Normal

takes for the object or condition of concern to be detected, the ease with which identification can be accomplished, and the complexity of the decision that the driver must make.

It is frustrating to have to use a qualitative expression like "longer" rather than time values in Table 9.5. The problem is that the time required to accomplish each step is enormously variable, since it depends on how much time it takes for the object or condition of concern to be detected, the ease with which identification can be accomplished, and the complexity of the decision that the driver must make. In addition, there is an unknown degree of overlap between the various steps that probably varies from situation to situation and from person to person.

In light of the difficulties just described, is it possible to make any firm recommendations concerning perception-response time in the real-world situations with which the readers of this chapter may be confronted? The answer is yes, to a degree. Given a reasonably clear stimulus and a fairly straightforward situation, there are good data indicating that most drivers (i.e., about 85 to 95%) will respond by about 1.5 seconds after the first appearance of the object or condition of concern. The evidence also indicates that the minimum perception-response time for this straightforward situation is about 0.75 second. Thus, the probable range of perception-response times for reasonably straightforward situations should be 0.75 to about 1.5 seconds. Please note these values are not chiseled in stone on tablets along with other commandments! The fact that an investigator may calculate that the perception-response time for a given individual under what is judged to be a straightforward situation is 1.6 seconds or even 1.7 seconds is not a basis for judging the driver's behavior to be unreasonable. The values from 0.75 to 1.5 seconds provide a basis for estimating what a reasonably alert driver should be capable of doing. The quality of the data and the uncertainty concerning individual situations does not permit accuracy to one or two tenths of a second, particularly where the welfare of real people is at stake.

The expression "reasonably straightforward" might seem to imply a minimal situation. Not so. Under some conditions shorter times may be possible. For example, a driver who finds the road completely blocked by a very large object such as a truck may respond faster because of the size of the stimulus (which ensures that it will be fixated foveally relatively soon), its intimidating nature, and the fact that braking is the only reasonable response. No data are available on this or a comparable situation because, for obvious reasons, it would be a difficult study to carry out.

Factors Complicating Perception-Response Time

The next question is what kinds of conditions can complicate matters and lead to longer perception-response times? There are a number of such conditions, and these will now be briefly discussed.

Driver Expectancy

Expectancy is discussed in some detail in Chapter 4. Briefly, expectancy refers to a predisposition on the part of drivers to believe that something will happen or be configured in a certain way. Violations of expectancy increase the likelihood that people will take longer to respond to a given situation and also increase the likelihood of error. For example, barring information to the contrary, drivers expect the road to be clear of obstacles. They also expect pedestrians and other drivers to follow the rules and yield right of way when appropriate. The situations with which reconstructionists are typically concerned involve violations of driver expectancy, and they must be approached as such.

Night vs. Day

Investigators commonly assign longer perception-response times for nighttime collisions. It may seem reasonable to do so, because visibility in general is degraded at night. The simple fact is, however, that there is no basis for arbitrarily increasing perception-response time simply because the investigation concerns an incident that occurred at night. The driver must go through the same information-processing as in daylight before a response will be elicited, and in many cases the situation is straightforward enough that perception-response times at night will be the same as in the day. The difference at night is that the detection and identification stages are more likely to be lengthened. As a matter of fact, in many cases it may make sense to simply eliminate the detection stage from consideration. A complete discussion of this issue will be found in Chapter 10. If we could collect all possible perception-response scenarios and study them night and day we would probably find that, on average, the times are longer at night. The investigator must think the issue through with some care. Hopefully, by this point in the chapter the reader will realize that not all perception-response times are equal during the day, because factors that affect one or more of the stages will result in longer or shorter times. Exactly the same logic applies at night. The difference is that complications in one or more of the stages are more likely at night.

Chemicals, Driver Fatigue

There are a number of chemicals that individuals may ingest that can affect perception-response time. The main substance that has attracted attention in this respect is alcohol. Many studies have investigated the relationship between perception-response time and blood alcohol concentration (BAC). While it is clear that perception-response time tends to increase with BAC, there is great variability in results concerning the degree of increase as well as the BAC level above which increases in perception-response time can be documented (Moskowitz and Robinson, 1987).

Some research has also focused on the effects of marijuana on a variety of driving skills, including perception-response time. One of the best of these is by Moskowitz et al. (1976). They found that marijuana increased error in recognition of signal lights, with consequent increase in response time.

There are a great number of other drugs, most of which are legal, that have an effect on the central nervous system and, potentially at least, on perception-response time. There is little research on most of these as concerns their effect on driving-related skills. A valuable reference is provided by Shinar (1978), who lists the supposed therapeutic as well as the side effects of a number of drugs. New drugs are being introduced all the time, however, and an investigator who has reason to believe that a given driver was taking some drug or other should check with a qualified toxicologist concerning its effects.

Fatigue is a fact of life in motor vehicle operation. It happens that very often driving is a fairly boring activity that can continue for many hours at a stretch. For this reason, there has been some interest in determining whether perception-response time increases with driving exposure and, presumably, fatigue. Based on several studies (Lisper, et al., 1968, Laurell and Lisper, 1976, Muto and Wierwille, 1982), response time does increase with driving exposure. There is also evidence that fatigue exacerbates the effects of alcohol (Corfitsen, 1982). Persons interested in a comprehensive review of the subject of fatigue and driving would find the volume edited by Hartley (1995) interesting.

It is, unfortunately, impossible to attach solid numbers to the effects just noted. Perception-response time will increase, on average, but some persons will be unaffected while others will be very much affected. The effects will vary depending on a number of possible variables as well, leaving the investigator in something of a quandary. It is generally not possible to provide an estimated perception-response time for a particular individual with some level of impairment. Sometimes, however, the facts of a case allow the investigator to approximate the actual perception-response time of an individual, based on the facts of a collision. Then the problem can be approached by pointing out that the perception-response time for a reasonably alert, unimpaired driver would fall within some range of values. If the calculated perception-response time is significantly outside the indicated range this may be attributable to the impairment.

Age and Sex

There is much information to suggest that perception-response time lengthens with age. Data in the context of driving (using a very simple simulator) are shown in Figure 9.2 (American Automobile Association, 1952). These data were collected from a sample of over 1400 persons of various ages by having them step on a brake pedal in response to a light signal. The averages range from 0.44 seconds in the 20-year-old group to 0.52 second in the 70-year-old group. An exception to this general trend has been reported in one study (Olson, et al., 1984), which found no difference between old and young subjects in responding to a

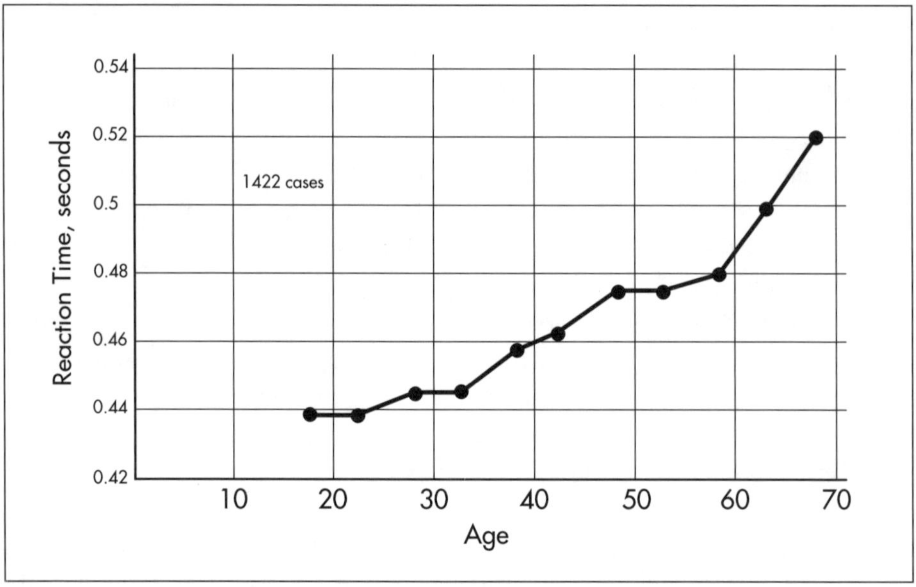

__Figure 9.2__ Perception-response time as a function of age. Reprinted with permission from 890731 ©1989, Society of Automotive Engineers, Inc.

surprise encounter with a roadway obstacle. In a follow-up test where the stimulus was a light mounted on the hood of the test car, the same two groups of subjects exhibited the characteristic age difference, with the median response time for the young subjects being 0.57, compared to 0.65 for the older subjects.

Not shown in Figure 9.2 are the distributions for each age group. There is great overlap in these distributions. In other words, some of the old folks will consistently have shorter perception-response times than some of the youngsters. Thus, there is no justification for adjusting a perception-response time estimate up or down knowing nothing more than a particular driver's age. On the other hand, if an analysis shows that the apparent perception-response time to a hazard in a given accident was somewhat beyond the expected range, and the driver was elderly, age effects may offer an explanation.

On average, women tend to respond slower than men in standard perception-response tests. Figure 9.3 (American Automobile Association, 1966) shows a distribution of perception-response time data as a function of sex. This was a choice-response-time study in which the subjects had to distinguish among three types of signals. The average difference between the two groups is about 0.08 second. Note the almost complete overlap in performance comparing the two groups. Hence, as in the case of age, nothing can be concluded about an individual's response-time potential knowing only their sex.

There are, in short, a number of factors that can affect perception-response time in a specific situation. This is definitely not a one-number-fits-all situation. It is a situation in which the investigator must have knowledge of the relevant research as well as the limitations of that research. Response-time estimates must be made with considerable care.

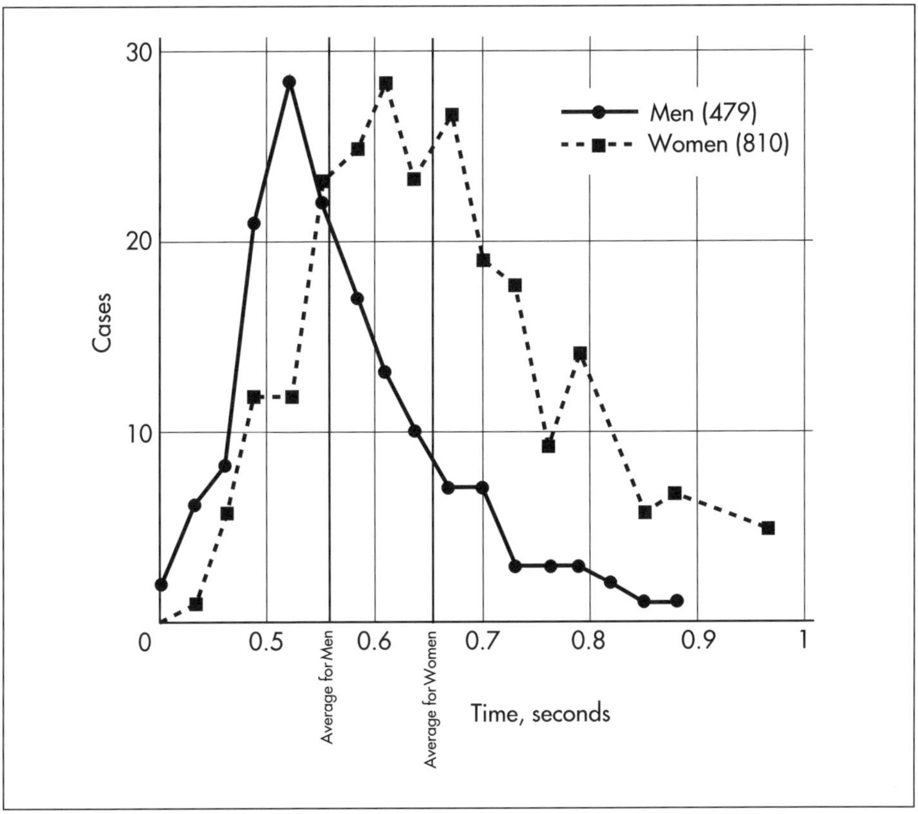

Figure 9.3 *Perception-response time as a function of sex. Reprinted with permission from 890731 ©1989, Society of Automotive Engineers, Inc.*

Chapter Overview

Perception-response time is the interval between the appearance of some object or condition in the driver's field of view and the initiation of a response. Between those two points the driver must become aware of the potential hazard (detection), reach some conclusion regarding what it is and what it is doing or likely to do in the near future (identification), decide what action, if any, is appropriate (decision), and put that action into effect (response). The time required to accomplish all of this in a driving situation is of considerable interest to accident investigators seeking to establish whether a given driver's performance falls within reasonable bounds. The following are the principal points covered in the chapter:

- While there is a great deal of research on perception-response time, very little of it is applicable to the driving situation. This work does make clear, however, that the time required for an individual to respond depends in large measure on the intensity of the stimulus, the amount of information that the individual is required to process and the complexity of the decision-making process.
- Several studies suggest that most drivers will begin to respond to a relatively straightforward situation in about 1.5 seconds. The minimum time to respond is unlikely to be much less than 0.75 second.
- There are a number of things that can affect perception-response time. Some of these are expectancy, driver fatigue, use of chemicals such as alcohol and certain drugs, age and sex.
- The first thing an investigator should do when estimating perception-response time for a given situation is to consider whether the specific scenario fits the general model. Many do not. If there is reason to believe that there are aspects of the situation that cause one or more of the processing steps to be lengthened or shortened, this will affect overall perception-response time. For example, if evidence suggests that a driver took 2.5-3.0 seconds to respond to a given situation, an analysis of this type might be used to argue that the time was within reason. However, any attempt to produce hard estimates of perception-response time for a situation that has some complicating features is fraught with uncertainty. The available information must be applied to specific situations with a measure of respect for its limitations.

References

American Association of State Highway and Transportation Officials (1984). *A Policy on Geometric Design of Highways and Streets.* Washington, D.C.

Alexander, G. J. and Lunenfeld, H. (1986). Driver Expectancy in Highway Design and Traffic Operations. Washington, D.C. The Federal Highway Administration. Report No. FHWA-TO-86-1.

American Automobile Association (1952). Traffic Engineering and Safety Department. Age and Complex Reaction Time. Report No. 41.

American Automobile Association (1966). Traffic Engineering and Safety Department. Reaction Time as Related to Age. Report No. 69.

Allen Corporation of America. (1978). Field Validation of Taillights - Report on Phase 1: Pilot Testing. Alexandria, Virginia. US Department of Transportation, NHTSA. Contract No. DOT-HS-7-01756.

Barrett, G. V., Kobayashi, M. and Fox, B. H. (1968). Feasibility of Studying Driver Reaction to Sudden Pedestrian Emergencies in an Automobile Simulator. *Human Factors*, 24, 19-24.

Corfitsen, M. T. (1982). Increased Viso-Mororic Reaction Time of Young, Tired, Drunk Drivers. *Forensic Science International*. 20(2), 121-125.

Damon, A., Stoudt, H. W., and McFarland, R. A. (1966). *The Human Body in Equipment Design*. Cambridge, Massachusetts. Harvard University Press.

DeSilva, H. R. and Forbes, T. W. (1937). Driver Testing Results. Cambridge, Massachusetts. Harvard Traffic Bureau.

Finnegan, P. and Green, P. (1990). The Time To Change Lanes: A Literature Review. Ann Arbor. The University of Michigan Transportation Research Institute. Report Number UMTRI-90-34.

Gazis, D., Herman, R. and Maradudin, A. (1960). The Problem of the Amber Signal Light on Traffic Flow. *Operations Research, 8,* 112-132.

Grime, G. (1952). Traffic and Road Safety Research at the Road Research Laboratory. *HRB Proceedings, 31*. 466-486.

Hartley, L. (1995). *Fatigue and Driving.* London. Taylor and Francis.

Hoffman, E. R. (1991). A Comparison of Hand and Foot Movement Times. *Ergonomics, 34*. 397-406.

Huffman, W. J. and Hummel, G. R. (1967). A Comparison of Accelerator Release and Brake Response Times of Ten Hand and Foot Braking Methods on a Simulator Under Three Experimental Conditions. Champaign, Illinois. Illinois University. Safety and Driver Education Laboratory.

Johansson, G. and Rumar, K. (1971). Drivers' Brake Reaction Times. *Human Factors*, *13*(1), 23-27.

Konz, S. and Daccarett, J. (1967). Controls for Automotive Brakes. Washington, D.C. *The Highway Research Record, 195*, 75-79.

Laurell, H. and Lisper, H. O. (1976). Changes in Subsidiary Reaction Time and Heart-Rate During Car Driving. Passenger Travel and Stationary Conditions. Uppsala University, Department of Psychology.

Lisper, H. O., Dureman, I., Ericsson, S. and Karisson, N. G. (1968). Effects of Prolonged Driving Upon a Subsidiary Serial Reaction Time. 1. Comparison With Brake Reaction Time to Stimuli on the Road. 2. Effects of Sleep Deprivation on Night Driving. Uppsala University, Department of Psychology.

Lister, R. D. (1950). The Reaction Time of Drivers in Moving and Stationary Vehicles. Road Research Laboratory Note No. RN/1324/RDL.

Massachusetts Institute of Technology. (1934). Report on Massachusetts Highway Accident Survey. Cambridge, Massachusetts.

McGee, H. W., Moore, W., Knapp, B. G. and Sanders, J. H. (1978). Decision Sight Distance for Highway Design and Traffic Control Requirements. Washington, D.C. U.S. Department of Transportation. Federal Highway Administration. Report No. FHWA-RD-78-78.

McGee, H. W., Hooper, K. G., Hughes, W. E. and Benson, W. (1983). Highway Design and Operations Standards Affected by Driver Characteristics. Volume II: Final Technical Report. Vienna, Virginia. Bellomo-McGee, Inc. Report No. FHWA-RD-83-015.

Moskowitz, H., Hulbert, S. and McGlothlin, W. H. (1976). Marijuana: Effects on Simulated Driving Performance. *Accident Analysis and Prevention*. 8(1), 45-50.

Moskowitz, H. and Robinson, C (1987). Driving-Related Skills Impairment at Low Blood Alcohol Levels. In: Noordzij, P., Roszbach, R. (Eds.) *Alcohol, Drugs and Traffic Safety*-T86. Amsterdam. Excerpta Medical Elsevier Science, 79-86.

Muto, W. H. and Wierwille, W. W. (1982). The Effect of Repeated Emergency Response Trials on Performance During Extended-Duration Simulated Driving. *Human Factors*. 24(6), 693-698.

Nagler, C. A. and Nagler, W. M. (1973). Reaction Time Measurements. *Forensic Science*, 2, 261-274.

Olson, P. L., Cleveland, D. E., Fancher, P. S., Kostyniuk, L. P. and Schneider, L. W. (1984). Parameters Affecting Stopping Sight Distance. Washington, D.C. The National Cooperative Highway Research Program. Report 270.

Perchonok, K. and Pollack, L. (1981). Luminous Requirements for Traffic Signs. Washington, D.C. Federal Highway Administration.. Contract No. FHWA-RD-81-158.

Postman, L. and Egan, J. P. (1949). *Experimental Psychology: An Introduction*. New York. Harper and Brothers.

Shinar, D. (1978). *Psychology on the Road-The Human Factor in Traffic Safety*. New York. John Wiley.

Sivak, M., Olson, P. L. and Post, D. V. (1979). Evaluation of Experimental (Including High-Mounted) Configurations of Brake Lamps in Actual Traffic. Ann Arbor, Michigan. The Highway Safety Research Institute. Report No. UM-HSRI-79-87.

Sivak, M., Olson, P. L. and Farmer, K. M. (1981). High-Mounted Brake Lights and the Behavior of Following Drivers. Ann Arbor, Michigan. The Highway Safety Research Institute. Report No. UM-HSRI-81-31.

Summala, H. (1981a). Driver's Steering Reaction to a Light Stimulus on a Dark Road. *Ergonomics*, *24*. 125-131.

Summala, H. (1981b). Driver/Vehicle Steering Response Latencies. *Human Factors*, *23*. 683-692.

Triggs, T. J. and Harris, E. G. (1982). Reaction Time of Drivers to Road Stimuli. Clayton, Victoria, Australia. Monash University Human Factors Group. Report No. HFR-12.

Wortman, R. H. and Matthias, J. S. (1983). An Evaluation of Driver Behavior at Signalized Intersections. Final Report. Tucson, Arizona. Arizona Transportation and Traffic Institute.

Chapter 10

Perception-Response Time in Non-Standard Situations

Introduction

For relatively straightforward situations, the material presented in Chapter 9 suggests that most perception-response times will fall within a range of 0.75 to 1.50 seconds. The key term is "relatively straightforward." It should be obvious that not all perception-response situations are created equal. There is some perceptual and cognitive activity going on, which takes time. If the complexity of the task is altered significantly, the amount of time required to process that information will change as well. Therefore, a careful evaluation of each specific situation is called for, with appropriate adjustments made where necessary.

It is easy to say that "adjustments should be made where necessary," but implementing those adjustments poses some difficulties. The problem is that there is not a great deal of good information about driver perception-response time to start with, and what is known is based on rather simple scenarios. There are no tables, equations, etc. to guide the expert who wants to know how much of an adjustment would be appropriate for a situation that is different from that upon which the available data are based. Under the assumption that the first step to solving a problem is to understand it, this chapter will discuss some of the conditions that may require an adjustment when estimating perception-response time. For the present at least it will be up to individual experts to exercise their own judgment regarding the magnitude of the adjustment.

From the discussion in Chapter 9 it will be recalled that perception-response time is the interval between the first appearance of some object or condition in the visual field and the initiation of a response on the part of the individual. For example, the interval starts when a pedestrian steps out from behind an obstacle or a hazard appears over a hill crest. The interval ends when the driver's foot contacts the brake pedal or he/she starts to turn the steering wheel. The definition is important because many situations do not fit this model. It is those situations that will form the basis for some of the discussion to follow.

The reader will also recall that several steps or activities take place between the entry of the object into the visual field and the ultimate response. Briefly these are:

- *Detection.* The detection interval starts when the object or condition of concern enters the field of view and ends when the individual becomes consciously aware that something is present.
- *Identification.* This is a step in which the driver acquires enough information about the hazard to be able to decide what, if anything, should be done about it.
- *Decision.* The driver must now decide what action is appropriate.
- *Response.* The brain issues orders to the necessary muscle groups to set the response in motion.

This chapter will be concerned with two classes of situations in which it may be necessary to alter perception-response time estimates from those given in Chapter 9. One of these arises when the fact situation indicates that the time required for one or more of the four steps should be lengthened or shortened. The other class of situation concerns scenarios in which it is appropriate to disregard one or more of the steps when estimating perception-response time.

Situations Requiring Adjustments in One or More of the Four Steps

The test situations from which the 0.75 to 1.50 second perception-response estimate were derived were characterized earlier as "straightforward." That is, the target object was fairly conspicuous, relatively easily identified, and the driver's decision was not especially complicated. Many situations are significantly different from that in one or more respects. Where that is the case adjustments in perception-response time estimates may be indicated. Examples follow.

Detection

The key concept in detection is conspicuity. Conspicuity relates to the ability of a given object or condition to call itself to the attention of an observer. The object of concern in a specific case may be more or less conspicuous than those used in the various studies. Conspicuity depends on a number of factors. For example, larger objects, objects whose color or brightness causes them to stand out well from their background, and objects that are moving are more conspicuous than objects lacking those characteristics, and will, on average, be detected sooner. Other factors being equal, an object that first enters the visual field in the far periphery will be less conspicuous than one that pops into view more centrally. The probability of detection is also affected by the amount of information being processed by the driver when the object first enters the field of view. For example, drivers struggling to find their way through a strange city in rush hour would be less likely to detect a given hazard than other drivers in the same situation who are familiar with the area.

Identification

Identification may be complicated by such things as poor visibility conditions and an unusual situation. Nighttime and fog are but two visibility conditions that may complicate identification of an object or condition that would otherwise present no difficulties. Unusual situations include a great many things, but often involve assessment of speed and trajectory.

A particularly difficult situation for any driver arises when another vehicle is seen to be on a collision course under ambiguous conditions. For example, an oncoming car may be seen drifting into one's lane for no apparent reason. What's going on? Will the drift continue? Will the driver suddenly realize the error and return to the proper lane? A response decision must be made quickly, and without answers to these questions. After the decision has been made and a compensatory action initiated the other driver may also make a correction that cancels out the first driver's action and results in a tragedy. The world of litigation being what it is, often enough an "expert" will be found who will be willing to testify that had the driver who made the evasive input to avoid the vehicle drifting out of its lane only behaved "reasonably" (i.e., done something else) the collision would have been avoided.

It is, of course, the height of absurdity to apply 20/20 hindsight to a situation in which a driver must make a quick decision under life-threatening circumstances. It is generally impossible to know with great precision what that individual perceived in the brief time interval before a decision had to be made. Therefore, it is generally impossible to pass judgment on their actions.

Decision

In most of the perception-response studies there was a choice between steering and braking. Sometimes there is no real choice available, so the decision interval may be shorter. On the other hand, the choice might be complex. For example, steering might be the obvious choice in some situation, but the driver has to be concerned about conflicts with other vehicles. Or, the possibility of braking might be tempered by the realization that the road is slippery.

In brief, the 0.75 to 1.50 second perception-response estimate applies to a limited range of driving situations. It is not a universal fit to all driving situations, although it is a reasonable estimate for many. The expert must evaluate each case with some care. Knowing how the model values were developed, it is appropriate to ask whether a particular case is a reasonable fit. If not, explain why not. Which step(s) need adjustment? Is a shorter or longer perception-response time indicated? Unfortunately, where an adjustment is seen as necessary, the degree of adjustment is a judgment call. All the expert can do is point out the problem, indicate what time value would normally apply, how much is being allowed on this occasion, and why.

Situations Requiring the Elimination of One or More Steps

Some cases do not fit the basic definition of perception response described earlier. It may be appropriate in these cases to drop one or more of the four processing steps when arriving at an estimate of perception-response time. These cases fall into two broad categories:

- There are many cases where there is no clearly-defined entry of the hazard into the driver's field of view. This is particularly true under low-visibility conditions. Since there is no way to define the start of the detection interval, it is best to drop it and start the perception-response time once detection has been accomplished.
- Also common are cases in which a potential hazard has been detected and identified, but the circumstances cause the driver to initially decide that no action was necessary. Realizing that the initial judgment was wrong constitutes the end of the identification interval, hence it is appropriate to drop both the detection and identification intervals from the perception-response time estimate. Examples of each of these cases follow.

A common instance in which there is no clearly-defined entry into the driver's field of view involves an encounter with a hazard such as a pedestrian while driving at night. In reviewing such a case an investigator might note that the skid marks start a certain number of feet from the area of impact, and will add the distance traveled during the perception-response interval to determine the detection point. For example, the pre-impact skid marks might be measured at 30 feet and speed estimated at 40 ft/sec. Using a perception-response time range of 0.75 to 1.5 seconds, the investigator would conclude that the driver first perceived the pedestrian between 60 and 90 feet from the area of impact.

Recall that the detection interval technically starts when the object of concern enters the field of view. In the example cited, the pedestrian may have been in the path of the approaching car, or at least in the roadway, for some time. Under daylight conditions the pedestrian might have been within the field of view of the driver for many seconds. He/she was not seen earlier in this instance due to the low illuminance received from the headlamps when the vehicle was at a distance. As the target gradually gained contrast while the car approached there came a time when it was detected by the car driver. Clearly, this is a bit different from the conventional definition of the detection interval.

There are two approaches to developing a perception-response time estimate for this situation. One would estimate the start of the detection interval using threshold detection data. As noted earlier, "threshold" is a statistical concept. In a threshold study an experimenter presents stimuli at various intensity levels. The stimulus that is detected a given percentage of the time (usually 50%) is the threshold. Clearly, this method will produce much scatter in the data, rendering uncertain the start of the detection interval for a given individual under given conditions. For this reason it is not a viable approach.

A simpler approach is to drop the detection interval from the perception-response estimate. Unfortunately, no one knows how long a detection interval is for the straightforward situations described in Chapter 9, so an estimate is necessary. A reasonable estimate of a perception-response range in the absence of a detection interval is probably about 0.60 to 1.25 seconds. Using this range for the example given at the start of this section, the expert would say that detection probably occurred when the driver was 54 to 80 feet from the pedestrian.

Nighttime collisions between vehicles and low-contrast hazards of various kinds are common enough that it would be very useful to have a better estimate of perception-response time. One way in which this might be accomplished is to arrange a surprise encounter with a low-contrast, pedestrian-sized object in a nighttime study. If this were done at two different speeds we would find that the response at the higher speed averaged closer to the target object. The difference in response distance associated with speed would be due to perception-response time, which could be calculated. The good news is that such a study has been reported (Roper and Howard, 1938), although not for the purpose of estimating perception-response time. In that study the average perception-response interval was 1.36 seconds. The bad news is that only thirteen subjects were used, far too few to draw meaningful conclusions.

Another common case that requires dropping steps from the perception-response model occurs when a driver makes an erroneous identification. Consider the following: car 1 is on a through street, approaching an intersection at which the cross street is controlled by a stop sign. Driver 1 sees car 2 on the cross street, approaching the intersection. Driver 1 also sees car 2 slow and come to a stop. Driver 2, however, fails to see car 1 and pulls out from the stop sign and into its path, precipitating a collision.

What is an appropriate estimate of perception-response time for Driver 1 in a case like this? The analysis should begin with the realization that there were actually two perception-response intervals. In the first of these car 2 was detected. Its actions, coupled with the knowledge on the part of Driver 1 that this was a stop-controlled intersection, led to an identification error on the part of Driver 1 (i.e., it will let me pass), and a decision that no action was called for. As car 2 accelerates forward it will eventually make Driver 1 aware that it is coming and is on a collision course. This realization on the part of Driver 1 constitutes the identification stage of perception-response. Therefore, it is appropriate to start the response-time estimate at the end of the identification interval. Having said that the next question a reasonable individual might ask is "how much time does the decision-response interval require?" Again, unfortunately, no one knows for sure. Lacking certainty, it seems reasonable to allow about half the "normal" perception-response interval, say a range of 0.40 to 0.75 second.

The real problem in cases such as that just described is identifying the point at which a reasonably attentive driver will perceive the hazardous situation. The vehicle had been detected, identified, and a decision reached that it would properly yield right of way. Thus, an expectation was established on the part of Driver 1. As noted in the discussion of expectancy in Chapter 4, it has an effect on perception, hence on perception-response time. Situations that violate expectancy are less likely to be detected, or likely to be detected later than those for which there are no special expectations. With the car on the cross street dismissed as a potential hazard, a driver may well take his/her eyes from it, placing it in peripheral vision where it is less well seen. Under these circumstances the intruding car may get well under way before the other driver becomes aware of the hazard.

A similar problem occurs when a vehicle simply blows a stop sign. This vehicle may be detected during the approach and initially excite no suspicion on the part of the driver who has the right of way. The expectation is that it will stop. Eventually, the combination of forward speed and proximity to the intersection will cause the driver on the through street to realize that it is not going to stop. As before, this realization constitutes identification, and it is appropriate to apply a time estimate only for the decision and response intervals.

Failure-to-yield crashes such as those described are common, but there is no information to assist in addressing the key question of when a reasonably alert driver should identify the hazardous condition. Research would be very helpful. It would seem perfectly feasible (and much safer) to employ a simulator in this work. One such study has, in fact, been reported (Lechner and Malaterre, 1991).

The study was conducted using a very sophisticated simulator. Subjects (49 total) drove the machine for about ten minutes, supposedly to become familiar with it. At the end of that period they found themselves approaching an intersection. Another vehicle approached from the right, stopped, and then moved forward again. The intruding vehicle accelerated forward for 1.9 seconds, then braked and stopped in the middle of the road after 2.6 seconds, having moved forward a total of 6 meters. About two-thirds of the subjects braked in response to this situation. Brake response times ranged from about 0.7 second at the 5th percentile to about 1.5 seconds at the 95th percentile. The median perception-response time was 1.0 second. These times are very close to those reported by Olson, et al. (1984), who measured subject response to a stationary roadway hazard. Steering response times in Lechner and Malaterre's study were somewhat faster, although the smaller number who steered resulted in less reliable estimates. The median steer response time, for example, was about 0.8 second.

The study of Lechner and Malaterre is very interesting and the only one of its kind in the literature at the moment. Given the fact that a vehicle accelerating at a moderate pace moves forward very little in the first second or so, the response times are surprisingly short. The authors do not state whether this is the first encounter with a vehicle at a cross road during the test run, which could have an effect on expectancy. It would be desirable to have a number of such encounters in which the crossing vehicle properly yielded right of way before the test encounter. Further work of this kind would be desirable, examining approaches from both right and left as well as different levels of acceleration on the part of the intruding vehicle.

There are other situations in which this truncated model of perception-response time applies. Generally any instance in which there is an initial identification error, whether reasonable or not, is appropriate. One fairly common application is the closing-speed issue discussed in Chapter 3. Because of the difficulties people have in assessing closing speed, the probable initial judgment when the vehicle ahead is first noted is that there is nothing unusual in the dynamic relationship. When the driver realizes that there is a high closing speed this constitutes the end of the identification interval, leaving only decision and response.

Chapter Overview

This chapter has explored some relatively common cases in which perception-response time is important, but the times derived from the basic model discussed in Chapter 9 may not be appropriate. There are certainly other instances where the same type of arguments would apply. The point is that reconstructionists should not rigidly apply a single number to all cases where perception-response time is an issue. The first question the expert should ask is: "does it fit the basic model?" If not, some thought should be given to the differences and what effect those differences would be expected to have on the time it would take the individual to respond. The investigator may conclude that adjustments are necessary because one or more of the components was affected by the circumstances of a particular collision. In other cases the investigator may deem it advisable to delete the detection interval or both the detection and identification intervals from consideration. Regretfully, there is an absence of hard data, so adjustments must be made using a measure of careful judgment. This, however, is better than a slavish application of values derived from research that does not fit the situation under investigation.

The following are the principal points covered in this chapter:

- The available data on perception-response time apply only to relatively straightforward situations. These are cases where the object of concern is relatively easily detected and identified and the decision is not particularly complicated. A specific case under consideration may lead the investigator to the conclusion that one or more of these steps is more or less complicated than in the available research and adjustments should be made.
- In some instances it is desirable to eliminate the detection stage. Mainly these would be in low-visibility situations, where there is no clear entry of the stimulus into the driver's field of view. In such a case the investigator would use a slightly shorter perception-response interval and speak of it as starting when detection has been accomplished.
- In cases characterized by an initial identification error on the part of the driver it is generally advisable to eliminate both the detection and identification intervals from the estimate. Episodes like these commonly arise from right-of-way violations. Such cases actually have two perception-response intervals, with the first resulting in an erroneous identification on the part of the driver. The real question in these instances is how long does it take the driver to overcome the misleading expectation resulting from the first perception?

References

Alexander, G. J. and Lunenfeld, H. (1975). Positive Guidance in Traffic Control. Washington, D.C. The Federal Highway Administration.

Lechner, D. and Malaterre, G. (1991). Emergency Maneuver Experimentation Using a Driving Simulator. The Society of Automotive Engineers. Technical Paper Number 910016.

Olson, P. L. (1989). Driver Perception-Response Time. The Society of Automotive Engineers. Technical Paper Number 890731.

Olson, P. L., Cleveland, D. E., Fancher, P. S., Kostyniuk, L. P., and Schneider, L. W. (1984). Parameters Affecting Stopping Sight Distance. The University of Michigan Transportation Research Institute. Report No. UMTRI-84-15.

Perchonok, K. and Pollack, L. (1981). Luminous Requirements for Traffic Signs. Contract No. FHWA-RD-81-158. Washington, D.C. The Federal Highway Administration.

Roper, V. J. and Howard, E. A. (1938). Seeing with Motor Car Headlamps. *Transactions of the Illumination Engineering Society,* Vol. XXXIII, No. 5, 417-438.

About the Author

Paul L. Olson received a Ph.D. in Industrial Psychology from Purdue University in 1959. Having an interest in Human Factors, he first went to work at the General Motors Research Laboratories in Warren, Michigan. While there he was involved in research in vehicle dynamics and traffic flow theory. He also participated in evaluations of vehicle lighting and signaling systems that GM had under development at the time. In 1971 he joined the Human Factors Division at the University of Michigan Transportation Research Institute (UMTRI). In 1975 he became head of that Division. At UMTRI most of his research was concerned with nighttime driver visual information processing. It covered areas such as vehicle lighting, marking and signaling systems, and the visibility and legibility of roadway signs. In addition, he has conducted research on driver perception-response time. He has authored many reports, publications and book chapters on these subjects. In 1993 he retired from the University and has since served as a consultant in litigation where issues on which he has carried out original research are at issue.

Mr. Olson is a member of several professional societies and has served on numerous committees and advisory groups. He is a fellow of both the Human Factors and Ergonomics Society and the American Psychological Association. He is a recipient of the A. R. Lauer Traffic Safety Award from the Human Factors and Ergonomics Society and the Ralph H. Isbrandt Automotive Safety Engineering Award from the Society of Automotive Engineers.

Index

Train Accident Reconstruction and FELA & Railroad Litigation, Second Edition #0969

by James R. Loumiet, BSME and William G. Jungbauer, Esq.

Train collisions usually result in serious injury or death to motorists and pedestrians, often resulting in litigation. Yet the railroad industry presents complexities not known to the average person, making it difficult for an attorney to prepare a successful case. Even experienced accident reconstructionists are usually unfamiliar with the operation of railroads and trains. Yet the ability to reconstruct train collisions is often vital to the successful conduct of railroad litigation.

This ground breaking reference text by Loumiet and Jungbauer is the first of its kind in the are of train accident reconstruction, FELA and Railroad litigation. It explains how the railroads operate, the design and operation of trains, how to calculate train speed and successfully conduct FELA and railroad litigation. This text is for both the novice and experienced litigator and reconstructionist. It contains information and formulas that can be found nowhere else. $6^{1}/_{8}$" x $9^{1}/_{4}$", 686 pages.

Aircraft Accident Reconstruction and Litigation #5155

by Dr. Barnes W. McCormick, Ph.D., P.E. and Myron P. Papadakis, Esq. (1996)

This book teaches you how to investigate accidents and discover evidence. Your ability to reconstruct aircraft accidents can make the difference between successful and failed aviation litigation. Yet even experienced accident reconstructionists are often unfamiliar with the myriad complexities of aircraft. Now, whether you're a reconstruction expert or an experienced litigator, you can access a wealth of information in this ground-breaking text. In fact, much of the data, formulas, illustrations and investigative tools available to translate wreckage reconstruction data into credible and probative evidence suitable for introduction in the courtroom are available here exclusively, saving you hours of tedious calculations and research. It's the most comprehensive listing of aviation state law and cases ever published. Written in a hands-on format to give you the vital tools needed to investigate, reconstruct, and litigate in the technical and sophisticated arena of aircraft accident reconstruction. 6" x 9", hardbound, 720 pages, also includes 84 page Addendum List of Experts.

Bicycle Accident Reconstruction and Litigation #0918

by James M. Green, Paul F. Hill and Douglas Hayduk (1996)

Your ability to reconstruct bicycle accidents can make the difference between successful and failed litigation. Yet even experienced accident reconstructionists are often unfamiliar with the myriad complexities of bicycles. Now, whether you're a novice or an experienced litigator, you can access a wealth of information in this ground-breaking text. In fact, much of the case research data and formulas are available here exclusively, saving you hours of tedious calculations and research. This book is divided into three sections: engineering analysis; bicycle metallurgy; and legal analysis. You'll have informative diagrams and drawings, plus a complete index, appendix and citations. 6" x 9", hardbound, 784 pages.

Motorcycle Accident Reconstruction: Understanding Motorcycles #5031

by Kenneth Obenski, P.E. (1994)

Riding a motorcycle has been estimated as five times more complex as driving an automobile...and reconstructing an accident can be equally difficult. This text, written by a professional engineer who has investigated over 170 motorcycle accidents—and has safely ridden motorcycles for more than 35 years—gives you the detailed information you need to reconstruct and litigate accidents. In clear, jargon-free language the text sets out the basics of motorcycle operation, and the unique interactions between riders, passengers, machines, and other traffic. You'll understand why motorcycles frequently leave less evidence at the scene of an accident, and how a trained reconstructionist can observe and translate even scant evidence.

Of special significance is the section that explains what motorcycle operators can and cannot do, as well as what they should and should not do. Also included is training information published by the State of California, which is a basic source of motorcycle safe operating instruction. Your single source for motorcycle safety standards because its supplemental appendix contains the Department of Transportation (D.O.T.) Motorcycle Safety Standards as well as the preambles and superseded standards. With this detailed history you'll understand D.O.T.'s philosophy in arriving at each standard. 6⅛" x 9¼", hardbound, 296 pages.

Snowmobile Accident Reconstruction: A Technical and Legal Guide #5023

by Richard Hermance, ACTAR (1995)

The increased popularity of snowmobiling over the past few years has resulted in a rise in snowmobile-related accidents and injuries, and reconstruction of these types of accidents poses a unique challenge for you. This ground-breaking reference and law text is the first of its kind in the area of snowmobile accident reconstruction and litigation. You'll find detailed reference material covering the technical aspects of snowmobile safety, trail design and administration, maintenance, mapping, accident investigation and reconstruction, as well as snowmobile law.

The author is a nationally recognized and accredited accident reconstruction expert who has been involved in over 50 snowmobile accident investigations and reconstructions. An avid snowmobiler for the past 25 years, Hermance has ridden extensively in the northeastern and northwestern United States and Canada. He also designed and taught the New York State Snowmobile Accident Reconstruction course given to New York's State Troopers, Forest Park Police, Sheriff's Department, and local police. 6" x 9", hardbound, 700 pages.

Pedestrian Accident Reconstruction with Videotape #0977

by Jerry Eubanks (1994)

Pedestrian accidents involving a motor vehicle vary in both nature and scope from accidents involving only passenger cars. Intensified collision damage and injuries frequently result, often due to the inherent disadvantages a pedestrian has in an accident. Reconstruction of these types of collisions pose a unique challenge for accident investigators, attorneys, and insurance professionals. The new Pedestrian Accident Reconstruction book and video set discusses, demonstrates, and teaches you the technical fundamentals and mechanics of collisions between motor vehicles and pedestrians; providing a single source of state-of-the-art research dealing with these types of collisions. This valuable set contains chapters on: history and statistics of motor vehicle/pedestrian collisions; pedestrian walking speeds and relative motion; vehicle speed and pedestrian collision formulas; human factors and conspicuity; photography of a motor vehicle/pedestrian collision; case discovery and preparation; and a workbook section covering the videotape of pedestrian accident investigation and reconstruction. 6⅛" x 9¼", 288 pages, hardbound, includes 60-minute VHS video cassette tape.

Boat Accident Reconstruction and Litigation #5082

by Roy Scott Hickman, P.E. (1996)

The clearest guide to understanding accidents on and in the water. Your capability to reconstruct boating accidents can make the difference between successful and failed litigation. Yet even experienced engineers and attorneys are often unaccustomed with the myriad complexities of boating accidents which involve concepts and methods not present in other types of accidents. Now, whether you're a beginner or experienced litigator, you can access a wealth of information in this 496 page ground-breaking text. In fact, much of the information at hand here will save you hours of research time hunting through numerous books and on-line services.

You'll start with the basics of how boats function and progress to the way boats are designed which is a key element in the reconstruction of most boat accidents. You'll be introduced to Fluid mechanics and the numerous formulae and methods normally used to analyze accidents. Of particular value is the extensive series of appendices which includes numerous Coast Guard Regulations and Rules controlling boating traffic and safety equipment. You can quickly access the most complete description of major boating accident case citations ever published. You'll be presented with chapters on safety equipment, transportation issues, boat descriptions and designs, and marina issues. All types of boats are covered including Personal Water Craft, Water-skiing and the sport of SCUBA diving. You'll also learn about the special problems of Carbon Monoxide Poisoning with boats. 6" x 9", hardbound, 496 pages.

Notes

Notes

Notes

Notes

Notes

Notes

Notes

Notes

Notes

Notes